By Lowell Reidenbaugh

FIRST PRINTING *December 1976*

THE SPORTING NEWS Publishing Company
1212 North Lindbergh Boulevard
St. Louis, Missouri 63166

Printed in the United States of America

⚛️

Foreword

One hundred years!

The world has changed drastically in the century since 1876. Our country has gone through many changes, too, but one institution—and you can use that word with accuracy—has stood solid against the vagaries of time.

Baseball is an inextricable part of America, and the National League is at the heart of this fabric. War or peace, depression or prosperity, it has always operated in the spirit that has made our nation great. It has offered us the heroes to enhance the fantasies of our youngsters and merit the admiration of our adults. It has no peer in sports.

The National League clubs do more than play games; they stir our emotions, they add to our pleasures, they stimulate our conversations and they make our vicarious dreams come true.

Lowell Reidenbaugh, managing editor of THE SPORTING NEWS, *delved deeply into the year-by-year story of the National League in writing the articles that make up this book. It is not a definitive history; that job can be left to the cut-and-dried scholars. Instead, it is a lively and interesting, but withal authoritative account of the men and events that shaped the National League and built it to its present eminence.*

One hundred years!

For the National League, it has been a century of glorious contribution to America.

C. C. Johnson Spink

The Formative Years

1876-1900

✕☻✕

Prospects for a long and distinguished career were mediocre at best in February, 1876, when William A. Hulbert announced to a somnolent sports world the arrival of a sprawling, squalling infant that he had christened the National League of Professional Base Ball Clubs.

Chances are that Hulbert, given the gift of vision, would have averted the prediction that the new amalgam, conceived and born in an unpropitious sports climate, would crawl uncertainly through its early years, then stride haltingly into a new century so that, in 1976, it would celebrate its 100th anniversary as an international, transcontinental behemoth.

Hulbert sauntered upon the baseball scene as a director of the Chicago club of the National Association which operated under a loose rein from 1871 to 1875.

A native of New York State and a Chicagoan by adoption, Hulbert, a graduate of Beloit College, demonstrated an early affection for baseball, but he abhorred the conditions under which it was played.

Gambling was rampant, betting was widespread, pool-selling was conducted openly, odds quoted freely and liquor dispensed conveniently, so that drunkenness was an accepted ally of the sport.

PLAYERS CONVICTED of throwing games experienced virtually no difficulty in obtaining employment with other clubs in the league, and contracts were broken almost at will.

Additionally, Hulbert was distressed by the practice of affluent clubs in the east blandishing lucrative contracts to members of western clubs which were unable to match the offers and consequently lost the services of the players they had developed. As a result, the western clubs were consigned to the role of second-class citizens. In flag races, they were constant also-rans.

In 1875, the National Association embraced 13 franchises, including three in Philadelphia, the Athletics, the Pearls and the Centennials; two in St. Louis, the Brown

Stockings and Red Stockings; the Washington Nationals, who had folded during the 1872 and '73 pennant races, but who were readmitted in succeeding seasons upon payment of $10 annual dues; the Mutuals of New York, Atlantics of Brooklyn, Boston, Hartford, New Haven, Chicago and Keokuk.

To attempt remedial measures on this unwieldy structure, with its assorted evils, was, was thought Hulbert, too onerous a chore for one such as he, possessed with uncommon energy and desire.

The logical solution, he concluded, was a new league, balanced geographically between the east and west, with higher entry fees, stringent regulations and the power of enforcement.

HULBERT'S INITIAL move in the restructuring of professional baseball was in the direction of Boston, then en route to its fourth consecutive pennant. The club was to finish the season with a record of 51 wins and only seven losses and a perfect season record on its home grounds.

The nucleus of the Boston club was the "Big Four," consisting of Albert Goodwill Spalding, a pitcher of superlative talents; second baseman Ross Barnes, who led the league hitters in 1875 with 1.79 hits per game; catcher Jim (Deacon) White, who compiled a 1.66 HPG mark in '75, and first baseman Cal McVey, with a 1.60 figure.

In addition to his extraordinary pitching, Spalding was a hitter of substance, collecting 1.40 hits per game.

The modern system of compiling batting averages was not introduced until 1876, when Barnes batted .404 to lead all hitters in the fledgling National League.

The "Big Four" were under contract to the Boston club for 1875, but, undeterred, Hulbert offered the quartet contracts for the following year. Among the arguments used by the budding entrepreneur was that all four were westerners by birth, hence owed a stout allegiance to their native area.

In lining up the foursome, Hulbert not only assured contending status for his Chi-

William A. Hulbert . . . A new concept spawned a new league.

cago club, but also created a solid building block for the anticipated new league.

IT WAS AT THIS stage that I first met Mr. Hulbert," wrote Spalding in his book AMERICA'S NATIONAL GAME in 1911.

"For myself, I felt the time was ripe for a change. I gave him (Hulbert) to understand I was not averse to such a move (to Chicago) and said that if I did come I would bring a team of pennant winners.

"Later in the season, in June 1875, he called upon me at Boston as president of the Chicago club. He there and then signed Barnes, McVey, White and myself, and I accompanied him to Philadelphia where (Adrian) Ansón and (Ezra) Sutton already had been signed through my efforts."

(Anson fulfilled his contract with the Chicago club, but Sutton reconsidered and remained with Philadelphia.)

Despite efforts to keep the signings a secret, wrote Spalding, they "lasted about two weeks when an announcement appeared in a Chicago paper that the four Boston and two Philadelphia players had been signed for the Chicago club for 1876."

In a master understatement, Spalding added, "This occasioned a great sensation in Boston and Philadelphia. For the remainder of the season we were caricatured, ridiculed and even accused of treason."

AT THE CLOSE OF the season, reports circulated that the six jumpers would be expelled from baseball for violating the rule that prohibited players from signing a future contract while still obligated to another club.

"I probably exhibited some uneasiness," wrote Spalding, "but Mr. Hulbert answered by assuring me that whatever happened Chicago would pay the salaries of her players in full. Chicago, he said, had been waiting for years to get a winning ball team and now that she had finally secured one, he proposed that Chicago should have what was coming to her."

According to Spalding, Hulbert exuded such a monumental civic ardor that he never dwelt on what he would do, but always expounded on what Chicago would do. One of his favorite expressions, the ballplayer noted, was: "I would rather be a lamp post in Chicago than a millionaire in any other city."

On christening his new organization, Hulbert departed from the earlier terminology, substituting the "National League of Professional Base Ball Clubs" for the "National Association of Professional Base Ball Players." The change, Spalding said, was well conceived.

The evils that wrecked the National Association had stemmed from the executive level of the game, not from the playing field, Spalding noted, adding:

"It began to be apparent that the system in vogue for the business management of the sport was defective; that means ought to be adopted to separate the control of the executive management from the players and the playing of the game. The idea was as old as the hills; but its application to Base Ball had not yet been made. It was, in fact, the irrepressible conflict between Labor and Capital asserting itself under a new guise.

"**THE EXPERIMENT** of business control of Base Ball by the men who played the game had been tested under several administrations. No further evidence of the inability of ballplayers, whether amateurs or professionals, to manage both ends of Base Ball enterprises at the same time was needed than was presented in conditions apparent to everybody—and especially in the overdrawn bank accounts of those who had undertaken to finance the sport.

"Now, this picture of the situation as it was carries with it no reflection whatever

Albert G. Spalding

Morgan G. Bulkeley . . . First president, by luck of the draw.

upon the business acumen or the executive ability of ballplayers as individuals. Scores of those who have won fame on the diamond have also won fortunes in business. But no ballplayer, in my recollection, ever made a success of any other business while he was building up his reputation as an artist on the diamond. The two branches are entirely unlike in their demands. One calls for the exercise of functions differing altogether from those which are required in the other. No man can do his best at ballplaying unless his whole soul is in the effort. The man whose whole soul is absorbed in the business of playing ball has no soul left for the other business—just as important in its way—of conducting the details of managing men, administering discipline, arranging schedules and finding ways and means of financing a team.

"And so," said Spalding, "certain men . . . desirous of the success of the national game . . . proposed an organization that should draw a sharp line of distinction between the terms 'club' and 'team.' Heretofore Base Ball clubs had won and lost games, matches, tournaments, trophies. The function of Base Ball Clubs in the future would be to manage Base Ball teams. Clubs would form leagues, secure grounds, erect grandstands, lease and own property, make schedules, fix dates, pay salaries, assess fines, relieving the players of all care and responsibility for the legitimate functions of management, require of them the very best performance of which they were capable, in the entertainment of the public, for which service they were to receive commensurate pay."

WITH THE NAME of the new league determined, Hulbert turned his attention toward the most effective strategy to be employed in his efforts to convince eastern organizations that a new league was urgently required.

By the mid-winter months of 1875-76, he had formulated his plan of attack and was ready to confide his strategy to Spalding.

"Let us anticipate the eastern clubs," Hulbert told his confidante. "Let us organize a new association before the March meeting (of the National Association) and then see who will do the expelling."

Hulbert's first move was to visit St. Louis, where he conferred with Charles Fowle, owner of the local club, and C. Orrick Bishop, an attorney who was vice-president of the Association club and a member of the Association's judiciary committee.

The St. Louisans were amenable to Hulbert's propositions and Bishop drafted a league constitution embracing all of Hulbert's specificiations. Hulbert, Spalding and Fowle then moved on to Louisville, where they conferred with William Haldeman,

Thomas Shirley and Charles Chase, representing that city's club, and John Joyce of Cincinnati.

Again Hulbert's suggestions were received favorably. At meeting's end, the Chicagoan and Fowle were empowered to visit New York where they should invite the four most attractive eastern clubs to join the new organization.

BECAUSE OF THE significance of the Louisville parlay, some historians are inclined to cite that city as the birthplace of the National League. Officially, however, New York is accorded the honor, because it was there, on February 2, 1876, that Hulbert met with G. W. Thompson, president of the Athletics, N. T. Appolonio, Boston; Morgan G. Bulkeley, Hartford, and W. H. Cammeyer, Mutuals of New York.

Resuming his narrative, Spalding, who was not present at the meeting, wrote: "One after another came until all had arrived. Then this aggressive Base Ball magnate from the west, who had never been present at a similar meeting in his life, went to the door of the room, locked it, put the key in his pocket, and, turning, addressed the astounded guests something after this manner:

"Gentlemen, you have no occasion for uneasiness. I have locked the door simply to prevent any intrusion from without, and incidentally, to make it impossible for any of you to go out until I have finished what I have to say to you, which, I promise, shall not take an hour."

The locked door episode receives scant credence from Dr. Harold Seymour in his scholarly work, BASEBALL, THE EARLY YEARS.

"Glorifiers of Hulbert," wrote Seymour, "have claimed for him the same tactics which tradition attributes to J. P. Morgan, who supposedly locked fellow financiers in his office during the panic of 1907 until they agreed to what he wanted. . . . The story is no doubt apocryphal. Most likely it was Hulbert's forceful personality, coupled with the appeal of his plan, which convinced the others."

Bound or free, the delegates adopted Hulbert's proposals, among which were:

A NEW CLUB MUST represent a city of 75,000, unless obtaining unanimous approval from the incumbents, and two blackballs could bar an applicant;

Dues would be $100 annually, 10 times what they had been in the Association;

Each team was to meet every other team 10 times between March 15 and November 15;

The team winning the most games would be declared champion and would receive a pennant costing not less than $100;

Nicholas Young . . . Between $300 and $500 annually.

If two teams finished with identical win totals, then the team with the fewest losses would be declared champion;

If a team used an ineligible player or was prevented from appearing for a game, that game should be forfeited;

Each club was to provide a sufficient number of police to preserve order;

After each game a complete score, with full particulars, was to be submitted to the league secretary, N. E. (Nick) Young, a holdover from the Association.

League by-laws stipulated that the secretary should be a gentleman of intelligence, honesty and good repute, versed in Base Ball but not connected with the press and not a member of any professional club."

FOR HIS SERVICES, Young was to receive not less than $300 nor more than $500 a year, plus traveling expenses.

A five-man board of directors was to be elected, it was agreed, with the names to be drawn from a hat. Moreover, the first name drawn was to serve one year as president.

By the luck of the draw, Morgan Bulkeley of Hartford was elevated to the president's chair. It also earned him a niche in the Hall of Fame, a distinction that has been denied Hulbert who, after one year, replaced Bulkeley, later a United States senator and governor of Connecticut, and served with distinction until his death in 1882.

Other decisions made at that New York meeting provided that clubs straying from the straight and narrow should be judged by their peers and a two-thirds majority was sufficient to convict.

Infractions sufficient for expulsion from the league included disbanding during the season or failing to obey a rule passed by the board, violating the constitution and breaking contracts with players, providing the athletes were not at fault.

The players, of course, had no voice in the operation of the league. Justice, for the hired hands, was at the indulgence of management.

NO CLUB WAS permitted to play an exhibition against another club, league or non-league, in a city where another N. L. club existed.

And when a player was suspended, he was required to wait for the regular league meeting in December to obtain a hearing.

Preston D. Orem, writing in BASEBALL 1845-1881, commented: "Perhaps no reporters were present or aware of the meeting (at the Grand Central). And most likely a press release was prepared for distribution. The first newspaper articles noted appeared on February 5, three days after the meeting, and are strikingly similar in their details."

Before the centennial year of 1876 would

run its course, George Armstrong Custer would have his bell rung in a battle along the Little Big Horn River.

And Rutherford B. Hayes would defeat Samuel Tilden in a Presidential election battle suffused with vitriol and charges of fraud.

William A. Hulbert, too, would wage his own battle in the theater of baseball, the details of which remained fresh in Spalding's memory 35 years later when he had long since passed from the athletic arena and was then the head of the sporting goods company bearing his name.

Recalling Hulbert's contributions to professional baseball, Spalding wrote:

"TO HIM CAME the great struggle that attended the early years of the league. Upon his shoulders were loaded many of the heavy burdens of formative and creative duty. Against him were directed the assaults of enemies of the league—and of the game. He was the recipient of the abuse of gamblers and of the innuendoes of their apologists.

"The struggles he encountered cheerfully because he was a born fighter; the duties he assumed willingly, for he was an industrious worker; the planning he undertook intelligently, for he was a master of business system, and the opposition of the rabble amused him while it injured him not at all.

"William A. Hulbert was not a purist. He was never charged with religious bigotry or fanatacism of any kind other than that which manifest itself in a great love for our national game. His name was not enrolled among the list of moral reformers. He thought this world was good enough for him—for anybody, and he enjoyed it in his own way. And yet this man stood like a stone wall, protecting this game of Base Ball in its integrity, and turning back the assaults of every foe who sought to introduce elements of dishonesty, discord or degeneration. He demanded always clean management, a clean game, and the best interest of manly sport."

Concluding his panegyric to the founder of the National League, Spalding commented:

"I ASK ALL living professional Base Ball players to join me in raising our hats to the memory of William A. Hulbert, the man who saved the game!"

When Hulbert and his associates departed the Grand Central Hotel 100 years ago, the groundwork had been laid, their calculated reckonings had been distilled into a new concept called the National League of Professional Base Ball Clubs.

Ahead lay countless heartaches and roadblocks, many more valleys than peaks.

But there also would be numberless thrills

and exultations on the playing field which, only 11 years after Appomattox, would help heal the wounds left by four years of intersectional strife, and provide, too, the escape valve for the excess energies welled up within a nation on the threshold of a second glorious century.

It happened this way:

1876

To Boston and Philadelphia fell the distinction of playing the first National League game. The two clubs met in Philadelphia, on April 22, with 3,000 attending the game under cloudy but favorable weather conditions. Boston won, 6-5, scoring two runs in the ninth inning.

The two teams met three days later with the Athletics an easy winner, 20-3.

In a primitive effort to identify the players, the Chicago club dressed its players in vari-colored caps: Spalding, red, white and blue; McVey, black and blue; Barnes, black and yellow; Peters, black and red; Anson, black and white; Hines, white; Bielaski, white and red; Addy, white and brown.

Harry Wright, manager of the Boston club, advocated a change in scoring rules to credit a pitcher with an assist on a strikeout. "Unfortunately," reported Orem, "Harry succeeded in establishing the idea, which endured for some time."

The first no-hitter in league history was recorded on July 15 by George Washington Bradley of St. Louis, who blanked Hartford, 2-0.

Philadelphia and New York were expelled from the league for failing to make their final western trip. The clubs, wrote Spalding, "argued that they were more important to the League than was the League to New York and Philadelphia. Very greatly to their surprise (they) were summarily expelled."

The order of finish in the inaugural N. L. pennant race was: Chicago, Hartford, St. Louis, Boston, Louisville, New York, Philadelphia and Cincinnati.

"It is worthy of note," reported Spalding, "that honors now were almost evenly divided, as between East and West, as shown by the alternating of the nines in the order of their standing in the race."

The star of the White Stockings may have been inspired to make this observation by the fact that the White Stockings won the pennant.

For the first season, the bat was limited to 42 inches in length, the pitcher's box, four feet by six feet, was 45 feet from the plate and a rule was adopted permitting a substitute to enter the game prior to the fourth inning.

1877

The "fair foul" rule was eliminated, making any ball that hit in fair territory and rolled foul between home plate and the bases an ordinary foul ball. The rule removed one of the favorite offensive weapons of Ross Barnes, the league's first batting champion, with an average of .404.

In the absence of a reserve clause, George Washington Bradley deserted St. Louis in favor of Chicago, for whom he won only 19 games, a sharp decline from his 45 victories of a year earlier.

Exhibition games with teams from the International Association and the League Alliance were played at such a rapid pace that on June 4, Hartford, which played all home games at Brooklyn, had played only eight games, Boston nine.

Canvas bases, 15 inches square, were introduced and home plate was placed squarely within the angle formed by the foul lines.

The first scandal of the new league developed late in the season when the Louisville club, which had been one of the strongest entries, failed to win a single game on its last trip to Boston and Hartford.

Diamond stickpins and rings indicated that four players had come into sudden affluence and reports of huge killings by New York gamblers combined to point the finger of suspicion at pitcher James Devlin, shortstop William Craver, outfielder George Hall and third baseman Al Nichols, all of whom were expelled after having been shown telegrams implicating them with gamblers. They confessed to their guilt.

Commenting on the banishment of the players, Spalding recalled a scene he witnessed in Hulbert's Chicago office some time later.

"I was sitting in the reception room and Mr. Hulbert was at his desk," Spalding recounted, "when the outer door opened and a sorry looking specimen of humanity entered. It was midwinter and very cold, but the poor fellow had no overcoat. His dust-covered garments were threadbare and seedy. His shoes were worn through with much tramping while the red flesh showing in places indicated that if stockings were present, they afforded not much protection to the feet. Everything about the man's appearance betokened weariness and woe. His face was a picture of abject misery. The visitor passed me without a glance. He walked straight to the chair where Mr. Hulbert sat and, dropping to his knees at the big man's feet, lifted his eyes in prayerful entreaty

Harry Wright . . . An 'unfortunate' scoring rule.

while his frame shook with the emotion so long restrained. Then his lips gave utterance to such a plea for mercy as might have come from one condemned to the gallows.

"The man was Devlin. He had been a personal friend of Mr. Hulbert, and knowing that man's kindly heart, felt that if he could only see him, face to face, his friendship and the memory of former days would cause him to relent in his purpose of punishment.

"How Devlin reached Chicago I never knew. There was everything in his appearance and condition to indicate that he may have walked all the way from Louisville. The situation, as he knelt there in abject humiliation, was beyond the realm of pathos. It was a scene of heart-rending tragedy. Devlin was in tears, Hulbert was in tears and if the mists of a tearful sympathy filled my eyes, I have no excuse to offer here.

"I heard Devlin's plea to have the stigma removed from his name. I heard him entreat, not on his own account—he acknowledged himself unworthy of consideration—but for the sake of his wife and child. I beheld the agony of humiliation depicted on his features as he confessed his guilt and begged for mercy. I saw the great bulk of Hulbert's frame tremble with the emotion he vainly sought to stifle. I saw the President's hand steal into his pocket as if seeking to conceal his intended act from the other hand. I saw him take a $50 bill and press it into the palm of the prostrate player. And then I heard him say, as he fairly writhed with the pain his own words caused him: 'That's what I think of you, personally; but, damn you, Devlin, you are dishonest; you have sold a game; and I can't trust you. Now go and let me never see your face again, for your act will not be condoned as long as I live.' "

Because Cincinnati failed to pay its annual dues of $100, its games were wiped out and the league finished the season with five members.

1878

Boston and Chicago were the only returning clubs. Cincinnati was given new life and with Indianapolis, Providence and Milwaukee, helped to round out the six-club circuit.

Because of the swift and firm action against the Louisville gamblers of the previous season, the league enjoyed a new respect from press and public alike at the start of its third campaign.

In an effort to improve the quality of umpiring, the league published an approved list of 20 arbiters from which the clubs could select the men to handle their games.

Boston offered season tickets from its new offices at 786 Washington Street, over George Wright's store.

Turnstiles were used for the first time, and at the new Providence park 6,000 spectators, many conveyed by two special trains from Boston, overflowed the grandstand, while 300 carriages rimmed the outfield, as the home club dropped a 1-0 decision to Boston.

Cincinnati, managed by Cal McVey, star of the all-conquering Reds of 1869, drew a crowd of 6,000 in Boston, the largest throng in that city in two years.

Injuries seldom sidelined players, but in such rare instances, the athletes were assigned to ticket-selling or ticket-taking chores. In Boston's 60-game schedule, only outfielders Jim O'Rourke and Jim Manning missed as many as four games. Frequently, a shorthanded team would sign a semi-pro player when it was on the road to fill out its roster.

Sunday baseball was a controversial issue, reported Dr. Harold Seymour. "In keeping with the avowed purpose of making baseball respectable, the League frowned on Sunday games. At first such games (played on Sunday) simply did not count toward the championship, but in 1878 the League clamped down harder with a rule expelling clubs that violated the sabbath or failed to get rid of any man who participated in such games, either as player, umpire or scorer."

The Cincinnati club was the particular target for the league purists, although St. Louis, too, was criticized for its "usual disregard for righteousness."

1879

With Indianapolis and Milwaukee having withdrawn from the league and Cleveland, Troy, Buffalo and Syracuse admitted, the circuit was again an eight-club organization.

The schedule was increased from 60 to 84 games and a staff of umpires was introduced. Unlike earlier seasons when a pitch was voided if it was not thrown where the batter specified, every pitch was now to be called a ball, strike or foul.

Also, a pitcher was required to face the batter before delivering a pitch, and nine balls were necessary for a base on balls.

A uniform baseball was adopted for the first time, furnished free by the Spalding company for the advertising value it would afford.

Perhaps the most significant innovation of the year was the reserve clause, guaranteeing a club a player's services for as long as it wished.

Fred Lieb in THE BASEBALL STORY, relates: "It was supposedly written by the thrifty Bostonian, Arthur Soden . . . (and)

Cal McVey . . . A 6,000-fan attraction in Boston.

sought to stop the player stealing by more opulent clubs and player jumping by more avaricious athletes. At first clubs reserved only five men; the number later was increased to 11, then to 14 and eventually covered the entire team. When we think that the present reserve clause often is referred to as a chain, holding the baseball peon in bondage, it is amusing to recall that the early players felt it a decided honor to be placed on his team's reserve list.

"At least, that is what John B. Foster, early Cleveland and New York baseball writer, once told me. 'The athlete eagerly scanned the winter reserve list to see whether his name was included,' said Foster. 'Only the stars and better players were reserved. If a player wasn't on the list, he was a baseball nobody.' "

1880

Syracuse, having disbanded before the close of the previous season, was replaced by Worcester, Mass.

Rules changes included: eight balls were required for a base on balls; playing of games on Sunday was prohibited; the catcher was required to catch the baseball on the fly to retire a batter on a third strike; a runner hit by a batted ball would be declared out, whether or not he attempted to avoid the ball.

When a Boston report indicated that "League authorities are complaining about the baseballs furnished by Spalding," the president of the firm furnished some balls that were harder and livelier, accounting, said a paper, "for the long hits."

In an exhibition game, Harry Wright, Boston manager, introduced a square bat and a new style baseball "its peculiarity being the presence of a small globe of cork wound round with string, rubber and yarn."

Because the bat chipped if the ball was hit even slightly off center, and because the impact of bat against ball produced a stinging sensation in the hands, it was discarded during the game.

The baseball went swift and far, but was too difficult for the infielders to handle, inspiring the comment: "When uniformly made, the league ball is the best."

The Chicago Tribune introduced the runs-batted-in feature, but when the readers greeted the innovation coolly, the paper discontinued the statistic.

When the Boston club was in Cleveland, September 2, player Charlie Jones demanded of Manager Wright his entire salary for the month of August. Under the custom of the time, clubs advanced players money away from home, but paid salaries only in their home city.

Jones, claiming the club also owed him $128 for July as well as $378 for August, was suspended, fined $100 and expelled from the league.

Boston executives refused to pay Jones any part of his salary, whereupon the player sued the club, obtained a judgment and attached the club's gate receipts on the road to obtain satisfaction.

Chicago clinched the pennant on September 15, with 10 games still to be played, and was reported to be the only club that made money during the season.

At a league meeting in Rochester, N. Y., October 4, Cincinnati, which finished last in the pennant race, was censured for having leased its park to a non-league club for Sunday baseball.

Moreover, the club sold beer at its park before and during games. When the Cincinnati representative refused to sign a pledge, arguing that Sunday rentals and beer sales netted the club $4,000 annually, the club was expelled.

The action was hailed in Chicago. Crowed the Tribune: "The League is well rid of that one-horse town."

Highlight of the season was the pitching of two perfect games within a five-day period.

On June 12, John Lee Richmond, Worchester lefthander, hurled professional baseball's first perfect game, blanking Cleveland, 1-0, in one hour and 27 minutes before a crowd of 700 at Worcester.

John Lee Richmond

John Montgomery Ward . . . A no-hitter against Buffalo.

On June 17, in a morning game, scheduled to avoid a conflict with afternoon boat races, John Montgomery Ward of Providence whitewashed Buffalo, 5-0, before 2,000 at Providence.

1881

Detroit replaced Cincinnati and drew the best opening day crowd, 1,500, but lost to Buffalo, 6-5.

A rule permitting "runners to be put out while returning to first base on called foul balls" was repealed. The pitching distance was lengthened from 45 to 50 feet.

Visiting clubs were required to submit their starting lineup by 9 a.m. on the day of the game, which could not be changed.

No substitution was allowed of any player after the start of a game except for illness or injury.

No substitute base-runner was permitted under any circumstances.

Umpires were prevented from reversing a decision under any circumstances, or from taking testimony of any player or bystander in making a decision. Umpires also were empowered to fine a pitcher for deliberately hitting a batter. The rule proved immensely unpopular and was repealed after one year.

After Chicago dropped a 7-1 decision to Worcester before 2,500, the Chicago Tribune volunteered this opinion: "Captain Anson, when his men are at bat or on the bases, should play the bench less and play base ball more."

The next day, after Tommy Burns' home run had produced a Chicago victory, the same daily commented: "Profiting by the sincere and well-intentioned advice of The Tribune, to the effect that better play and more earnest work was due in order to meet the requirements of the liberal patronage according to Base Ball in Chicago, the White Stockings yesterday buckled down and played a magnificent game."

A few days after Boston friends presented a gold watch to Lew Brown, the Detroit player was given his release and spent the night behind bars (for debt). Shortly thereafter he signed with Providence.

At its winter meeting, the league adopted a rule requiring the various clubs to wear different colored stockings as follows: Chicago white, Cleveland dark blue, Providence light blue, Worcester brown, Buffalo gray, Troy green, Boston red, Detroit yellow. Shirts, belts and caps were specified for each position: catcher scarlet; pitcher light blue, first baseman scarlet and white, second baseman orange and blue, third baseman blue and white, shortstop maroon, left fielder white, center fielder red and black, right fielder gray, substitutes green and brown. All pants and ties were to be white and shoes of leather.

1882

For the first time there was no change in franchises.

Providence offered season tickets at $15 apiece until March 15, then the price went up to $20 each until April 15. Boston season tickets also were $15, with ladies' ducats selling for $10.

On the eve of the league's seventh pennant race, William A. Hulbert, league founder, died in Chicago. Contrary to expectations, Albert G. Spalding was overlooked in the election of a successor. After Arthur Soden was elected interim president, Col. Abraham G. Mills of Washington, former player and official of the Olympic club, was elevated to the office.

The only known instance of an umpire's dishonesty occurred in June when Dick Higham was barred from the league. Earlier in the season, Higham had appeared on the field wearing a mask. The innovation was not immediately approved, many fans believing the arbiter could see better without a "muzzle" and, furthermore, many of the spectators looking forward eagerly to the ump getting "a smack on the kisser" from a foul tip.

On June 30, directors met in Detroit and confronted Higham with evidence of his collusion with gamblers. At first he denied the charges, but when handwriting experts linked him with the authorship of letters to gamblers, he confessed.

When an umpire appeared on the field at Providence attired in pantaloons, a green shirt and wide suspenders Owner Winship refused to permit him to work the game. In the words of a Providence reporter: "Mr. Winship is nothing if not aesthetic."

On an eastern trip, at the rate of 50 cents per admission, Detroit's share of the gate came to $112 for three games in Worcester, $196 for three games in Troy, $496 for three games in Providence, and $481 for three games at Boston.

On the same tour Detroit played five exhibition games with the Phillies of the American Association, for which it received 25 cents a head, and came away with $1,356, more than for the other 12 games at a higher admission price.

In mid-September, the largest non-holiday crowd ever to see a game in Chicago, 7,000, watched the White Stockings complete the sweep of a three-game series with Providence by winning, 6-1. The crowd overflowed the "bleaching seats" and was remarkably quiet "submitting to two or

Adrian (Cap) Anson . . . "Should play baseball more."

three grossly unfair decisions by umpire Howes with nothing more than a few moderate expressions of disapproval."

On September 22, the league held a special meeting in Philadelphia, at which time Worcester and Troy delegates were advised that their cities were not supporting the clubs adequately and that they were, therefore, invited to withdraw so that Philadelphia, owned by A. J. Reach, and New York, owned by John B. Day, could enter the league.

The Boston club, one of the best franchises in the league, issued these figures for the year:

Gross receipts, $42,224.42; expenditures, $38,473.50; gross gate receipts, $37,917.45; net gate receipts, $29,847.23; paid visiting clubs, $8,060.22; home receipts, $30,000; league abroad, $7,200; against Metropolitans at New York, $3,700; at Philadelphia, $1,300; attendance at home, 50,971; league-abroad, 48,066; New York City, 29,584; Philadelphia, 10,994.

Although ridiculing the rival American Association as a "Beer and Whiskey Circuit," league executives recognized the urgency for a peace agreement that would guarantee survival. Accordingly, President Mills arranged a meeting at the Hotel Victoria in New York, February 17, to which he invited representatives of both leagues, as well as those from the Northwestern League, which operated in Michigan, Ohio and Illinois.

From this "Harmony Meeting" came the Tripartite Pact, forerunner of the National Agreement, in which Mills had proposed an 11-player reserve limit, territorial rights and minimum salaries of $1,000 for the N. L. and A. A. and $750 for the minor Northwestern.

In a tribute to his success in unifying baseball, Col. Mills soon was being referred to as "The Bismarck of Baseball."

A staff of umpires with fixed salaries was

Alfred J. Reach

John B. Day

Abraham G. Mills . . . "The Bismarck of Baseball."

appointed for the first time and, also for the first time, a pitcher was permitted to raise his arm above his waist while delivering the baseball, paving the way for harder throwing.

The season opened on May 1, with New York making its debut before a crowd estimated as high as 15,000. Many spectators were unable to see the game as the overflow gathered in front of the grandstand and free seats at the Polo Grounds.

Among those who watched the New Yorks beat Boston, 7-5, was Ulysses S. Grant, Civil War hero and 18th President of the United States, who, according to one account, "applauded the good plays of both teams" while smoking one large cigar after another.

Rookie umpire George Burnham encountered frequent difficulties during the season, once being denounced for making "more unjust decisions in Chicago in three days than all the errors made in Chicago by all the other umpires all season."

Cleveland fans, on July 25, however, gained a fresh appreciation of the arbiter when, in pregame ceremonies, he was presented a watch bearing the inscription:

"Presented to George W. Burnham by his Cleveland friends, July 25, 1883."

Later, it was disclosed that Burnham had purchased the watch himself, paid for the inscription and arranged for the presentation. Thereafter he was known as "Watch" Burnham.

In a game at Detroit on July 15, Black Jack Burdock of Boston hit a grounder to first baseman Martin Powell. As Powell prepared to throw to the plate to retire the runner from third, Burdock pinned Powell's arms to his body. Ezra Sutton, the runner at third, was so amazed he stood transfixed. Burnham, despite hisses from the home crowd, called Sutton out and fined Burdock $20.

Boston engineered the surprise of the pennant race by dethroning Cap Anson's three-time champion White Stockings. The Red Sox, in seventh place in June, brought back John Morrill, fired at the close of the previous season, to replace Burdock, and the club won 75 percent of its remaining games, beating out Chicago by four games. James (Grasshopper) Whitney, inelegantly described by a newspaperman of the era as having "a head about the size of a wart with a forehead slanting at an angle of 45 degrees," won 38 games for the new champions.

Prospects for a world series between Boston and the Philadelphia Athletics, champions of the Association, appeared auspicious until the A's lost seven of eight postseason exhibitions, and declined the invitation.

1884

On opening day in New York, the crowd of 12,000 grew ecstatic when the home club annihilated Chicago, 15-3. Giving vent to their jubilation, the grandstand spectators bombarded the standees with cushions, which were promptly returned, making the air black with missiles.

A change in ground rules at Lake Park in Chicago focused attention on home runs for the first time.

The White Stockings were forced to open the season on the road because the Illinois Central Railroad, which had offered the city $800,000 for the property on which it planned to build a depot, had obtained an injunction against the ball club playing in its home park.

Eventually, on promise of finding another site for 1885, the White Stockings were allowed to play in Lake Park, where a ball driven over the left field fence would now count as a home run instead of a double, as previously.

In the third home contest, Ed Williamson powdered three drives over the fence, thus gaining the honor of being the first major

Ed Williamson

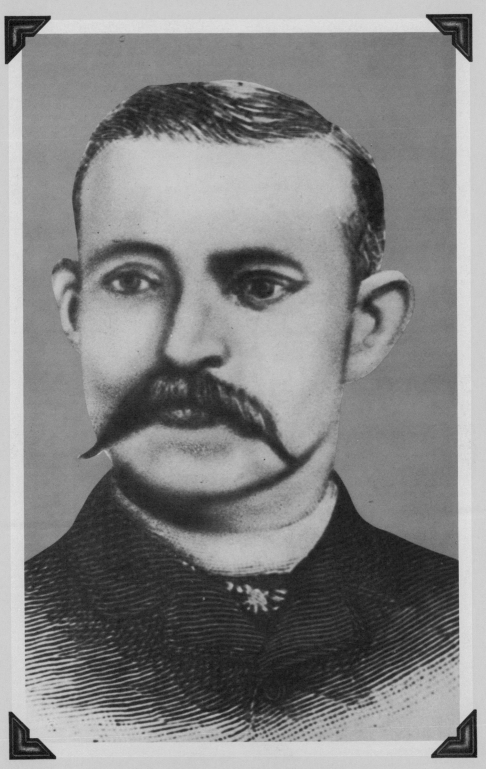

Charles (Hoss) Radbourn . . . 60 wins and 11 shutouts.

leaguer to hit three home runs in one game. Before the season ended, Williamson had hit 27 homers, 25 in Chicago, and ranked as the all-time season homer king until Babe Ruth clouted 29 in 1919.

But pitching was not without its luminaries, particularly Charles (Old Hoss) Radbourn, who pitched 73 complete games out of 74 starts for Providence, winning 60, 11 by shutouts, and losing only 12.

One of the new umpires was Eugene Van Court of San Francisco. The newcomer experienced his share of hassles, being overshadowed by the taller athletes, and eventually took up a profession for which he had been endowed by nature—he became a jockey.

Cap Anson, Chicago manager, and his third baseman, Ed Williamson, got into a scrap at Buffalo, July 21, when Williamson, holding four aces, won a $95 pot from his boss, who was betting four queens.

Williamson grabbed a water pitcher and threatened to test Anson's skull before peace was restored. Sizing up his captain, Williamson observed: "Cap's okay as a player, but don't count for cornstalks as a man."

Charley Sweeney won 19 games for Providence before July 22, but on that date he got into a rhubarb with Manager Frank Bancroft and was suspended, whereupon he joined St. Louis of the Union Association.

Providence won the pennant, beating out Boston by 9½ games, and was challenged to a three-game series by the New York Metropolitans, champions of the American Association.

Radbourn made short work of the series, winning on successive days, 6-0, 3-1 and 12-2.

At the league's annual meeting, in New York, November 19, Col. Mills submitted his resignation as president. Among the reasons for his action was the strong sentiment among club owners to pardon the players who had jumped to the Union Association, a feeling that was not shared by Mills. The league voted to combine the offices of president and secretary, and elected Nick Young, longtime secretary, to the double-duty position.

1885

St. Louis replaced Cleveland and the rules-makers now permitted a portion of the bat's surface to be flat, while home plate could be made of marble or white rubber. Chest protectors for catchers and umpires came into common use.

In his rookie season as president, Nick Young was forced to settle a sticky problem engendered by the Detroit club, which bought the Buffalo franchise for $7,000. The object of the deal was the acquisition of Buf-

James White

Hardy Richardson

falo's "Big Four," Deacon White, Dan Brouthers, Jack Rowe and Hardie Richardson, a clear violation of the rule prohibiting the signing of players before October.

Young ordered the quartet back to Buffalo, an order they ignored, and the following year they were permitted to play for Detroit.

The Big Four also had been coveted by Arthur Soden, but, knowing he had no chance to obtain them, the Boston owner bought the Providence franchise for $6,000 in order to acquire Radbourn and his catcher, Con Daily.

The New York club was being referred to as the Giants, one source attributing the nickname to the uncommon size of the players, another to the fact that the club got off to a fast start, winning 16 of its first 20 games.

Henry Lucas, owner of the St. Louis Maroons, whose uniforms were greatly admired around the circuit, was highly popular with his players as the result of his generosity.

When three of his players were blacklisted, Lucas held a benefit, consisting of field events, a ball game and a fox chase. The affair drew 5,000 spectators and netted $400 for each player.

On Saturday nights, Lucas would seek out his players, who usually were short of funds by that time, and ask if they could use some financial assistance. "Here, take this," Lucas told them, "clear out, have a good time and come around sober and ready to play ball."

One of the season's biggest rhubarbs occurred at St. Louis June 24 and involved umpire Decker, who "was at his worst and his best is gross incompetence." A baserunner failed to get out of the way of a fielder, who tripped over the runner and fell to the ground as the ball struck him. Decker solved the dilemma by ordering the runner back to third base and the batter back to the plate to bat again.

Later in the same game, Decker strolled into the stands to obtain a rule book from a spectator to settle a dispute about pitching regulations.

Lucas announced the Maroons never again would play a game officiated by Decker, who, not too surprisingly, did not survive the season.

The White Stockings won the pennant and opposed the St. Louis Browns, Association champs, in the World Series.

A. J. Reach, editor of the Official American Association Base Ball Guide, described the action:

"The first game, which was played in Chicago, resulted in a tie (5-5). The second meeting (in St. Louis) resulted in a wrangle

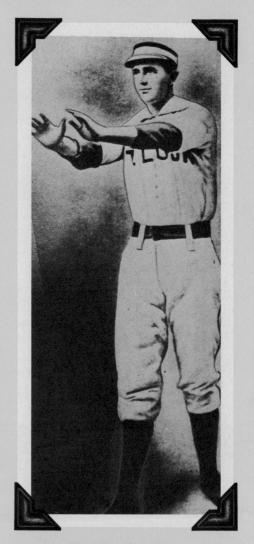

Charles A. Comiskey

in the sixth inning during which the spectators crowded upon the field and stopped the game. The St. Louis club led at the end of the fifth inning, but the Chicagoans were one run ahead when the game was stopped. The second game was won by St. Louis by a score of 7 to 4, and the third by a still closer score of 3 to 2. Both were played in St. Louis.

The fourth game was played in Pittsburgh and resulted 9 to 2 in Chicago's favor. The fifth game came off on the Cincinnatis' grounds and was won by Chicago by the same score of 9 to 2.

"When the two clubs met for the sixth game on the Cincinnati grounds on October 24, it was announced by umpire John Kelly in hearing of over one thousand spectators just preceding the beginning of the game that it had been agreed between the St. Louis and Chicago clubs that the game of that day would end their series, and as each club had won two games the result of the contest that afternoon would decide the Series and the question of the championship. Captains Anson and Comiskey of the two clubs stood close by while the announcement was being proclaimed and neither, by word or gesture, affirmed or denied it. The game proceeded and resulted in an overwhelming victory (13-4) for the American Association Champions.

"The Chicagos accepted their defeat philosophically and returned to Chicago. The press next day announced that the championship of America had been won by the St. Louis club. Later, however, the Chicagos laid claim to the unfinished game at St. Louis and declared the Series had been a draw. There are, however, one thousand witnesses in Cincinnati who will readily testify that umpire Kelly made the statement before the last game as above noted. Mr. Kelly, the oldest and best known umpire in the country, also will testify that he made the announcement at the request of both club captains."

The Spalding Guide reported that, because the Series ended in a deadlock, each club received $500, just half of what had been agreed upon if there had been a clearcut champion.

1886

Kansas City and Washington joined the league, replacing Buffalo and Providence.

A rule was introduced requiring that two baseballs be placed in the hands of the umpire at the start of a game and the umpire was able to call for a new ball any time he thought it necessary.

Doubleheaders were introduced, with Philadelphia and Detroit engaging in the first one, at Detroit, October 9.

The schedule was expanded from 112 games to 126 games, with each club meeting every opponent 18 times instead of 16.

Chicago won its second consecutive pennant, and fifth in seven years, spearheaded by Mike (King) Kelly. The versatile Kelly, whose flamboyant manners endeared him to the fans, stole 53 bases and inspired the cry "Slide, Kelly, Slide," which later became the title for a song.

Kelly, acknowledged as the inventor of the hit-and-run play, batted .388 as the White Stockings edged out Detroit for the pennant.

Possessed of a trigger-quick mind, Kelly,

noticing in one game that the Chicago catcher was unable to reach a high pop foul, stepped off the bench, announced, "Kelly now substituting," and caught the ball to retire the side in a crucial spot.

After the White Stockings lost the World Series to St. Louis, four games to two, with the winners taking all of the gate receipts, Chicago fans were benumbed to learn that Kelly had been sold to Boston for the unheard-of sum of $10,000. The salary limit, imposed by owners at the time, was $2,000, but The King was given an additional $3,000 "for the use of his picture."

One newspaperman reported that the Boston players were allowed only one pair of shoestrings a season. If a player could make a pair last two years, his fare on the horse cars would be paid one way either to or from the ball park.

Scoring rules were far from uniform. Some scorers understood that "battery errors," bases on balls, wild pitches and passed balls, were to be placed in the summary only. But about mid-season President Young issued instructions to "place bases on balls in the error column."

In Detroit, when property owners outside the park erected seats which they sold for cut-rate prices, the club attempted to bring legal action, which was refused. The club then erected a 50-foot fence to curb the practice.

In Philadelphia, New York catcher Tim Deasley, in full uniform, and three friends, all in an advanced state of inebriation, were refused admittance to the dressing room by the elderly attendant, Dave Brooks, during a game. Deasley assaulted Brooks, who started to choke the athlete. Deasley called for help, breaking up the game, bringing fans out of the stands and a squad of police officers, who restored order. New York Manager Jim Mutrie emphatically denied he had fined Deasley $100.

In New York, as a game was about to start, umpire John Gaffney announced he would not take the field unless John Montgomery Ward of the Giants apologized for an incident of the previous day. Ward refused, so Pud Galvin, Pittsburgh pitcher who was in the stands, called the game.

Of St. Louis it was written: "St. Louis plods wearily along. It is a surprise when they win and they do so only when Gaffney umpires or the opposing players are lame and sick."

Gaffney eventually resigned as an umpire and became manager of the Washington club.

The league still followed the old custom of tossing a coin before the game, with the winner given the choice of batting first or last. Anson of Chicago usually chose to bat

Mike Kelly . . . They all bowed to the King.

last, feeling that it gave his club an advantage.

1887

Pittsburgh and Indianapolis were new members, replacing St. Louis and Kansas City.

A new arrangement giving visiting clubs only a $125 guarantee instead of a percentage of the gate caused early dissatisfaction as the rich clubs grew wealthier and the less affluent clubs grew poorer.

King Kelly, coaching for Boston, called to a young visiting pitcher to "let me see the ball." When the pitcher complied, Kelly stepped aside, let the ball roll free and a Boston run scored.

At another time, The King called the Boston club off the field in protesting a decision. He later ordered his players back to their positions and, it was reported, Boston received all the better of the decisions thereafter.

When Ebenezer Beatin, the "Allentown Wonder," signed with Detroit, Cincinnati, Indianapolis and a few other clubs, the Board of Arbitration went into action, assigning the pitcher to Detroit, which had signed him first.

Philadelphia opened its new $80,000 park on April 30, drawing 14,500 and winning, 15-9, from New York which "caused consternation in New York as it played like minor leaguers."

When the Giants released Joe Gerhardt, Manager Jim Mutrie answered reporters'

Jim Mutrie

questions of why with, "Because I just felt like it."

President Young's instructions to umpires pointed out that "no pitcher was to lift his rear foot off the ground while delivering the baseball, not even to raise his heel or toes." Trying to comply, many pitchers strained their backs.

In Philadelphia one evening, the entire Indianapolis club "tied one on" and police made several arrests. During the disturbance, catcher Tug Arundel clouted a teammate on the head with a loaded cane and was sentenced to 30 days in the workhouse, which he was forced to serve.

When Governor David Hill of New York attended a game, an observant newsman reported: "A smile of Jeffersonian simplicity overspread the Governor's classic features as the New York players became greatly rattled and Chicago added four more runs to the list." Score: Chicago 9, New York 4.

Chicago fans complained loudly of the White Stockings' failure to overhaul Detroit, blaming it all on the sale of King Kelly. Spalding and Anson chose to blame it on the players. Anson fined James Ryan $100 for a trivial offense and Spalding fined Fred Pfeffer $125 for a "careless error."

But with it all, national interest in baseball was mushrooming. According to the Spalding Guide ". . . there never having been so many people at a ball match in either New York or Brooklyn, since the national game was established, as there were on Decoration Day when over thirty thousand people entered the Polo Grounds to see the championship matches between the Chicago and New York teams and over twenty-thousand saw the matches at Washington Park (Brooklyn) the same day between the St. Louis champions and the Brooklyn club team, each of the local clubs being defeated handsomely by the visiting club teams."

Detroit, N. L. champions, challenged the Browns to a World Series to consist of 15 games. The Series, reported the Reach Guide, was "carried forward on a scale of magnificence never heard of before in the baseball world."

The umpires were J. H. Gaffney, manager of the Washington (N. L.) club, and John Kelly, Louisville (A. A.) pilot.

The Series started in St. Louis, where two games were played on October 10, and shifted to Detroit for one game on October 13. From there the troupe moved to Pittsburgh, Brooklyn, New York, Philadelphia, Boston, Philadelphia, Washington, Baltimore, Brooklyn, Detroit, Chicago and St. Louis, where it concluded, October 26.

Detroit clinched the Series at Baltimore, 13-3, and finished with 10 victories.

Tim Keefe

The 15 games attracted 51,455 spectators, topped by 6,796 in Brooklyn. Receipts totaled $42,000 and expenses $18,000, the remaining $24,000 divided equally between the competing clubs.

1888

The White Stockings broke out in their new uniforms which were to be worn in the first game of each series. The new duds, costing $45 a copy, were of black broadcloth cut in full dress style and featured button-hole bouquets.

Sporting Life, popular weekly of the time, editorialized against one segment of the uniform. "The white pants should be discarded or made looser. As it is now they are skin-tight and positively indecent. Otherwise the new Chicago uniforms are the prettiest in the league."

The uniforms were laundered nightly and Cap Anson required his players to wear neckties on the field.

When the White Stockings marched from their clubhouse in the Polo Grounds prior to their first game, the Giants, in their regular uniforms, followed behind, attired in linen dusters and high white hats as a burlesque on their opponents' dress.

When umpires Phil Powers and Bill Furlong showed up to umpire a Chicago-New York game, both were pressed into service, signalling the start of the two-arbiter system which, it was reported, proved very unsatisfactory.

Honest John Kelly, former manager of Louisville, joined the league staff of umpires and immediately made headlines. At Louisville, Kelly had been reputed to be a teetotaler. As an arbiter, he left no doubts about his affinity for spiritous stimulants.

In Washington, Kelly went out on the town with two Congressmen, Hoss Radbourn and King Kelly. He arrived at the ballpark at 2 o'clock, slept for two hours, was given the "John L. Sullivan treatment," consisting of water in the face and a brisk rubdown, and strutted onto the field, to his customary round of applause, just slightly past the 4:30 starting time.

On September 21, Kelly failed to appear in Detroit, but he was on the job the next day after writing lurid headlines in the city's dailies.

With a Detroit gambler, a saloonkeeper and an unnamed New York player, Kelly visited a house of carnal delight on Bates Street, where Kelly jingled his money, ordered wine and sang a song: "I'm a Swell, You Bet."

Kelly shattered some furniture, then fell asleep, whereupon his friends grew quarrelsome and were asked to leave. Kelly roused and commenced throwing beer bottles at the girls. When the madam threatened to call gendarmes, Kelly hit an inmate, Emma Gordon, in the mouth with a water pitcher, dislodging two teeth.

At midnight, the revelers departed for another house of pleasure on Antonio Street, where they were admitted by the housekeeper, who was unaware of their condition.

Here Kelly shattered furniture and glassware, then hopped on a piano, where he did a can-can dance to the applause of his pals. Policemen, summoned to the scene, refused to arrest Kelly because they had not witnessed the misdemeanor.

Still going strong, Kelly and his cohorts left for still a third bordello, where everyone, including the girls, proceeded to get raging drunk. Kelly, falling against some furniture, suffered a bad gash in his head. The wound was bandaged and the umpire put to bed in the Hotel Cadillac. At noon, on complaint of Miss Gordon, he was arrested on charges of assault and battery and locked up. Friends heard of his troubles, looked up Miss Gordon and settled for $25, permitting Kelly to walk free in time to officiate at that afternoon's game.

The World Series format again was designed by the contending clubs and matched the Giants against the Browns, four-time A. A. winners. The tournament consisted of 10 games, starting in New York, October 16, when Tim Keefe defeated Silver King, 2-1. The Browns knotted the series the next day, 3-0. The Giants won the third game, in New York, the fourth game, in Brooklyn, the fifth in New York and the sixth in Philadelphia, before the series transferred to St. Louis for the final four contests.

St. Louis, trailing five games to one at that point, won the seventh game, but Keefe chalked up his fourth series win in the eighth game, 11-3. St. Louis won the two remaining games, but gate receipts of $411 and $212, respectively, reflected a pathetic lack of interest. Total receipts for the 10 games came to $24,362.

At the close of the season, A. G. Spalding, then owner of the Chicago club, arranged baseball's first international tour. Starting in Chicago, October 20, the White Stockings and a team of N. L. Stars played games at St. Paul, Minneapolis, Cedar Rapids, Des Moines, Omaha, Hastings, Denver, Colorado Springs and Salt Lake City, en route to the West Coast, where they played at Los Angeles and San Francisco.

Overseas, games were played at Hawaii, Sydney, Melbourne, Cairo, Naples, Egypt (where a Pyramid was used for a backstop), Rome, Paris and London.

1889

When the players on Spalding's world tour returned to the United States shortly before the opening of the season, they were appalled to learn that owners had adopted the Brush Classification Plan, designed by John T. Brush, Indianapolis owner, in which players were graded from A to E, with salaries ranging from $1,500 to $2,500.

Because the season was about to start, the players, many of whom were members of the Brotherhood of Professional Base Ball Players, were unable to fight the new system immediately.

However, John Montgomery Ward, Giant shortstop who held a law degree from Columbia and was president of the Brotherhood, called on the representatives from the various clubs to meet at the Fifth Avenue Hotel in New York, July 14.

At the conference, the players were instructed to return to their cities and attempt to secure funds to bankroll a new league. The results, Ward reported later, were encouraging.

On November 6, the players announced their withdrawal from the N. L. to form the Players League which, despite the lateness of the hour, was able to build parks in Boston, Brooklyn, New York, Chicago, Philadelphia, Pittsburgh, Cleveland and Buffalo before the start of the next season.

Lamenting the athletes' action, the Spalding Guide commented: "The fact that the secession movement had its origin in the New York team, which club had petted its players for years, only emphasized the fact of the ingratitude for personal favors done, which marks the average professional ball player."

By contrast, THE SPORTING NEWS hailed Ward as "the St. George of baseball, for he has slain the dragon of oppression."

Because the Polo Grounds was closed due to impending extension of 111th street through the property, the Giants opened the season in Jersey City and then played home games on Staten Island.

The "new Polo Grounds" at 155th street and 8th Avenue was dedicated on July 8, with more than 10,000 in attendance to see the Giants defeat Pittsburgh, 7-5. The visitors were attired in their new road uniforms consisting of black pants and shirt, that contained one orange cord, an orange belt and orange and black striped stockings.

The Indianapolis club, which had scheduled an exhibition game at Johnstown, Pa., May 31, was persuaded by Manager Harry Wright of Philadelphia to play a rained-out game of May 27 instead. At about the time the Indianapolis club would have been leaving the Hurlbut House for the ballpark, the hotel was struck by the rampaging waters of the Johnstown flood, drowning all the guests. Among the flood victims was Joseph Borden, who had pitched under the name of Josephs for the Boston club in 1876.

When the Giants defeated Cleveland to clinch the pennant, Owner John Day wired the folks at home: "The People will arrive at the Chambers Street Depot at 4:30 p.m. tomorrow via the Erie Road," giving birth to the cry, "We are the People."

The Boston Globe, which had promised to give $1,000 to the Boston players if they won the flag, gave the money to the Giants instead.

The Giants played Brooklyn in the World Series. The Giants captured the championship in nine games, with Hank O'Day, later an N. L. umpire, winning the clincher, 3-2. The Series attracted 47,256 spectators, 24,702 for four games in Brooklyn and 22,554 for five games in New York.

1890

War between the National League and the insurrectionist Players League erupted in full-scale fury early in the year, spewing

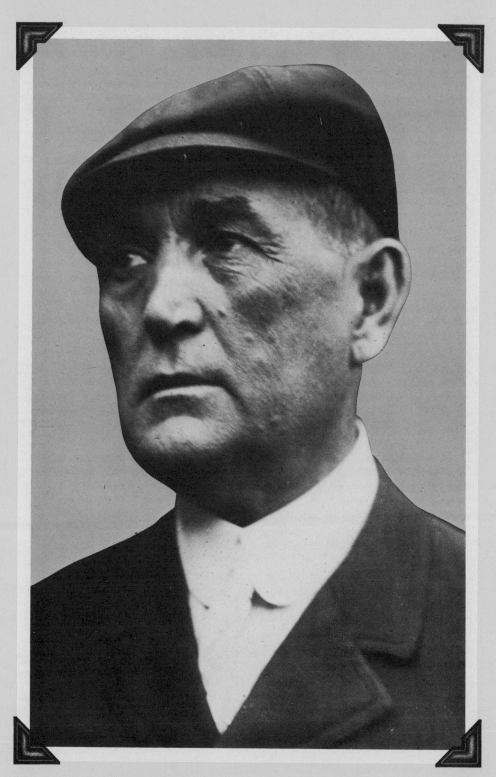

Hank O'Day . . . Payoff pitcher for the Giants.

court suits, slander, chaos and impoverishment.

An estimated 80 percent of the N. L. players jumped to the new circuit, including the entire Washington team, which moved to the Buffalo club of the Players League. Among the jumpers was an angular catcher by the name of Connie Mack.

To combat the outlaws, the N. L. dropped the Washington and Indianapolis franchises, replacing them with Brooklyn and Cincinnati. As a result, the two leagues went head-to-head in seven cities, the only one-club cities being Cincinnati in the N. L. and Buffalo in the P. L.

After the National League published its schedule, the P. L. issued its own schedule, whereupon the N. L. released a revised slate in which its teams competed almost daily with rival clubs for hometown patronage.

Shocked to their senses by the trend of events, N. L. owners appointed a "War Committee," consisting of A. G. Spalding of Chicago, John B. Day of New York and Col. John I. Rogers of Philadelphia, to launch an all-out campaign for survival.

Through press releases, friendly sportswriters and undercover tactics, the committee sought to undermine the P. L. Once Spalding offered King Kelly $10,000 and a three-year contract at Kelly's terms to desert the Boston P. L. club. The King asked for time to take a walk and think over the matter. On his return, he refused the offer because "I couldn't let the boys down," and then borrowed $500 from the Chicago club president.

When the P. L. issued suspiciously high attendance figures, Spalding stationed agents at the turnstiles to compile their own totals, which he subsequently published to the embarrassment of the P. L.

Gate figures for the season were listed as 980,687 for the P. L. and 813,678 for the N. L., but in view of the leagues' contest of one-upmanship, the figures have little validity.

As the P. L. playing season progressed, Buffalo and Cleveland fell from contention quickly. In the N. L., Pittsburgh and Cincinnati encountered difficulties. Pittsburgh used 50 players during the season that produced 113 defeats, including 23 in a row. On Labor Day, it dropped a triple-header to Brooklyn and the turnstile count for one game came to 26.

Perhaps the sorriest figure in the sanguine struggle was John B. Day, the Giants' owner. A dedicated baseball man, he rejected a $25,000 offer to serve as president of the Brotherhood. Day chose to remain loyal to the N. L., and borrowed nearly $90,000, including $25,000 each from Spalding, Soden and Brush, before tossing in the towel and selling the club.

In 1923, Day was discovered, paralyzed and broke, living with his wife, dying of cancer, in a furnished room in lower Manhattan, bereft of funds to buy food.

At the close of the season, the Players League, battered and bruised, sued for peace, a consummation readily granted by the older circuit. The Players League deficit was placed at $340,000, which included $215,000 in park investment. The N. L. losses were estimated as high as $500,000.

With most of the headline players in the Players League, the World Series between Brooklyn and Louisville created minimal interest. Each team won three of seven games, with one contest ending in a tie.

1891

Peace did not come immediately to the warring factions. Time was required to hammer out the articles of agreement and many a temper was thrown over alleged inequities in the re-assignment of players.

According to peace terms, all the players who had been reserved by National League clubs for the 1890 season should now report to those clubs.

One of the sharpest controversies raged over Louis Bierbauer, a second baseman, and Harry Stovey, fleet-footed and heavy-hitting outfielder, both of whom had been with the Athletics in 1889 before jumping to Brooklyn and Boston, respectively, in the Players League.

Unfortunately for the Athletics, neither player had been reserved, paving the way for Pittsburgh of the N. L. to sign Bierbauer, thereby earning the nickname of Pirates, which survives to 1976.

The American Association intended to assign Stovey to its new Boston club, but the athlete chose the Boston N. L. club instead.

The dispute was referred to the National Board, the new governing body for professional baseball, consisting of representatives of the three leagues in the new National Agreement, John I. Rogers of the National League; Allan W. Thurman of the American Association and L. C. Krauthoff of the Western Association.

"Reluctantly," the Board voted to permit the athletes to play with their new clubs. The deciding vote was cast by the A. A. representative, who was instantly branded a traitor.

On August 25, when a six-man peace committee (three from each league) was about to convene in Washington to forge terms of a truce, word arrived that King Kelly, ever the headline grabber, had jumped his Boston N. L. club and joined the A. A. club in the same city. One term of the inducement was a trip to Europe for him and his wife.

Connie Mack . . . He answered the call of the Players League.

Kelly's action threw a wrench into truce talks for several months, but on December 15, at Indianapolis, details were worked out for the N. L. to absorb four A. A. franchises, Baltimore, Washington, St. Louis and Louisville, thus expanding to 12 clubs.

The remaining A. A. clubs, Boston, Philadelphia, Columbus, Milwaukee and Chicago, were bought out for varying amounts that totaled $130,000.

After Chicago beat Cincinnati on April 30, umpire Phil Powers approached Tony Mullane of the Reds and asked: "You don't think I was going to rob the Chicagos just to please you, do you?"

Mullane answered: "No, you did nothing but rob us."

The remark cost Mullane $100 on the spot.

"I don't care if you make it $1,000, you pea-headed chump," said Mullane, making a pass at the arbiter and grazing his chin.

More fists were swung, and Powers levied more fines totaling $250. The league, however, ruled that Powers had exceeded his authority after the game and had made the first remark, so no fines were assessed.

Pittsburgh released pitcher Henry Staley for "lushing," but pitcher Jim Galvin, who had 15 children, corrected his habits and was retained by the same club.

The Giants were ordered by the Board of Aldermen to cover their "bleaching boards with awnings" at the Polo Grounds within 30 days or face a fine of $100 per day.

Pete Browning, the Gladiator, drew a $50 fine for playing with spikeless shoes at Pittsburgh. The Pirates bought Pete a pair of cloth shoes, but released him shortly thereafter and he caught on with Cincinnati, breaking in with a triple and single on July 1.

In mid-season, 39-year-old Cap Anson appeared on the field wearing a flowing beard and hair, played the entire game and helped Chicago defeat Boston, 5-3.

Boston, the league's best-paying club, with salaries totalling $57,000, won the pennant, beating Chicago by 3½ games.

Harry Stovey

James Galvin

Tony Mullane . . . 'Robbery' cost him $100.

1892

With the American Association dead and buried and all competition for talent eliminated, the players' bonanza in the National League quickly deteriorated. Conditions grew more intolerable than what they had been before the birth of the Players League.

In June, the owners reduced club rosters from 15 to 13 players and simultaneously slashed salaries from 30 to 40 percent.

All clubs engaged in paring their payroll except Brooklyn and Philadelphia, which had taken care of the matter before the start of the season.

Louisville cut the pay of half its players, Boston cut everyone, although it was leading the league at the time. Tony Mullane, who already had won 21 games for Cincinnati, was asked to take a cut from $4,200 to $3,500. He refused and joined Butte of the Montana State League. The following January, he signed for $2,100.

Tommy Lovett, a Brooklyn pitcher, remained out of the game all season rather than accept a cut, losing $3,000. His teammate, George Haddock, a 34-game winner in 1891, capitulated after a two-month holdout, and Charles Buffinton, a 28-game winner the previous season, came to terms in time to win five games.

Tom Burns enjoyed better luck. When the Pirates sought to fire their player-manager, who had a three-year contract for $4,500 a year, he took them to court and won a $1,500 settlement.

Recounting the club owners' get-tough policy, Dr. Harold Seymour, in BASEBALL, THE EARLY YEARS, wrote:

"By October nearly all clubs gave their players 10 days notice that they would be released at the end of the playing season. Since the contracts ran to November 1, the players would lose two weeks' pay. But the men were really not free agents, because the clubs . . . acted in collusion by agreeing not to hire each other's men. As the New York World said, these were 'releases that did not release.' The whole thing was simply an expedient to save on salaries. It also softened up the players for further salary cuts in 1893."

There were three exceptions to the early "release" policy, Boston and Cleveland, which, as winners of the split-season schedule had to remain intact for the championship Series, and Chicago, which, according to Cap Anson, would wait and talk salary reduction in a determined manner.

In New York, John B. Day announced to his players that he was strapped for funds, and offered them 25 cents on the dollar, with promissory notes for the balance, a deal which they accepted. Philadelphia players protested vehemently to the loss of two weeks' pay so John I. Rogers arranged a two-week exhibition schedule whereby the players would not lose any income.

One of the major accomplishments of the season was Wilbert Robinson's seven-for-seven hitting performance for Baltimore on June 10 in the first game of a doubleheader. Curiously, little attention was paid to the achievement either in the daily papers or the weekly sports publications. Robinson's feat occurred in the Orioles' 25-4 victory over St. Louis, a game that was completed in the surprising fast time of one hour and 50 minutes.

There was a new rule that permitted a change in personnel at any point of the game.

The championship series between Boston and Cleveland called for nine games, three in Cleveland, as many in Boston and the remainder, if needed, on neutral grounds.

The opener wound up in an 11-inning scoreless tie, after which the Beaneaters swept the next five contests.

James Buffinton

Wilbert Robinson . . . Seven hits in one game.

1893

Rules changes lengthened the pitching distance from 50 feet to the current 60 feet, six inches, the pitcher's box was replaced by a rubber slab, 12 by four inches, and a batter who sacrificed was excused from a time at bat.

The revised rules produced an abundance of .300 hitters as pitchers experienced difficulty adjusting to the new regulations. A total of 65 players batted more than .300, led by Hugh Duffy, the league champion, at .378, Sam Thompson, .377, George Davis, .373, Jesse Burkett, .372, and Buck Ewing, .371.

Fred Lieb, in THE BASEBALL STORY, explains how the six inches came to be added to the pitching distance.

"The original intent was to increase the distance 10 feet—to 60 feet—and one of the National League rules committeemen handed a surveyor the new specifications, reading 60 feet, 0 inches. The surveyor took the '0' inches to be '6' inches and made the new infield accordingly. And there it has remained."

If the athletes thought they suffered severe salary slashes in 1892, they were in for an even greater shock the following season.

A salary comparison of four Philadelphia players showed that lefthanded catcher John Clements, who earned $2,450 before the Players League entered the fight for talent, and $3,000 in 1892, when the American Association was still operating, was now playing for $1,800 annually.

Ed Delahanty went from $1,750 to $2,100 to $1,800; George Hallman, from $1,400 to $3,500 to $1,800, and Sam Thompson from $2,500 to $3,000 to $1,800.

Although the salary limit was not spelled out, it was generally understood that a $2,400 ceiling was in effect, with a club limit of $30,000.

When the owners, attempting to justify their retrenchment policy, asked lamely what the players would earn if they were forced to seek a livelihood in another line of endeavor, THE SPORTING NEWS replied: "What would anyone earn outside his line? Sportswriters, for instance?"

Commenting on the position of the players in this unilateral situation, Dr. Seymour wrote:

"There was little the players could do except take their cuts. Unionism had died among them as the result of the Brotherhood defeat. Now there was nothing for it but to take what was offered, or else, as Jim Hart said, 'Retire from the business.' The players' weakened bargaining power is demonstrated by a letter from the Brooklyn manager, the same John Ward who led the players' revolt, to Bill Joyce, one of his players, who had wired requesting $200 advance money. Ward's reply, while composed in a humorous vein, still brings out the changes in the players' position:

Either you are joking, William, or you are away behind the times. Haven't you heard yet of the consolidation of the League and Association into one big league? And if so, don't you understand the days of advance money are past? Why, my innocent William, hereafter it is the players who are to pay advance money to the magnates . . . Your inning is over, my boy,. Wake up . . . Get a move on you, William.

Later Joyce was traded by Brooklyn to Washington, which offered him a $1,800 contract, compared with one calling for $2,800 in 1892. He sat out the entire season, but signed for 1894.

Although clubs were not required to pay injured or sick players, they did so on occasion. When Cleveland paid an ailing athlete, it was hailed for being "humane."

Baltimore acted in a similar lofty manner, giving John McGraw $1,200 when the future Hall of Famer returned from a long idleness produced by typhoid fever.

Boston won its third consecutive pennant under Frank Selee, beating out Pittsburgh by 4½ games.

Frank Selee

John McGraw . . . Typhoid fever, and then $1,200.

Ed Delahanty   **Sam Thompson**

1894

Pitchers still were encountering difficulty in adjusting to the longer mound-to-plate distance and batting averages skyrocketed.

Four players posted averages in the .400 class, including Hugh Duffy, .438, and the entire Philadelphia outfield, George Turner, .423, Ed Delahanty, .408, and Sam Thompson, .400.

Cap Anson, 40 years old and in his 24th season, batted .395.

Three clubs suffered heavy fire damage to their facilities during the season.

On May 14, during the third inning of the game between Baltimore and Boston, a conflagration started in a pile of rubbish beneath the stands at Boston. In less than three hours, flames consumed structures on 12 acres, including the grandstand and bleachers, a large school house, an engine house and 164 wooden buildings. Loss was estimated between $300,000 and $1,000,000.

During the last half of the sixth inning at Chicago August 5, fire broke out in the 50-cent seats, which was chronicled by the Reach Guide as follows:

"Anson was at the bat and all eyes were directed toward him. One man cried, 'Fire!' but he didn't seem to attract any attention except from those near him. Persons began to move away from the spot and the crowd thought there was a fight in progress. The flames made great headway, however, and the alarm was given by hundreds of voices. This caused great excitement and everyone wanted to get out first. The players, meanwhile, paid no attention to the cries, and Anson held his position at the home plate, bat in hand, and would not turn his head. Four strands of barbed wire had been placed in front of the grandstand and the bleachers, to keep the people from crowding out into the field. Escape for a time was cut off in that direction. The stairways proved entirely inadequate to accommodate the hurrying throng, and the fire was making such rapid strides that the crowd turned again to the barbed wire. Seats were wrenched from the reserved section and the wires were broken down. Then a perfect flood of humanity went over into the field. Men and women were trampled under foot and jumped upon and several hundred persons received injuries of a more or less serious character. Before the fire could be controlled, one half of the grandstand was destroyed and all the bleachers and 50-cent seats. The improvements were new and had been made at a cost of $45,000. The loss was about $18,000. Later on, the same grounds was visited by another fire which destroyed nearly all of the buildings left by the first conflagration."

The third fire of the season occurred in Philadelphia, August 6, while the team was practicing and within an hour had levelled what was described as "the finest baseball stands in the United States" to a mass of smouldering ruins. The fire was believed to have started in the ladies rest room from inflammables left by some plumbers. The stands had been built at a cost of $80,000 and were replaced immediately by the club.

Hugh Duffy . . . .438-hitting outfielder for Boston.

In a Memorial Day afternoon game, Bobby Lowe, Boston second baseman, gained the distinction of being the first player to hit four homers in one game, performing the feat in a 20-11 victory over Cincinnati.

The Baltimore Orioles won the first of three successive pennants, edging New York by three games, and were overwhelming favorites to defeat the runners-up in the post-season series for the Temple Cup, which had been placed in competition by William Chase Temple, former president and still stockholder of the Pittsburgh club.

When the Orioles, who had celebrated their championship roisterously, lost the series in four straight games, Temple grew so disgusted he sold his 200 shares of Pittsburgh stock and left baseball.

Later it was disclosed that five Baltimore players had agreed to split their shares with as many New Yorkers. A split share was worth $564. When the New York players refused to honor their agreement, the story became public knowledge.

Harry Von Der Horst, brewer-owner of the Orioles, was convinced that "the whole Temple Cup business has been a farce and I shall offer a resolution at the coming meeting that the trophy be returned to Mr. Temple with thanks."

League directors rejected Von Der Horst's proposal and the cup remained in competition for three more years.

Entering the season, the treasurer's report at the annual meeting showed that the league had paid off its $140,000 indebtedness, incurred in the consolidation with the American Association, and had a balance of $25,000. Treasurer Nick Young proposed a dividend, reducing the surplus to $5,000, but the suggestion was rejected.

Only one of the 12 clubs finished the 1894 season in the red, one or two clubs broke even and the remainder reported profits ranging from $5,000 to $40,000.

Horizons were limitless for the baseball monopoly, particularly since an attempt to revive the American Association had been squelched ruthlessly. Three of the organizers of the aborted loop were National Leaguers who, for their disloyalty, were hailed before the high tribunal, where they and all of baseball were warned that future efforts to organize a rival league would result in permanent disbarment.

1895

The Orioles, rapidly becoming the most famous and feared of baseball clubs, slashed, stomped and stormed their way to a second pennant, finishing three lengths ahead of Cleveland.

Managed by Ned Hanlon and featuring Hall of Famers-to-be like John McGraw, Hughie Jennings, Willie Keeler, Wilbert Robinson and Joe Kelly, the Orioles supplemented their baseball talents with fists and spikes to subdue the opposition.

Honus Wagner, great Pittsburgh shortstop, once recalled that he had made a triple out of what should have been a home run because the first baseman gave him the hip as he rounded the bag, the second baseman "almost killed me, Jennings tripped me at shortstop and when I got around to third, McGraw was waiting for me with a shotgun."

Appraising the Orioles in later years, John A. Heydler, an umpire in the '90s and subsequently president of the league, told Fred Lieb:

"They (the Orioles) were mean, vicious, ready at any time to maim a rival player or an umpire if it helped their cause. The things they would say to an umpire were unbelievably vile, and they broke the spirits of some very fine men. I've seen umpires bathe their feet by the hour after McGraw and others spiked them through their shoes. The club never was a constructive force in the game. The worst of it was that they got by with much of their browbeating and hooliganism. Other clubs patterned after them,

William Chase Temple

Bobby Lowe . . . First with four homers in one game.

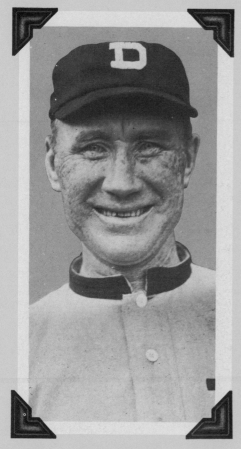

Hugh Jennings

Willie Keeler

and I feel the lot of the umpire never was worse than in the years when the Orioles were flying high."

In the Temple Cup Series against Cleveland, however, the Orioles fared only slightly better than in 1894, winning one of the five games, a 5-0 decision in the fourth contest. Cy Young won three games for the Spiders, 5-4, 7-1 and the clincher, 5-2.

Gross receipts exceeded $15,000 and the player shares, computed on a 60-40 basis, rather than 65-35 as in 1894, amounted to $528 for the winners and $316 for the losers.

On their return home, the Spiders were guests at a huge civic banquet sponsored by the Elks. The editor of the Spalding Baseball Guide, duly impressed with the opulence of the occasion, reported:

"A feature of the table ornamentation was a design about four feet square, representing a baseball diamond, with a spider on each base, a spider for pitcher and an open oyster, symbolic of the Baltimores, lying open midway between home plate and first base, with four spiders walking over it and eating it up. . . . Among the special guests were the Mayor of the city, the Treasurer and the sheriff. Mr. Temple was invited, but was unable to be present. He sent a nice letter of congratulations, however."

Harry Wright, the British cricketeer who managed baseball's first professional team, the Cincinnati Red Stockings of 1869, died of cerebral pneumonia at Atlantic City, October 8.

And Cap Anson, Chicago manager, made his dramatic debut at Syracuse, N. Y., in November, when he starred in a play written especially for him entitled, "A Runaway Colt."

1896

A $200 fine, the result of a breach of team discipline, resulted in Amos Rusie, great New York pitcher, remaining out of baseball for the entire season.

Cy Young . . . Trimmed the Oriole feathers three times.

When the righthander, winner of 22 games in '95, received his contract, calling for a $200 deduction, he refused to sign unless he was reimbursed, which the club flatly refused to do.

A deadlock developed and Rusie presented his case to the National Board, which refused to rule on the grounds that it had no jurisdiction in such matters.

Rusie then appealed to the National League Board of Directors, which met on June 29 and voted unanimously in approval of the New York club's action.

In November, Rusie filed two suits in the Federal Court in Chicago, one seeking $5,000 in damages, the other enjoining the Giants from reserving the pitcher for 1897. Because neither party to the suits was a resident of Illinois, both were dismissed.

Later Rusie filed the suits in New Jersey, but before they could be heard, N. L. directors, uneasy over growing public sympathy for the pitcher and eager to avoid a court test of the player contract, collected a reported $3,000 to reimburse Rusie for the 1895 salary he did not receive.

An early-season incident at Louisville resulted in fines to four Cleveland players for disorderly conduct and assaulting an umpire.

Manager Pat Tebeau was assessed $100, Jimmy McAleer and Jess Burkett $75 apiece and Ed McKean $50. The league Board of Directors, at its June meeting, took up Tebeau's case and ordered President Nick Young to fine the Cleveland firebrand $200, with the stipulation that the fine be paid within 10 days.

As time was about to expire, Tebeau went to court, seeking to restrain Young from collecting the fine on the grounds that the N. L. constitution granted an accused player the right of notice before trial and a chance to

Amos Rusie

Jimmy McAleer

defend himself before the Board, a right that had been denied him. The court upheld Tebeau and issued a permanent injunction against the National League collecting the fine.

Late in the season, according to the editor of the Reach Baseball Guide, the four players "appeared before the Louisville court by counsel and confessed judgment for $10 each, which was accepted and the whole case ended."

On July 13, at Chicago, Ed Delahanty of Philadelphia clouted four home runs and a single, thereby duplicating Bobby Lowe's four-homer feat of two years earlier for Boston.

Baltimore made a runaway of the pennant race, beating out Cleveland by 9½ games, and atoned for past post-season transgressions by sweeping the Spiders in four games, beating Cy Young, 7-1, in the opener and following up with 7-2, 6-2 and 5-0 victories.

Total attendance came to 14,300 and net receipts only $12,000. A winning share was worth about $200, each loser's $115.

1897

Twenty games during the season resulted in ties and eight were forfeited. Among the reasons for forfeits were: a balk decision, delay of game because of an approaching rainstorm, a pitcher soiled a new baseball, a player refused to leave the field when ejected by an umpire and one player was not in uniform when inserted into the lineup.

When Louisville and New York played a doubleheader at the Polo Grounds on July 3, league directors voided the result of the first game, maintaining that the twin-bill violated a league rule permitting doubleheaders only in the last series of the season between two clubs.

One of the season's lustier brawls occurred at Cincinnati, August 4, when fans, protesting a call by Tim Hurst, threw beer glasses at the arbiter, who promptly threw the missiles back from whence they had come.

One of Hurst's projectiles struck an off-duty fireman on the head, badly injuring him. Hurst was arrested, released on bond, re-arrested two days later in St. Louis, released on habeas corpus proceedings, umpired the game under surveillance, returned to Cincinnati, was tried and fined $200.

One of baseball's most glittering careers came to an end when Adrian Constantine (Cap) Anson, 45 years old and a major leaguer since 1872, called it quits after batting .303 for Chicago.

At the same time, a career that could have been among the foremost of all time flared brightly, then terminated in sodden ruination.

Louis Sockalexis, a Penobscot Indian from Old Town, Me., batted .331 in half a season with Cleveland. The future appeared unlimited until Sockalexis discovered whiskey and plummeted as rapidly as he had soared. He was reduced to beggary on the streets of Cleveland, found his way back to Maine and died there at age 42 in 1913.

Willie Keeler established a league record by hitting safely in his first 44 games before Frank Killen of Pittsburgh shut him out on June 18.

Baltimore made a determined bid to win its fourth consecutive pennant and led Boston by one point .707 to .706, at the start of the season-ending series between the two clubs.

Tim Hurst

Boston won the opener, 6-4, and Baltimore the second, 6-3, delaying the outcome of the race until the final game.

When the Oriole management sold 25,390 tickets for the finale, far exceeding the park's capacity, fans rimmed the playing field, shoving the outfielders to positions just behind the infield. Any ball hit into the crowd was an automatic double. In a game that was no true test for either club, Boston triumphed, 19-10.

With fan interest drained by the pulsating climax, few cared that the Orioles won the Temple Cup from the Beaneaters, four games to one.

It marked the third time in four years that a second-place club had won the big prize, after which it was abandoned.

1898

One of the most controversial figures in the early years of the National League was Andrew Freedman, owner of the New York Giants.

Freedman purchased the club in January, 1895, and almost immediately became a storm center of frequent clashes involving players and fellow owners. It was Freedman whose fining of Amos Rusie led to the pitcher remaining out of baseball the entire season of 1896.

Freedman was at his controversial worst in 1898, the year of the lobster incident at the Polo Grounds.

As described by Lee Allen in THE NATIONAL LEAGUE STORY:

"A typical example of Freedman in action was provided by the Ducky Holmes riot. Holmes, who had played in the outfield for the Giants in 1897, was a member of the Baltimore team that visited the Polo Grounds, July 13, 1898. In the fourth inning, with the score tied, 1-1, he struck out.

" 'Oh, Ducky, you're a lobster. That is why you were chased off the New York team,' a fan yelled.

" 'I'm glad I don't have to work for that Sheeny any more,' Holmes shouted.

"That vulgar but rather trifling exchange should have ended the matter. But as the teams were changing sides at the end of the inning, Freedman charged down on the field with a group of police and tried to remove Holmes from the game. The umpire, Thomas J. Lynch, said he did not hear the remark that Holmes addressed to the fan and threatened to forfeit the game to Baltimore if Freedman and the police did not stop interfering with play. But Freedman would not leave and Lynch forfeited the game.

"Freedman's arrogant violation of league rules in interfering with play on the field and his deliberate forfeiture of the game indicated a singular fatuity. Only one New York newspaper agreed with his stand, and in other cities the papers were unanimous in condemnation of him.

"When the row with Holmes started, the Baltimore club had received its share of the gate receipts. After the incident, Freedman reimbursed the spectators deprived of a game because of his folly and then demanded that the Baltimore club, which had done nothing to cause the forfeit, return its share of the receipts. Baltimore refused to do this and Freedman stopped payment on the check.

"Baltimore then demanded that the New York club be fined $1,000 for deliberately forfeiting a game as provided for by league rules. Freedman deposited the money with the league president, Nick Young, pending disposition of the case and sailed for Europe. He also announced that Holmes would never be permitted to play in another game at the Polo Grounds, but failed to say how he would accomplish this."

League directors voted that the forfeit and the fine should stand, but also suspended Holmes for the remainder of the season. Holmes obtained an injunction in Baltimore permitting him to play and the directors hurriedly reinstated Holmes by a vote of four to one.

The directors also refunded the $1,000 fine to Freedman at their meeting in December, 1899.

Although victims of no-hit pitching twice during the season, Boston repeated as league champions, beating out Baltimore by six lengths. Jim Hughes of Baltimore turned the no-hit trick on April 22 and Frank Donohue of Philadelphia on July 8. Walter Thornton duplicated the feat on August 21 against Brooklyn. The season's fourth no-hitter was achieved by Theo Breitenstein of Cincinnati against Pittsburgh on April 22, the same day as Hughes' feat.

From the Reach Guide: One of the queerest complications of baseball occurred in a game between Pittsburgh and St. Louis. In the eighth inning, Pittsburgh scored four runs and made the tally 7-7 with the side not out. Darkness was coming on. Swartwood was umpiring. He turned and asked Padden of the Pittsburgh club if the innings were even. The player, thinking he had been asked concerning the score replied, "Yes," and Swartwood called the game, imagining it a tie. The score reverted and St. Louis won.

1899

Syndicate ownership came into prominence and developed into a major concern for many as the result of deals involving Cleveland and St. Louis and Baltimore and Brooklyn.

In St. Louis, where the one-time "Poss Bresident," Chris Von der Ahe, had fallen on evil times, the Browns passed through several ownerships before they caught the eyes of Frank and Stanley Robison, Cleveland owners.

Unsuccessful in his efforts to sell the Spiders, Robison bought the Browns, which he stocked with some of the leading Cleveland players, including Jess Burkett and Cy Young. He also changed the color of the club's stockings, from brown to flaming red, prompting Willie McHale, a newspaperman, to call the club Cardinals, which soon became the official nickname.

Cleveland, weighted with all manner of nondescript talent, won only 20 games and lost 134, the poorest record in major league history. Six times it lost 11 consecutive games or more, and once dropped 24 in a row. Because of lack of support at home, the club played 113 of its 154 games on the road and was accorded nicknames such as Wanderers, Barnstormers and Exiles.

In the East, Harry Von Der Horst and Ned Hanlon of the Orioles purchased the controlling interest in the Brooklyn club, formerly held by the late Charles Byrne.

When Hanlon was named manager of the Dodgers, he presented the unique situation of serving as president of one club while managing another.

To strengthen the 10th-place club of '98, Von Der Horst and Hanlon switched Hughie Jennings, Willie Keeler and Joe Kelley to Flatbush, where they paid immediate dividends with a pennant-winner, while John McGraw was named manager of the Orioles.

Transferring games to other cities became a prevalent practice in a bid to increase revenue. The Washington club, after cutting in on a rich gate during a series in Philadelphia, switched all of its remaining home games with the Phillies to the Quaker City. For their action, the Washington owners were fined $1,000.

Although rowdyism was on the decline, umpires levied 184 fines at $5 apiece, or a total of $920 paid into the league treasury.

As the result of using an ineligible player, the champion Brooklyn club had 16 games wiped off its record, including 10 wins and six losses.

George (Zeke) Wrigley had completed his season with Syracuse and, while Brooklyn was negotiating with the Eastern League club for his purchase, the player signed with the Giants, for whom he played several games.

Andrew Freedman

On completion of the purchase, Brooklyn ordered Wrigley to join the Dodgers, for whom he played 16 games.

When the Giants appealed, the league board of directors ruled that the Dodgers had acted illegally in inducing Wrigley to leave the Giants and fined Brooklyn $500, in addition to erasing the 16 games in which Wrigley had played.

1900

Convinced that a 12-club league was too unwieldy and that top-to-bottom competition was nigh impossible, the league voted to reduce to an eight-club organization.

Acting on the recommendations of a committee, the league dropped Louisville, Cleveland, Washington and Baltimore.

The four clubs chosen for extermination demanded a total indemnification of $150,000, which would include about 70 players and the franchises.

The four clubs, moreover, suggested ways for the N.L. to raise the money, including an auction of the players.

Baltimore-Brooklyn delayed a decision at first, preferring to dispose of its own players. By March, the details were agreed upon and consisted of a $10,000 payment to Louisville, most of whose outstanding players, including Honus Wagner and Fred Clarke, had been transferred by Owner Barney Dreyfuss to Pittsburgh; $25,000 to Frank Robison for the Cleveland franchise; $30,000 to Baltimore, with the right to dispose of its own players, and $46,500 to Washington, minus $7,500, which it already had received for three players sold to Boston.

To raise the $104,000, the league agreed to set aside five percent of its gross receipts for the next two seasons.

In disposing of its players, Baltimore struck a snag; John McGraw, Wilbert Robinson and Billy Kiester refused to report to Brooklyn. The season was approximately one-third gone when Frank Robison, in St. Louis, obtained permission from the Brooklyn management to negotiate with the recalcitrants. He eventually paid $15,000 for the trio.

McGraw, cool to playing in St. Louis, signed a no-reserve clause contract calling for $100 a game, far above the going scale for that era. After playing 98 games for the Cardinals, and batting .337, McGraw jumped to Baltimore of the new American League, and then to the Giants.

National League players, who had been without organization since the collapse of the Brotherhood 10 years earlier, organized the Players' Protective Association and elected Chief Zimmer, Pittsburgh catcher, as president. At the first meeting of player and management committees, which was held in public at the players' request, three demands were submitted:

1.—The abolition of "farming" and claiming;

2.—The abolition of sales and assignments of players without their consent;

3.—The limitation of players' reservation to a fixed period of three, four or five years.

The Reach Guide reported: "The meeting adjourned with minimal expressions of good feelings."

Subsequently, the demands were softened in exchange for a new player contract.

A series between the championship Brooklyn and runner-up Pittsburgh clubs was played in Brooklyn. The Dodgers won three of the four games and were awarded the silver cup presented by the Pittsburgh Chronicle-Telegraph. Players of both teams earned about $400 apiece.

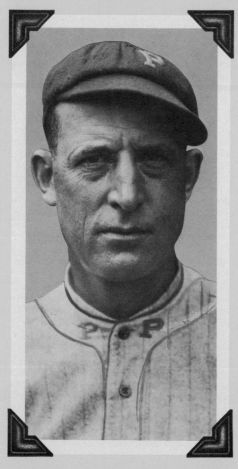

Fred Clarke

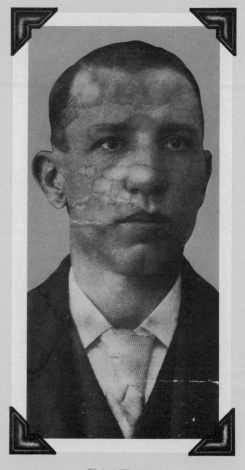

Chief Zimmer

The Toddling Years
1901-1925

✕⊖✕

William McKinley had been reelected to a second term in the White House. His Vice-President, Theodore Roosevelt, hero of the Spanish American War and the charge up San Juan Hill, was breathing a fresh vigor into American politics, although, to some, that animation portended evil.

One concerned politico allegedly inquired of delegates at the Republican national convention: "Don't any of you realize there is only one life between this mad man and the Presidency?"

The year 1901 would witness the first Nobel Prize in physics, presented to William Roentgen for his discovery of X-rays in 1895. Newspapers, as large as 40 pages and profusely illustrated with photographs, were being hawked on street corners and the gigantic United States Steel Corporation was created from the merger of 12 companies, partly because Andrew Carnegie was preparing to sell out for $492 million.

At the other end of the economic scale, immigrant children were working 10 to 12 hours a day as breaker boys in coal mines for as little as 35 cents.

During the year, the Yellow Fever Commission would discover the manner in which the disease was transmitted, the first wireless communication overseas would be established and oil would be found in Texas.

In New Orleans, a new type of music was germinating, a music combining plantation work songs, revival hymns, aboriginal voodoo, the new ragtime and street cries—something called jazz.

All the while Henry Ford continued to work on a gasoline engine in Detroit and Thomas Edison tinkered around the clock to perfect a new entertainment medium featuring pictures that moved.

While a few sophisticates discussed a German book, "The Interpretation of Dreams," published in 1900 by a Viennese doctor named Sigmund Freud, the National League, with its muscles rippling significantly, strolled clear-eyed and pur-

posefully into its second quarter century.

In the first season of the 20th century, the eight clubs would attract 1,920,031 spectators, nearly a quarter million more than the total registered by its new major league rival, the American League.

"For this good result," (the attendance superiority), reported the Reach Guide, "the National League was indebted first to a strict adherence to its policy of going along as though there were no war (with the American League), and second to the splendid showing made by the St. Louis, New York and Pittsburgh clubs, which enjoyed a monopoly of their productive territory."

1901

The National League encountered two powerful opponents in the first year of the new century, one from without, the other from within.

The American League, under dynamic and imaginative Ban Johnson, moved onto the scene, ignoring N. L. territorial rights, stealing players with finanical inducements in excess of the N. L.'s salary limits, and promising a brand of baseball in which umpires would receive complete league support and rowdyism would be extinguished so that more ladies could attend games.

More insidious than the external menace, and certainly more deadly, was the force working from within the league, a force that A. G. Spalding termed "Freedmanism."

Since entering the league as president of the Giants in 1895, Andrew Freedman had been conspicuous with his vile tongue and his ability to ruffle feathers.

By 1901, Freedman, Arthur Soden of Boston, John T. Brush of Cincinnati and Frank Robison of St. Louis formed a solid bloc against James Hart, Chicago; Charles Ebbets, Brooklyn; Barney Dreyfuss, Pittsburgh, and John I. Rogers and A. J. Reach, Philadelphia.

The factionalism exploded in full fury in late August after word leaked out that

Barney Dreyfuss . . . Stood tough against the syndicate.

Freedman and his cronies had met at Freedman's summer home in Red Bank, N. J., where they decided to toss out the National Agreement, under which baseball had functioned peacefully for many years, and institute syndicate baseball.

In this system, baseball would be operated as a trust, preferred and common stock would be issued and the operation of the league would be placed in the hands of a board of regents.

The anti-Freedman group appealed to Spalding for leadership. At the annual meeting in New York, December 11, Spalding was elected president by the Freedman opposition to replace Nick Young, by that time no more than a rubber stamp executive.

Freedman's group did not participate in the election, absenting itself from the hall, and when Spalding seized the league records from Young, Freedman obtained an injuction against the Chicagoan.

When harmony was finally restored, Freedman was forced to sell his interest in the Giants, Spalding resigned from the presidency which he never really held, and Harry Clay Pulliam was elected to the office.

Among the foremost players who jumped N. L. contracts in the interleague war were Nap Lajoie, Jimmy Collins, Clark Griffith and Cy Young, all future Hall of Famers.

One star who resisted Johnson's blandishments was Honus Wagner, the famous

Honus Wagner . . . Resisted new league's blandishments.

"Flying Dutchman," who batted .353 and led the Pirates to their first of three consecutive pennants under Manager Fred Clarke.

Willie Keeler, diminutive Brooklyn outfielder, coined his memorable contribution to baseball lore during a summer interview. Asked for a treatise on the science of hitting, the .345-lifetime hitter replied: "Keep your eyes clear and hit 'em where they ain't."

A new league rule prescribed a 16-player limit after May 15. To discourage "farming," a club was required to release a player every time it signed one in excess of the limit, and failure to do so was punishable at the rate of $500 a day.

1902

John J. McGraw, firebrand of the old Orioles, executed his second interleague "jump" within two years when, on July 19, he quit the Orioles to accept the position of manager of the New York Giants.

At the time of his second leap, McGraw was under indefinite suspension by Ban Johnson for umpire baiting. The maneuver brought down Johnson's full wrath on McGraw and the two never spoke again.

McGraw took with him to strengthen the last-place Giants five Baltimore players: pitchers Joe McGinnity and Jack Cronin, catcher Roger Bresnahan, first baseman Dan McGann and second baseman Billy Gilbert.

At the time, McGraw explained that he had obtained his release from the Orioles in exchange for "the club's substantial debt to me," but years later, considerably mellowed, he explained to Fred Lieb:

"I knew what Ban Johnson was up to. As far back as midseason of 1902, he made secret plans to drop Baltimore and move the franchise to New York. That was all right with me, as I expected to go along as manager, with a share in the club. But when I learned that I didn't enter into Johnson's New York plans, and that he was ready to ditch me at the end of the season, I acted fast. He planned to run out on me, so I ran out on him, and beat him to New York by nearly a year."

The Pirates raced roughshod through the 140-game schedule, beating Brooklyn by 27½ games, the largest margin by a winner in major league history.

Winning 103 games and losing only 36, the Pirates featured the hitting of Ginger Beaumont, the league batting king, Wagner and Clarke, but more impressive was their

Joe McGinnity   Roger Bresnahan

Jack Chesbro . . . 28 victories for the 1902 Pirates.

pitching staff that produced 130 complete games in 141 starts.

Jack Chesbro led the staff with a 28-6 record, followed by Deacon Phillippe, 20-9, Jess Tannehill, 20-6, and Sam Leever 16-7.

The Cincinnati club underwent a change in ownership, John T. Brush accepting $150,000 from a local syndicate consisting of the Fleischmanns, Max and Julius, who had amassed a fortune in gin and yeast, and George B. Cox, political boss of the city. When Julius Fleischmann was elected mayor, August (Garry) Herrmann, a rising politician in the city, was placed in charge of club operations.

With his $150,000, Brush went to New York where he purchased the Giants from Freedman.

At the league's annual meeting in New York in December, members voted to seek a peace agreement with the American League and appointed a committee to work out recommendations.

At a second meeting, in Cincinnati in January, earlier opposition by the Brooklyn and New York clubs was eliminated and the treaty was ratified.

1903

For the first time, the league president was invested with complete authority in the operation of the league.

At their meeting in New York, March 4-5, directors empowered President Harry Pulliam to discipline any manager or player at his discretion for violation of the rules or misbehavior of any kind.

At the same meeting, James Potter was introduced as a new owner of the Phillies, Potter and associates having purchased the club from A. J. Reach and John I. Rogers for $170,000.

Tragedy marked Potter's first year in office. On August 8, the overhanging gallery in the left field bleachers collapsed during a doubleheader with Boston, killing 12 spectators and injuring 282. As a result, remaining home games were transferred to the American League park of the Athletics.

Almost two months earlier, on June 9, the Phillies scored the run that snapped the Pirates' record streak of six consecutive shutouts (56 innings), in which Deacon Phillippe and Sam Leever blanked opponents twice, and Irwin (Kaiser) Wilhelm and Ed Doheny once each.

Pittsburgh was a big draw throughout the league and when Frank Bowerman, Giant catcher, assaulted Pirate Manager Fred Clarke at the Polo Grounds on June 26, the incident helped attract a record 32,240 the next day. On July 15, Bowerman was fined $100 by Pulliam.

With the two major leagues operating in

Harry Pulliam

Garry Herrmann

Deacon Phillippe

Sam Leever

harmony, Barney Dreyfuss, Pittsburgh owner, proposed a nine-game post-season series between his N. L. champions and the Boston Pilgrims, champions of the American League.

Before accepting the offer, Henry Killilea, Boston owner, sought the advice of Ban Johnson. "If you think you can beat 'em," replied Johnson, "play 'em."

After a formal agreement was signed, the Boston players refused to go along with the plan unless they received all the money given to the Boston club. Killilea appeased the athletes by granting them all the receipts, except a small portion for himself, and extending their contracts an additional two weeks.

Pittsburgh, handicapped by the absence of Doheny, who had suffered a complete mental breakdown, and a sore arm of Leever, nevertheless won three of the first four games, all by Phillippe. The Pirates never

won another game, however, Boston running off four consecutive victories to clinch the series. Bill Dinneen hurled the deciding game, spacing four hits, in a 3-0 triumph.

When Dreyfuss tossed the entire Pittsburgh share of the gate into the players' pot, he created the curious situation of the losers receiving a larger cut ($1,316) than the winners ($1,182). Phillippe received an extra check, plus 10 shares of Pirate stock, from Dreyfuss.

After the first modern World Series, Dreyfuss remarked: "I hope to win the pennant next year again. This would make it four in a row, one more than any other team ever won. This done, I will have enough. A baseball team is an expensive luxury, not a source of wealth, as is thought by many. The general impression seems to be that a great fortune is made each year by a winning ball team. I would like to say that if I depended on baseball for my living, I would be hungry often. I will trade my stock at par for a similar amount of stock at par in any good business at Pittsburgh."

The sportsman never fulfilled his promise.

1904

Sunday baseball, which was slowly moving into the strongholds of Puritanism, claimed another convert in April when the Brooklyn club announced its intentions of playing Sabbath games at Washington Park.

The first Sunday game was played on April 17 without incident, but when the Dodgers repeated a week later, catcher Fred Jacklitsch and pitcher Ed Poole of Brooklyn and catcher Frank Roth of Philadelphia were arrested as a test case. All were released under $200 bail.

On May 2, a New York judge declared Sunday baseball legal and ordered charges against the three players dropped. When the Dodgers met the Giants at Washington Park on May 29, another Sabbath, they attracted 20,000.

On June 18, however, the same Judge reversed himself, declaring that baseball on Sunday was illegal.

Because Pennsylvania banned Sunday ball, Barney Dreyfuss chartered a special train for $1,000 to convey the Pirates and Cardinals to St. Louis for a game in June. The distance was covered in the record-breaking time of 13 hours and 15 minutes.

When Iron-Man Joe McGinnity, winner of his first 12 decisions, went for No. 13 on June 11, a crowd of 40,000 jammed the Polo Grounds. McGinnity's streak was snapped when Bob Wicker of Chicago hurled an 11-inning, one-hit, 1-0 victory.

The New York Giants, who had finished last only four years earlier, won the pennant, beating out Chicago by 13 games, under the managership of John J. McGraw.

Philadelphia, which finished second three years previously, suffered in favor and at the gate when so many newcomers and regulars had poor seasons. James Potter stepped down and, on December 1, the club organized under a new charter with William Shettsline as the new president.

Giant Owner John T. Brush and Manager McGraw, who had announced as early as midseason that the club would not meet the American League champions if New York should win the pennant, held true to their promise. The club went on a two-week barnstorming trip with Jack Davis serving as manager, and then disbanded.

Explaining his decision to reject the World Series challenge, Brush said: "There is nothing in the constitution or playing rules of the National League which requires its victorious club to submit its championship honors to a contest with a victorious club in a minor league."

At their annual meeting in December, N. L. directors re-elected Pulliam as president, and endorsed a World Series for future seasons.

1905

Although the owners had vested the league president with full authority to run the game on the field as he deemed proper, this power was not always what it seemed to be.

John McGraw, for one, tested the authority and made a mockery of it.

On May 19, in a game at the Polo Grounds, McGraw, in a dispute with an umpire, accused the arbiter of being under the influence of Barney Dreyfuss. The Pirate owner was in the stands and overheard the allegation.

The next day, McGraw again ran afoul of the arbiters and was ejected. As he walked toward the clubhouse, Mac encountered Dreyfuss, chatting with friends, and accosted him with, "Hey, Barney."

Not content with this unwonted familiarity, McGraw ribbed Dreyfuss about alleged race track gambling, accused him of welshing on bets and tried to entice him into a $10,000 wager on the outcome of the game.

Dreyfuss filed a complaint and Pulliam called a directors' meeting for June 1 to consider the charges of crookedness against Dreyfuss.

McGraw denied that he had accused Dreyfuss of welshing on bets and then contacted Pulliam by telephone to protest that he was entitled to a hearing.

The Giant manager grew so abusive that Pulliam suspended him for 15 days and fined him $150 at the rate of $10 per day.

The directors, meeting on June 1, acquitted McGraw of wrong-doing in charging crookedness of Dreyfuss, and chided Barney for "indulging in an open controversy" with Mac.

McGraw and Giant Owner John Brush still were not appeased. Insisting that McGraw should have been offered an opportunity to present his side, they took the case to court and won a favorable decision from a Boston judge. Pulliam was restrained from enforcing the fine, and the umpires from keeping McGraw off the field.

Pulliam, crushed, declared that he would not observe two separate codes, "one for McGraw and the other for Dan McGann" (a Giant first baseman whom he had recently fined), and forthwith returned all fines in excess of $10 to earlier transgressors, a total of $490.

With Christy Mathewson winning 31

Christy Mathewson . . . Three shutouts in 1905 Series.

games, the Giants breezed to the pennant, beating Pittsburgh by nine games.

The first World Series under the auspices of the National Commission would have been an ideal showcase for a matchup between Matty and the Philadelphia Athletics' eccentric lefthander, Rube Waddell, who won 26 games and struck out 286 batters before September 1.

On that date, however, Rube engaged in some horseplay with a teammate on the railroad platform at Providence. He fell awkwardly on his shoulder and suffered an injury that sidelined him for the remainder of the season.

The championships turned into the "Shutout Series," with Matty winning three and Joe McGinnity one for the Giants and Chief Bender one for the A's.

A winner's share was worth $1,142, a loser's $832.

1906

John McGraw, driving the Giants toward what he hoped would be a third consecutive pennant, frequently ran afoul of authority, as did his players.

On August 6, the New York manager engaged in a verbal feud with umpire James

Dan McGann

Johnstone and was ejected from the game against the Cubs at the Polo Grounds. For his actions, McGraw was suspended by League President Pulliam.

The next day, when Johnstone arrived at the Polo Grounds, he was refused admittance by attendants and forfeited the game to the Cubs.

On August 8, the Giants protested the forfeiture, but were turned down by Pulliam, who reassigned Johnstone to the Polo Grounds. "The umpire," reported the Reach Guide, "was admitted without further protest and cordially received by the spectators."

The adverse decision did not stop the Giants, however. On August 19, they filed a civil suit against the Cubs, seeking $8,500 in damages for the Cubs' refusal to play the game on the day Johnstone was barred.

At its annual meeting in December, the league adopted a rule requiring all clubs to build separate dressing quarters for visiting teams. At the same time, Pulliam was re-elected president, with full disciplinary powers as in the past, and John A. Heydler was elected secretary-treasurer at an annual salary of $4,000.

At Pittsburgh on July 24, pitcher Joe McGinnity of the Giants took exception to "coaching" by Heinie Peitz and attacked the Pirate catcher. Iron Man Joe was arrested and hauled to the police station in a paddy wagon. He posted $50 bond for a hearing, but forfeited it the following day when he left the city with the Giants.

On July 31, McGinnity was fined $100 and suspended 10 days by Pulliam, Peitz was docked $50 and banned five days while umpire Hank O'Day was assessed $50 for failing to clamp down on Peitz.

Sunday baseball in Brooklyn continued to be a pressing issue. On April 15, the Dodgers played a voluntary-contribution contest at Washington Park without police interference.

On June 17, the gendarmes arrested Charles Ebbets, Dodger owner, Managers Patsy Donovan, Brooklyn, and Ned Hanlon, Cincinnati, and two players to make a test case of the Sabbath blue law.

Two days later, charges were dropped on the grounds that the law does not cover a "contributions plan."

On July 30, however, a justice of the New York Supreme Court issued a contrary decision, terminating Sunday ball in Brooklyn, at least for the time being.

The Cubs made a shambles of the pennant race, finishing 20 lengths ahead of the Giants, but then were beaten in the World Series by the "Hitless Wonder" White Sox, with a team batting average of .228. In six games, utility infielder George Rohe had

Charles Ebbets . . . A powerful voice in the council chambers.

Frank Chance . . . A "Peerless Leader" of matchless Cubs.

game-deciding triples in two games, a double and four RBIs.

On November 25, Arthur Soden sold the Boston Braves to George and John Dovey for $275,000.

1907

Although failing to match their record total of 116 victories of the previous season, the Cubs made it two pennants in succession by winning 107 games, finishing 17 lengths ahead of the Pirates.

Frank Chance, the celebrated Peerless Leader, topped Chicago batters with a .293 average. In July, Chance was suspended for four games by President Pulliam as the result of a rhubarb in Brooklyn. Target of a pop-bottle barrage from bleacherites, Chance tossed a bottle back at his tormentors, the missile striking a fan on the leg.

Mordecai (Three Finger) Brown followed up his 26-6 record of the previous season with a 20-6 mark while Orval Overall posted 23-8 and Ed Reulbach 17-4.

On March 10, Reulbach appealed to the

Mordecai Brown . . . Three-fingered Giant Killer.

National Commission, the game's ruling body, asking that he be released from reservation and his three-year contract because the Cubs had failed to tender him a contract before March 1. The appeal was denied on the grounds that the multi-year contract took precedence over the contract deadline.

John McGraw was relatively inactive as Peck's Bad Boy, being involved only in a scrap with a private guard in Cincinnati after a game, and tossing a cup of water in umpire Bill Klem's face at another time.

On January 10, while in Los Angeles, where the Giants trained, McGraw was hailed as a hero for stopping a runaway team of horses and saving two women from injury and possible death. McGraw was slightly injured.

The first damage suit growing out of the Philadelphia ballpark disaster of 1903 went to trial in Common Pleas Court in that city, March 6, with George L. Cunningham suing former Owners A. J. Reach and Col. John I. Rogers. The judge gave the jury binding instructions for acquittal, after which the case was appealed.

On April 11, the Police Commissioner of New York City informed the major league clubs that he would no longer furnish police for games in the metropolitan area. The same day, in the eighth inning of a game at the Polo Grounds, the crowd overran the field, forcing umpire Klem to forfeit the game to Philadelphia.

On May 18, Pulliam announced that the league, after a seven-year struggle, was out of debt. Three days later, he took official notice of an unusual squawk by Manager Fred Clarke of the Pirates, ruling that the new-fangled shinguards worn by catcher Roger Bresnahan of the Giants were not sufficient grounds on which to protest a game.

The Cubs needed only five games to defeat the Tigers in the World Series, including a tie in the opening game. A missed third strike with two out in the ninth inning helped Chicago score the tying run and umpire Hank O'Day called the game because of darkness after 12 innings.

Jack Pfiester, Reulbach, Overall and Brown then racked up the next four games, limiting, in the process, Ty Cobb, the A. L. batting champion, to four hits in 20 at-bats, a .200 average.

1908

Exactly what happened at the Polo Grounds on September 23 never will be determined, but there is no disputing the fact that what appeared to be a routine game-ending base-hit exerted a far-reaching influence on the lives of numerous people as well as on the history of the National League.

The Cubs and Giants, who battled the Pirates throughout the season for first place, were separated by only a few percentage points when they clashed before a crowd of 25,000. Jack (The Giant Killer) Pfeister drew the pitching assignment for the Cubs, future Hall of Famer Christy Mathewson for the Giants.

The visitors scored the game's first run when Joe Tinker, who had uncommon success against Matty, homered in the fifth inning, his low line drive eluding center fielder Mike Donlin, who attempted a shoestring catch, and rolling to the bleachers.

The Giants deadlocked the score in the sixth when Donlin singled to drive home Buck Herzog, who reached second base on an error.

The score remained 1-1 until the last half of the ninth inning when, with Moose McCormick on third base and Fred Merkle on first with two out, Al Bridwell hit what should have been a game-winning single to center field.

As was the practice of the day, Merkle headed for the clubhouse, disdaining the jog to second base.

As the exuberant crowd poured onto the

Bill Klem

field, Chicago second baseman Johnny Evers signaled frantically to center fielder Artie Hoffman to throw him the baseball.

Versions of what happened thereafter are in total disagreement. From somewhere Evers obtained a baseball. Whether it came from a young pitcher, Floyd Kroh, or another teammate, or whether it was the game ball, Evers gripped a baseball in his right hand, held it aloft for umpire Hank O'Day's attention and planted his foot on second base, maintaining that this constituted a forceout of Merkle.

At some point later in the day, O'Day announced that Merkle was retired and, because the crowd overran the field, making it impossible to continue the game, the score would remain a tie.

Giant tempers immediately shot skyward. Manager John McGraw maintained, not illogically, that Kroh had no license to be on the field, and as soon as he touched the baseball, it was dead. Furthermore, said McGraw, Cub outfielder Jack Hayden thought the game was over and left the field. Inasmuch as the Cubs did not have nine players on the field, added McGraw, further play was not possible.

Late that evening, after learning of O'Day's pronouncement, McGraw roused Merkle from a deep slumber at his hotel on Coney Island. At the request of the Little Napoleon, Merkle returned to the Polo Grounds and stepped on second base so that he could swear in an affidavit that he had, in truth, touched second base on September 23.

While the Giants were railing against O'Day, the Cubs worked up their own head of steam. Manager Frank Chance demanded that the Cubs be declared winner of the game by forfeit because the Giants, as the home club, had failed to provide the necessary number of attendants to clear the field so that the game could continue after the Merkle "forceout."

Rebuffed in that, Chance tried another approach. The next day, the Peerless Leader escorted his club to the Polo Grounds a couple of hours before the scheduled start of the game. At 1:30, the Cubs took the field and pitcher Andy Coakley threw four pitches to catcher Johnny Kling.

When the Giants and the umpires arrived later, Chance insisted that the Cubs be declared a forfeit winner because the Giants had failed to appear for the playoff of the previous day's tie. O'Day and Emslie ignored the demand.

A couple of weeks before the Merkle incident, O'Day had been challenged on a similar play between the Cubs and Pirates, with Evers insisting that the base-runner was out. On reflection, O'Day agreed with Evers and declared publicly that in the future he

Ed Reulbach

Jack Pfeister

would insist that a base-runner touch the next base under similar circumstances.

League President Harry Pulliam sustained O'Day's decision and, in turn, was backed by the league directors.

When the Cubs and Giants finished the regular season in a dead heat, a replay of the tie was ordered for October 8 at the Polo Grounds. Again Pfeister and Mathewson were the starting pitchers.

Pfeister failed to survive the first inning, departing after the Giants scored one run, in favor of Mordecai Brown, who had pitched in 11 of the Cubs' last 14 games, but had enough stamina left to pitch the remainder of the game and pick up the 4-2 victory that was highlighted by a Tinker home run and run-scoring doubles by Frank Schulte and Frank Chance.

As a result of the "Merkle incident," the 19-year-old first baseman was branded the remainder of his career with the nickname of "Bonehead."

McGraw stoutly absolved the youngster of all blame, pointing out that Merkle did

only what others had done for years, but few were willing to listen and Merkle played out a 14-year career under the cloud of his early misadventure.

The season was marked by renewed opposition to the spitball. Arguments against the freak delivery emphasized the unsanitary aspects, the unsightliness and the frequent errors committed by fielders on balls hit off the moist pitch.

At the league meeting in New York in February, a rule was adopted compelling all clubs to play out their complete schedule with all other clubs.

Honus Wagner, who had decided to sit out a season, was persuaded to rejoin the Pirates on April 19, five days after the start of the season, and was accorded a standing ovation.

On July 17, Pirate fans honored the great shortstop with a "Wagner Day," presenting him with numerous gifts that included a $700 watch.

Eight days later, on July 25, playing before a record crowd estimated at 34,000 at the Polo Grounds, Honus collected five hits, including two doubles, in five at-bats to help the Bucs beat the Giants, 7-2.

The league retained supremacy in the World Series, again defeating Detroit in five games as Brown and Overall notched two victories each and Pfiester suffered the only loss. Cub pitchers were less successful against Cobb, the two-time A. L. batting champion hitting .368 and stealing two bases.

After the Series, the Reach Guide reported, "Manager Frank Chance of the Chicago champions, with his wife, left Chicago for California without saying good-bye to President (Charlie) Murphy. It was announced the two had become seriously estranged." Chance retained his position until the end of the 1912 season.

In November, the Reds toured Havana, winning five games and losing seven against the Havana and Almendares teams.

1909

Harry C. Pulliam, who had succeeded Nick Young as league president at the start of the 1903 season, collapsed under the weight of the office after a six-year reign.

Speaking at a dinner of major league executives in Chicago in February, Pulliam announced, "My days as a baseball man are numbered. The National League doesn't want me as president any more. It longs to go back to the days of dealing from the bottom of the deck, hiding the cards under the table and to the days when the trademark was the gumshoe. Because I am for dealing above board and playing in the open, my

Fred Merkle . . . A dunce cap for a routine play.

days are numbered . . . I will have to quit at the end of this year for the owners want to revert to the old methods."

Recognizing the delicate state of Pulliam's health, friends obtained a leave of absence for Pulliam and turned direction of the league over to John A. Heydler, secretary-treasurer.

After several months, which included a tour of the southern states with Garry Herrmann, Pulliam returned to his office, apparently recovered. On July 29, however, Pulliam returned to his room at the New York Athletic Club and fired a bullet through his brain.

Heydler finished the season as operating head of the league, but refused to enter the race for the position at the winter meetings in New York. Giant Owner John T. Brush championed Thomas J. Lynch, one-time "King of Umpires" and now a theater owner in Connecticut, who was elected.

On April 23, Honus Wagner was the storm center of a huge rhubarb that resulted in a protested game and an admission from Bill Klem, the famous "old arbitrator," that he had missed a play, contrary to what he liked to tell folks in later life.

With Pittsburgh leading, 1-0, in the sixth inning, Wagner stepped across the plate while the pitcher was in the process of delivering the ball. Klem refused to call Wagner out, although very distinctly Honus had violated a rule.

When Clark Griffith, manager of the Reds, protested to Pulliam, the league president, who had not granted a protest previously, referred the matter to the board of directors—Herrmann, Charles Ebbets and George Dovey.

Klem defended his action by saying that to have called Wagner out would have been "ridiculous under the circumstances."

Herrmann replied that no "decision in accordance with the rules is ridiculous" and the board awarded the protest to the Reds. In the replay, the Reds lost, just as in the original game, but the Cincinnati club had the satisfaction of catching Klem in an improper call.

For the first time à President attended a ball game, William Howard Taft accepting an invitation to "President's Day" in Chicago, September 16. A special box had been constructed for the Chief Executive, who declined the honor. "Let me sit with the fans," requested Taft, one of 30,000 there.

Asked if he favored the Giants, 2-1 winners, or the Cubs, Taft replied, amid laughter, "I'm for the Reds." In his youth, Taft was an outstanding semi-pro player in Cincinnati and maintained a life-long interest in the game.

Barney Dreyfuss, on June 30, opened the league's newest showplace, his triple-decked steel ballpark, Forbes Field, Pittsburgh, attracting 30,338 for the occasion.

The Pirates made it a perfect year for Dreyfuss by ending the Cubs' domination with a 6½-game margin in the pennant race, followed by a victory, in seven games, over the Tigers in the World Series. Babe Adams, climaxing his first complete major league season, won three games for the Pirates. Wagner batted .333 for the winners, Cobb .231 for the losers.

Bill Abstein fanned 10 times during the Series, and was fired by Dreyfuss immediately thereafter.

1910

The thirty-fifth year of the senior circuit marked the debut of Horace Fogel as a major league executive.

Fogel, a Philadelphia newspaperman whose prior claim to fame was his attempt to convert Christy Mathewson into a first baseman during a brief spell as manager of the Giants in 1902, had headed a group that purchased the Phillies for $350,000 in the previous November.

To queries about his new-found affluence, the sportswriter asserted that "not a single dollar of outside money is invested in the club."

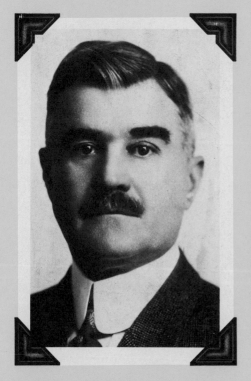

Thomas Lynch

Charles Webb Murphy

Horace Fogel

Shortly, however, it was disclosed that Charles Webb Murphy, owner of the Cubs, owned some of the action. The situation was identical to that of some years earlier when Andrew Freedman of New York attempted to install syndicate ball.

As a tool of Murphy, Fogel became an outspoken owner at league meetings and a bitter critic of umpires throughout the season.

Lynch encountered a lot of flak from other owners as well in his rookie season. When he fined Charles Ebbets $500 for "covering up" a player, the Brooklyn owner refused to pay, a stand in which he was supported by other directors.

For the first time, a cork-center baseball became available for major league play and made its influence felt immediately. Patented by A. J. Reach from an invention by Ben Shibe, owner of the Philadelphia Athletics, the new baseball boosted batting averages and led to the popularization of the hit-and-run play as a replacement for the sacrifice bunt, which had produced an abundance of pitching duels so displeasing to fans.

President William Howard Taft, who tossed out the first baseball at the Washington opener on April 14, thereby starting a practice that developed into a tradition, attended games at Pittsburgh and St. Louis, May 2 and 4, respectively.

William Howard Taft

In July, a piece of verse appeared in the New York Mail that was destined to find an enduring place in baseball literature. Composed by Franklin Pierce Adams, the rhyme immortalized the Cubs' double-play combination of Joe Tinker, Johnny Evers and Frank Chance, as follows:

These are the saddest of possible words
—Tinker to Evers to Chance.
Trio of Bear Cubs and fleeter than birds
—Tinker to Evers to Chance.
Thoughtlessly pricking our gonfalon bubble,
Making a Giant hit into a double,
Words that are weighty with nothing but trouble—
Tinker to Evers to Chance.

After sitting out the 1909 season, because Owner Charles Murphy offered him only a repeat $7,000 salary instead of the $8,500 he demanded, Johnny Kling signed with the Cubs on May 2. The pact covered three years, but, under a National Commission ruling, the catcher was not permitted to receive more than $4,500 for the first year. It was reported that Kling also received some money from the 1908 World Series pool.

Kling caught his first game on May 8, and batted .269 for the season as the Cubs returned to the winner's circle with a 13-game edge over the Giants.

The Cubs entered the World Series without Evers, sidelined with a fractured leg,

but it was doubtful if "The Crab" could have made a difference. The Cubs lost in five games to Connie Mack's youthful A's. Chicago's only victory was Mordecai Brown's 10-inning, 4-3 decision over Chief Bender in the fourth contest.

1911

Umpire baiting, which had increased in 1910, took another step upward under the endorsement and encouragement of Horace Fogel.

It attained new heights on July 10, during a game at St. Louis, when Sherry Magee, the Phils' left fielder, was tossed out of a game by umpire Bill Finneran for flipping his bat over a called third strike.

Magee, the league's defending batting champion, socked Finneran on the mouth, knocking out some teeth and inflicting numerous cuts, so that the arbiter was rushed to the hospital.

Magee was suspended by Lynch for the remainder of the season and fined $200. On August 16, however, Lynch reinstated the offending player on the grounds that the Phillies, a pennant contender, had been severely handicapped by injuries and had need for Magee's services. Magee's return, coupled with 28 victories by rookie Grover Cleveland Alexander, was unable to make champions out of the Phils, who again finished fourth.

After five years as a World Series specta-

Johnny Kling

Franklin P. Adams

Joe Tinker . . . Ruthlessly pricked Giant bubble.

Johnny Evers . . . Sharp wits led to pennant.

tor, John McGraw returned to the post-season show with the Giants, 7½-game winners over the Cubs.

The season was highlighted by a fire that razed the Polo Grounds after the second home game, the arrival of Rube Marquard as a full-fledged major league pitcher and the antics of pitcher Bugs Raymond.

After the wooden stands were consumed by the blaze, the Giants were invited to play in Hilltop Park, home of the city's American League club, an invitation that was quickly accepted.

When the Polo Grounds stands were rebuilt, the general impression was that the park capacity was 50,000. For World Series games, however, the attendance, which included thousands of standees, was announced as 38,281.

Convinced that they were being swindled out of a large share of their receipts, the players dispatched a committee to the National Commission to investigate. Eventually they accepted the figures.

Marquard, christened LaMarquis but known as Marquard after a young sportswriter mistook his patronymic, had been "the $11,000 lemon," after winning five games and losing 13 for the 1909 Giants following his purchase from Indianapolis.

In 1911, however, the lefthander blossomed into a 24-game winner, falling only two victories short of Matty's total.

Raymond, the talented righthander with an equally-talented thirst, finally wore out John McGraw's patience. The breaking point occurred when the manager gave the pitcher a new baseball with instructions to warm up in the bullpen. Instead, Raymond strolled out of the park to the nearest saloon, where he swapped the ball for three quick belts. When he was called into the game with two on, he fired two pitches over the batter's head, whereupon McGraw discovered Raymond's inebriated condition.

Like the Cubs the previous year, the Giants succumbed before the A's in the World Series, four games to two, as J. Franklin Baker, Philadelphia third baseman, earned the nickname of "Home Run" with round-trippers at crucial spots in the second and third games.

In November, McGraw took the Giants to Cuba for a series against local clubs. Even though it was a vacation-type trip, McGraw took early defeats seriously and scheduled a morning workout at which he announced that the players who did not go all out would be sent home on the first boat. The Giants won all the remaining games.

1912

After three malevolent seasons, the curtain fell with a sickening thud on the career of abrasive Horace Fogel.

The Phillies' front man, in a letter to the Chicago Post, accused Manager Roger Bresnahan of instructing his Cardinal players to lie down on the job when playing the Giants, Bresnahan's former club.

Later, talking with New York writers, Fogel accused Lynch and the umpires of fixing the race for the Giants, an accusation he

Bugs Raymond

Rube Marquard . . . From a lemon to a peach.

Charles Rigler   **Bill Dahlen**

repeated in a telegram to National Commission Chairman Garry Herrmann.

In a special meeting in New York, November 27, Fogel was found guilty on five of the seven charges preferred by Lynch and drummed out of baseball.

Subsequently it was revealed that Fogel had sent his story accusing Bresnahan to Charles Murphy and that the Cub owner relayed the missive to the Post for publication. No charges, however, ever were filed against Murphy.

Marquard had an even bigger season for the Giants than in 1911, winning 26 games, 19 of them in a row, to tie a mark set by Tim Keefe, also of the Giants, in 1888.

Under present scoring rules, Marquard would have been credited with 20 successive victories. On April 20, the lefthander replaced Jeff Tesreau in the ninth inning and retired the Dodgers, but not before the visitors had gained a 3-2 lead. The Giants won the game, 4-3, with Tesreau getting the victory under existing rules that governed awarding victories.

The game-winning hit was disputed so heatedly by the Dodgers that a fist fight erupted between umpire Charlie Rigler and

Manager Bill Dahlen of the losers. Wilbert Robinson, then a Giant coach, separated the combatants. McGraw was not on the field at the time, having been suspended for five games because of a run-in with umpire Finneran.

The Giants repeated as league champions, beating out Pittsburgh by 10 games, and faced the Red Sox in what was regarded as the most exciting World Series up to that time.

Two games went into extra-innings, including the second contest that was halted by darkness after 11 innings with the teams deadlocked, 6-6.

The eighth and deciding game went into the 10th inning and the Giants were only three outs away from the world title when misfortune struck.

Opening the inning, center fielder Fred Snodgrass made a two-base error on pinch-hitter Clyde Engle's easy fly ball. With one out, Steve Yerkes walked and Tris Speaker lifted a Mathewson pitch just outside first base. Catcher Chief Meyers or first baseman Fred Merkle could have caught the ball, but it fell untouched. Speaker then singled home the tying run and moved Yerkes to third, from where he scored on Larry Gardner's outfield fly, giving the Red Sox a 3-2 victory.

After the series, McGraw went on a vaudeville tour that included a stop in Chicago. After one night's performance, McGraw and Charles Comiskey, owner of the White Sox, shared dinner from which came plans for a world tour by the two clubs the following fall.

Shortly after McGraw's return to New York, he received word of the death of John T. Brush. The Giant owner, a near-invalid for years, was en route to California when he was stricken fatally near St. Charles, Mo. Brush's son-in-law, Harry N. Hempstead, was elected club president.

1913

The Giants captured their third consecutive pennant, scoring a 12½-length victory over the Phillies, but for the third successive season they finished second best in the World Series, losing in five games to the Athletics.

The Giants' only victory was a 10-inning, 3-0 triumph by Christy Mathewson in the second game.

The Series marked a parting of the ways for McGraw and his old Baltimore buddy, Wilbert Robinson. Robbie, who had served as pitching coach for the Giants, and McGraw had not spoken for a month or more as the result of a long-forgotten difference, and drifted farther apart despite numerous efforts of friends to patch up the enmity.

Robinson was named manager of the Dodgers.

On October 18 the Giants, under McGraw, and the White Sox, under Comiskey, opened their celebrated world tour. The trip started in Cincinnati and ended in London, February 26, in time for the players to return home for the start of spring training.

A total of 44 games was played in the United States, Japan, China, the Philippines, Australia, Ceylon, Egypt, Italy, France and England, where King George V was one of the spectators.

At the league's winter meeting, held in New York City in December, Tom Lynch, who had knuckled down to no special interests, was fired as president and succeeded by John K. Tener, who had one year to go on his term as Governor of Pennsylvania.

Tener received a four-year contract at $25,000 annually, in contrast to Lynch's one-year pacts at $9,000 per.

In leaving the councils of the N. L., Lynch told the club owners:

"In choosing your next president, you have gone on record as wanting a man who

Fred Snodgrass

Chief Meyers

will lend dignity and prestige to the office, and, in your selection of Governor Tener, you have the right man. But I hope you will inject some of the dignity expected of him into yourselves and be a help instead of a hindrance to him.''

League directors also greased the skids for Charles W. Murphy, head of the Cubs. During the City series of 1912, Murphy, furious at the White Sox scoring six first-inning runs against the Cubs, rushed to the dugout and fired Frank Chance, opening the way for the pilot to accept a $25,000-a-year job as manager of the New York A. L. club.

Now, Murphy was at it again, trading or releasing such old Cub favorites as Brown, Kling and Tinker. When he swapped Evers to the Braves for Bill Sweeney, Evers threatened to jump to the outlaw Federal League, then under organization.

The league intervened and permitted The Crab to sell his services to the Braves for $40,000.

At a special meeting in Cincinnati, attended by Tener and Charles Taft, who had bankrolled Murphy in the Cub venture, it was arranged for Taft to buy out Murphy's estimated 53 percent interest in the ball club, for $503,500. Charles H. Thomas was named to look after the Taft interests as Cub president.

1914

Last in the pennant race on July 4, still last on July 19, and then flag winners by 10½ games over the Giants. . . . That's the incredible tale of the Miracle Braves, whose accomplishment would be the yardstick against which all future pennant drives would be judged.

George Stallings, a model of refinement off the field but a profane demon in the dugout, made the Braves happen. Early in the season, Stallings announced: ''I have 16 pitchers, all of them rotten,'' yet it was pitching, chiefly, that carried the Braves to the title.

From last place on July 19, they climbed to second on August 10, 6½ games astern the Giants. They moved into first place on September 2, slipped briefly to third, and then regained the top spot on September 8, never to yield it again.

Despite Stallings' low evaluation of his pitchers, Dick Rudolph posted a 27-10 record, Bill James 26-7 and George Tyler 16-14. Joe Connolly was the only regular to bat over .300, finishing at .306. A second major factor was the double-play combination of

John K. Tener

George Stallings

Bill James . . . Worked wonders for Miracle Braves.

Dick Rudolph . . . Top winner for George Stallings' team.

George Tyler . . . Third member of a star-studded staff.

Rabbit Maranville at shortstop and Evers at second base, both future Hall of Famers.

Against Connie Mack's powerful defending world champions, the Braves were rated as decided underdogs, but again shocked the sports world by eliminating the Athletics in four games as Hank Gowdy batted .545 and Evers .438, while James and Rudolph won two games apiece.

On December 14, Stallings was rewarded with a five-year contract.

A strike by the Baseball Players Fraternity was narrowly averted in July when pitcher Clarence Kraft was optioned by Brooklyn to Newark, but was claimed by Nashville on a waiver technicality. Kraft refused to report to Nashville, asserting that he should be permitted to play for the club of higher classification.

Dave Fultz, president of the Fraternity, notified Garry Herrmann, chairman of the National Commission, that members would consider themselves no longer under contract because of the violation of a player's rights.

Everything came to a peaceful conclusion when Charles Ebbets, Brooklyn owner, purchased the player's contract and assigned him to Newark.

On July 17, in the longest game ever

played in the league at that time, New York defeated Pittsburgh, 3-1, in 21 innings. Larry Doyle's homer gave Marquard, who issued two bases on balls, one intentionally, the decision over Babe Adams, who walked none.

A post-season tour of All-National and All-American League stars engaged in a 44-game tour through the states and Hawaii. The Nationals, under Frank Bancroft of Cincinnati, won 23 games, and the Americans, under Mack, won 21.

When the tour disbanded at San Diego on December 27, each player received $1,321.95 as his share of the profits.

At the annual meeting in December, directors adopted a 21-player limit and set March 1 as the start for spring training.

1915

The outlaw Federal League, which had caused some waves in 1914, claimed full major league status in '15, with franchises in Chicago, St. Louis, Pittsburgh, Brooklyn, Kansas City, Buffalo, Newark and Baltimore.

The league, boasting such affluent backers as James A. Gilmore, a Chicago stationer, Harry Sinclair, the oil tycoon, and the Ward Brothers, Brooklyn baking barons, attracted a number of major league stars, including Joe Tinker.

After the Feds sued the majors for violating the Sherman Anti-Trust Law, and Sinclair announced his intentions of moving his Newark club to New York City, the N. L. appointed a committee of Tener, Dreyfuss and Jim Gaffney of the Braves to negotiate a peace settlement.

Treaty stipulations awarded $400,000 to the Wards, spread over 10 years, $100,000 to Sinclair in 10 payments and lesser indemnities to other club owners.

N. L. clubs also were required to buy back some of the contract jumpers, with McGraw one of the most active shoppers. The Giants paid $30,000 for outfielder Benny Kauff, called "the Ty Cobb of the Feds," and $7,500 for Edd Roush, who was traded to the Reds, for whom he played 10 seasons in his Hall of Fame career.

A giant rhubarb in the game's high councils developed over the rights to a young University of Michigan pitcher-first baseman, George Sisler. As a teenager in Akron, O., Sisler signed a contract with his hometown club, although he never played professionally. His contract subsequently was sold to Columbus, which sold it to the Pirates.

Sisler, meanwhile, blossomed into a college star at Michigan and signed to play for Branch Rickey, managing the Browns.

In the ensuing struggle, Sisler expressed a desire to play for Rickey and Garry Herrmann, as chairman of the National Commission, cast the deciding vote in awarding the player to the A. L. club. Dreyfuss screamed bitterly and started a campaign to do away with the three-man governing system of baseball.

The season also marked the major league debut of another future Hall of Famer, Rogers Hornsby, who batted .246 in 18 games as a shortstop for the Cardinals.

Like the Braves of the previous season, the pennant race produced another surprise winner, the Phillies, who, under freshman Manager Pat Moran, scored a seven-game victory over the Braves.

Grover Alexander, with 31 wins, and Gavvy Cravath, with a record-setting 24 home runs, sparked the Phils to the championship.

For the first and only time in his New York managerial career, John McGraw finished in the cellar, just two years after he won the pennant. The embarrassment was not as severe as it might have been, however, because the Giants were only 3½ games behind the fourth-place Cubs.

In the World Series, the Phils were wiped out by the Red Sox, even though Alex got them off on the right foot with a 3-1 triumph. After that the A. L. champs won four one-run decisions, three by a 2-1 score and the finale, 5-4. In three of those four games, the winning run crossed the plate in the ninth inning.

1916

Winning streaks and a superior pitching performance failed to pay off in a pennant for the Giants or Phillies.

McGraw's club peeled off two long winning streaks, 17 victories, all on the road in May, and 26, still a major record, in September.

All of the 26 victories were registered at the Polo Grounds and included six against the Cardinals, five against the Pirates, four over the Phils and Reds, three over the Cubs and Braves and one over the Dodgers. Jeff Tesreau accounted for seven victories and Ferdie Schupp six.

The streak ended on September 30 when George Tyler of the Braves outdueled Slim Sallee, 8-3.

Despite the two extended streaks, the Giants finished fourth as the result of inconsistent play in between.

In Philadelphia, Alexander posted another extraordinary season, winning 33 games, 16 of which were shutouts. The righthander blanked the Reds five times in his record streak, which included nine whitewashings in Philadelphia's band box Baker Bowl.

Grover Cleveland Alexander . . . 31 victories for champions.

Gavvy Cravath . . . A record 24 home runs in Philadelphia.

On July 20, the Giants said good-bye to one of their most illustrious heroes, Christy Mathewson, who, realizing that his pitching career was over, asked McGraw to help him find a managerial position.

Mac, desperately in need of a second baseman to solidify his infield, swapped his fading hurler to Cincinnati with Bill McKechnie and Edd Roush for playing manager Buck Herzog and outfielder Wade Killefer.

Herzog had been traded away twice previously by McGraw and disliked the manager with a fervor, which was heartily reciprocated. But each appreciated the other's value to a ball club and they avoided open hostility.

Mathewson was given a three-year contract to pilot the Reds. On his first appearance at the Polo Grounds in enemy uniform, Matty managed the Reds to a 4-2 victory.

Late in the season, before the Dodgers had clinched the pennant, a sticky situation developed in a game between the Giants and Dodgers, who were managed by McGraw's estranged pal, Wilbert Robinson, and which featured such ex-Giants as Fred Merkle, Chief Meyers and Rube Marquard.

After Giant pitcher Poll Perritt took a long windup with a runner on base, and the Giants committed some other suspicious plays, McGraw walked out of Ebbets Field, yelling to the press box: "I'll be no part to this."

Headlines screamed that McGraw had accused his players of lying down on the job and Pat Moran, Phil manager, demanded an investigation by Tener. The league president looked into the charges, but found them groundless and the Dodgers captured the pennant by 2½ games over Philadelphia. Boston was third and New York fourth, providing an all-East flavor to the first division.

The Dodgers had no better luck against the Red Sox in the World Series than did the Phillies a year earlier. Brooklyn captured only one game, the third, in which Jack Coombs defeated Carl Mays, 4-3. Ernie Shore won two games for the Red Sox and Babe Ruth and Hub Leonard one each.

1917

War guns were booming louder and patriotic fervor was mounting when the season opened a few days after Congress declared war on the Central Powers of Europe.

Although no clubs went to the extremes of the Minneapolis team, which adopted a khaki-colored uniform and a cap featuring red, white and blue stripes, some clubs engaged in close-order drills before games and invited spectators to participate.

An unprecedented feat occurred in Chicago on May 2 when Hippo Jim Vaughn of the Cubs and Fred Toney of the Reds engaged in the only double no-hitter in major league history.

After nine innings, during which each pitcher issued two bases on balls, the spell was broken with one out in the 10th inning when Larry Kopf of the Reds singled. The Cincinnati shortstop raced to third with two out when center fielder Cy Williams dropped Hal Chase's fly ball and scored when Jim Thorpe beat out a high hopper to the mound. Toney retired the Cubs in order in the last of the 10th, striking out Larry Doyle and Williams in a final flourish.

On a day in June, while the Boston club was in Cincinnati, Hank Gowdy, Brave catcher, enlisted in the United States Army, the first major leaguer to do so. "I had no excuses for not offering my services," was the laconic explanation of the 1914 World Series hero.

John McGraw again made fistic headlines with one of the largest rhubarbs of his

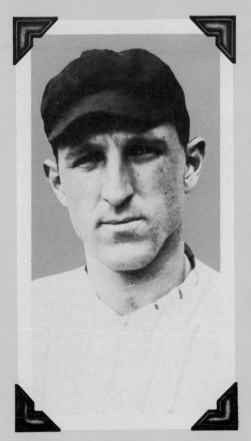

Buck Herzog

Fred Toney . . . A no-hit winner in 10 innings.

Jim (Hippo) Vaughn . . . Helped write history in defeat.

stormy career. Leaving the Cincinnati ballpark on June 8, McGraw resumed a running word battle with umpire Bill Byron, the upshot of which was a McGraw uppercut to Byron's jaw. A $500 fine and 16-day suspension followed.

When New York writer Sid Mercer notified McGraw of his penalty, the manager fired all barrels at league President Tener, accusing him of being a tool of the Phillies,

Hank Gowdy

and adding that the umpires were of the poorest quality he had ever seen.

Mercer asked if he could quote McGraw, and was told, "I want to see the quotes in every newspaper in New York."

Summoned before a meeting of the league directors, McGraw repudiated everything, even signing a statement in which he denied it all.

When Mercer and his fellow newsmen demanded a showdown, Tener called a meeting, after which Tener announced he was convinced that the manager had been quoted accurately. An additional $1,000 fine was levied.

Mercer, a devoted Giant writer until then, never covered another Giant game; nor did he speak to McGraw thereafter.

McGraw's luck was just as bad in the World Series as it had been in three previous classics—he lost again—this time to the White Sox in six games.

After the White Sox won two games in Chicago, the Giants won shutouts in New York, but then blew a 5-2 lead in the fifth game, during which McGraw refused to lift starter Slim Sallee until the Sox had gained a 7-5 lead.

The final game was decided in the fourth inning when Chicago scored three times on two hits, one of the runs scoring when third baseman Heinie Zimmerman chased Eddie Collins across the plate, which had been left unguarded.

1918

The nation's increased involvement in World War I was reflected in baseball's participation in the military effort.

N. L. clubs set aside one day in which each club would contribute 25 percent of its gross receipts to the Clark Griffith Bat and Ball Fund, which supplied baseball equipment to soldiers and sailors.

When General Enoch Crowder issued his "Work or Fight" order, designed to force non-essential persons into the armed forces, the National Commission asked Secretary of War Newton Baker for an opinion on baseball's role.

Baker suggested that the season be ended on September 1 and baseball, in essence, complied, terminating the season on Labor Day, September 2.

On August 6, John K. Tener resigned as president of the league, following a collapse in the National Commission's authority.

The ruckus started when the Athletics and Braves claimed rights to Scott Perry, a Philadelphia pitcher. The Commission awarded Perry to Boston, but the A's ignored the ruling, obtaining an injunction against the Commission enforcing the decision.

John Heydler . . . Stepped into Tener's shoes.

At that Tener resigned, paving the way for the directors, on December 10, to elect John A. Heydler as his successor at $12,000 annually for three years.

Until the war-shortened season, World Series monies were divided only between pennant-winning clubs. Early in the season, Tener devised an incentive plan for runner-up clubs to go all out in the final weeks, by allotting lesser amounts to their players. Tener was not on the scene when his plan went into operation during the Series between the Cubs and Red Sox.

Realizing that the receipts, already low because of poor attendance, would be even lower as a result of the Tener share-the-wealth plan, the contending Series players announced before the fifth game that they would not take the field unless the Commission granted their demand for a $1,500 share to the winning players and a $1,000 share to the losers.

Garry Herrmann of the commission met with player representatives and explained that the players, by terms of their contracts, were obliged to play in all of their clubs' games, a fact readily understood by the players, who took the field an hour after the scheduled start of the game.

Carl Mays and Babe Ruth won two games apiece in the Red Sox' six-game Series victory over the Cubs, and the Bambino also chipped in with a triple.

Before peace terms were signed in Europe on November 11, the N. L. had contributed 103 men to the armed forces, including Christy Mathewson, Cincinnati manager, and Branch Rickey, executive of the Cardinals, both of whom obtained commissions.

The foremost baseball casualty of the conflict was a National Leaguer, Captain Eddie Grant, a third baseman on the reserved list of the Giants who was killed by a shell fragment while leading his infantry battalion to

Hal Chase

Heinie Zimmerman

the rescue of the famous "Lost Battalion" in the Argonne Forest, near Verdun, on October 4. For years, a monument to Captain Grant's memory stood in center field at the Polo Grounds.

1919

Uncertain over the national economy in the immediate post-war era, the league reduced the schedule from 154 games to 140, and caused Harry Hempstead, on January 14, to sell the Giants to Charles Stoneham, John McGraw and Judge Francis X. McQuade.

The Phillies, who finished a dismal last, seven games out of seventh place, twice lost 13 games in a row, but participated in a record-setting accomplishment, September 28, when they dropped a 6-1 decision to the Giants in only 51 minutes, at the Polo Grounds.

The big headlines of the year were written for the shoddy developments that resulted in the banishment from Organized Baseball of Hal Chase, Lee Magee and Heinie Zimmerman.

The case against Chase went back to August 9, 1918, when the first baseman was suspended by the Reds for "indifferent playing," despite the fact that he was batting .301. Fielding lapses on easy plays were reported responsible for the action.

Chase sued the Reds for the remainder of his salary, but in the meantime reports were circulating that Chase had tried to influence players to throw games. John A. Heydler, not yet elected president of the league, called a hearing, but announced that there was insufficient evidence and acquitted the player, who signed with the Giants.

In September of the first post-war season, in which he played 107 games, Chase began to disappear mysteriously. The Giants reported Chase had returned to California, but suspicions of his here-again, gone-again actions remained.

Later, in the following season, in June of 1920, outfielder-infielder Lee Magee was released by the Cubs in the middle of a two-year contract. When Magee sued for his remaining salary, the suit was heard in Cincinnati. There, Magee spilled everything about Chase, mentioning names, places, dates, bets and a bookmaker. At the finish, his suit was dismissed and both he and Chase were through with Organized Baseball.

The once smooth-fielding first baseman drifted westward into Arizona and Mexico, where he played in copper mining towns with flashes of the skill that made him king of his position. He died of beriberi in California in 1947.

McGraw testified before Heydler that Zimmerman had attempted to bribe Fred Toney and Benny Kauff into throwing games, but that the Giant players had reported the matter to him and Zimmerman confessed to Stoneham. Like Chase and Magee, Zim was blacklisted from baseball.

The N. L. pennant race produced a surprise winner in the Reds, who, under Pat Moran, finished nine games ahead of the Giants. In the World Series, the Reds were even bigger surprises as they defeated the powerful White Sox, five games to three, with Hod Eller winning two games and Dutch Ruether, Slim Sallee and Jimmy Ring one apiece.

A year later, it was determined that eight Chicago players had connived with gamblers to throw the Series, resulting in lifetime banishment for Eddie Cicotte, Claude Williams, Chick Gandil, Swede Risberg, Buck Weaver, Joe Jackson, Happy Felsch and Fred McMullin.

1920

The National Commission, which had governed baseball since 1903 and had rendered approximately 1,600 decisions, most of them as the Reach Guide said, "with fairness and ability," was dissolved late in 1920, and replaced by a one-man rule, Judge Kenesaw Mountain Landis, who was given a seven-year contract at $50,000 annually.

Opposition to the Commission type of government had grown steadily, starting with Barney Dreyfuss' clamor against the Sisler decision in 1915. The Scott Perry case in 1918 further undermined the three-man authority and the Black Sox Scandal applied the finishing blow. Much opposition was leveled against Garry Herrmann's dual role as president of the Reds and chairman of the Commission.

With Babe Ruth creating widespread interest in hitting by clouting a record total of 29 home runs for the 1919 Red Sox, rules makers decided to cash in on the new craze by outlawing all freak pitches. Any pitch that involved tampering, like the application of sandpaper, emery or spit, to the surface of the ball, was outlawed. A violation was punishable with a 10-day suspension.

The rules committee did permit, however, 17 established major league spitballers to continue to use the moist pitch. National leaguers in this category included Bill Doak, Cardinals; Phil Douglas, Giants; Dana Fillingim, Braves; Ray Fisher, Reds; Marvin Goodwin, Cardinals; Burleigh Grimes, Dodgers; Clarence Mitchell, Dodgers, and Dick Rudolph, Braves.

Despite the efforts to improve hitting, the game's all-time record pitching duel took place at Boston, May 1, when Leon Cadore of Brooklyn and Joe Oeschger pitched a 26-inning, 1-1 tie. Oeschger allowed nine hits, Cadore 15 and Walter Holke, Boston first baseman, had 42 putouts. The Dodgers scored in the fifth inning, the Braves in the sixth, following which there was an uninterrupted string of 20 goose eggs.

For the first, and only, time in the 20th century, two clubs, the Reds and Pirates, played three games in one day at Pittsburgh. The Reds won the first two games,

Hod Eller

Judge Kenesaw M. Landis . . . Strong hand at a weak period.

Leon Cadore . . . May Day was long work day.

Joe Oeschger . . . 26 Innings to nowhere.

13-4 and 7-3, while the Pirates took the ~~third~~ game, in six innings, 6-0.

The three-game bargain bill was staged through a special dispensation of league officials, and was necessary to settle third place, the last spot to figure in World Series money. The first game started at noon on the final day of the season and the nightcap was halted by darkness.

Wilbert Robinson enjoyed the pennant edge over his one-time buddy, John McGraw, as the Dodgers scored a seven-game victory over the Giants.

The Dodgers won two of the first three World Series games, but then dropped four in a row in the nine-game set-up. The Series was featured by Bill Wambsganss' unassisted triple play for the Indians, on a line drive by Clarence Mitchell, Brooklyn pitcher, and the first grand-slam homer in Series play, by Elmer Smith, Cleveland outfielder, both in the fifth game. Mitchell also hit into a double play, giving him the dubious distinction of accounting for five putouts in two trips to the plate.

1921

In his first year as Commissioner, Judge Landis cracked down hard on National Leaguers.

First off, he informed Charles Stoneham and John McGraw that they must either get out of baseball or sell the Oriental Racetrack, Jockey Club and Casino in Havana. They chose the latter.

Next Landis banned Benny Kauff, the Ty Cobb of the Federal League and now a Giant outfielder. Kauff was accused of stealing an automobile in New York and receiving stolen goods, but was acquitted. When Landis saw a copy of the trial, he declared the verdict "one of the worst miscarriages of justice" he had ever seen and barred Kauff, who obtained an injunction against Landis and Heydler, then thought better of it and withdrew the action.

Gene Paulette, Phillies' first baseman, also felt the Judge's wrath, being declared ineligible for consorting with gamblers while with the Cardinals several years earlier.

When McGraw tried to buy Heinie Groh, holdout third baseman, from the Reds, Landis raised objections, so the Giant manager went to the Phillies, buying not only infielder Johnny Rawlings but also outfielders Emil (Irish) Meusel and Casey Stengel.

Despite these strengthening moves, the Giants trailed the Pirates by 7½ games when the Buccos moved into the Polo Grounds for a five-game series in late August.

The Giants swept the series and the Pi-

rates never recovered. The Giants finished four games in front.

Home-run hitting continued to captivate the fans and the league home-run total, which had climbed from 138 to 261 in the three previous seasons, now shot upward to 460.

Asked about the escalated distance hitting, league President Heydler replied:

"I took occasion to visit the plant where the Spalding baseball is manufactured. I found that the methods in use were precisely the same as heretofore. Only the wool yarn was a better quality and in my opinion more firmly bound."

As much a factor as the improved quality of the yarn, perhaps, was the success of Babe Ruth, which prompted immediate imitation by other hitters to the exclusion of sacrifices and stolen bases.

The World Series was the first to be played in one park, the Polo Grounds, as well as the first in which the winner lost the first two games.

The Giants were blanked in the opener, 3-0, on five hits by Carl Mays, and 3-0 again on two hits by Waite Hoyt. After the Giants won, 13-5, scoring eight runs in the seventh inning, and 4-2 behind Phil Douglas, the Yankees triumphed again behind Hoyt, 3-1. The Giants then ran off three consecutive victories climaxing the Series, 1-0, on Art Nehf's four-hit masterpiece over Hoyt.

The Series concluded on a spectacular note when second baseman Johnny Rawlings, fielding Frank Baker's smash on the outfield grass, threw the batter out at first base from where George Kelly fired across the diamond to third baseman Frank Frisch to retire Aaron Ward, attempting to advance two bases on the play.

1922

A decision that would be referred to thousands of times over the years was rendered in Washington in March when the Supreme Court ruled that baseball is not subject to Sherman Anti-Trust Laws.

Hailing the decision, league President John Heydler said: "After years of litigation, we finally have the clear-cut ruling that baseball is a sport and not a trade . . . (the decision) is a tribute to the foresight and wisdom of the men who laid the foundation for the sport."

The season was marked by a heart-shattering incident that resulted in ruin for Phil Douglas. The Giant righthander, given much to drink, was taken to task by McGraw in front of the other players following one of his escapades. Still in a muddled condition, Douglas wrote a letter to Leslie Mann of the Cardinals, suggesting he could

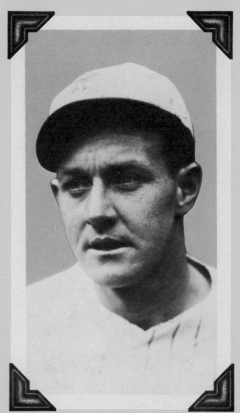

Jack Scott   **Hugh McQuillan**

"go fishing" for the rest of the season if the price was right, thereby making it easier for the Cards to win the flag.

Later, in command of all his faculties again, Douglas telephoned Mann and asked that the letter be destroyed. Unfortunately for him, Mann had shown the letter to his manager, Branch Rickey, who notified Judge Landis.

Confronted with the evidence, Douglas readily confessed and was banished from the game.

Two other pitchers, however, turned out much better for McGraw. Hugh McQuillan, purchased from Boston, won six games, and Jack Scott, released by the Reds as washed up, won eight games.

Scott, a North Carolina tobacco farmer, convinced McGraw that he still could pitch and Mac, impressed by his sincerity, gave him an opportunity.

Rogers Hornsby captured his third consecutive batting championship, posting a .401 figure.

One of the season's most memorable con-

tests was played at Pittsburgh, July 7, when the Pirates lost to the Giants, 9-8, in 18 innings. The day's batting honors went to Max Carey, who, in nine at-bats, collected three walks and six hits. The league's champion base-stealer also swiped three sacks, including home once.

The pennant again was won by the Giants, who finished seven games in front of Cincinnati and once more it was a subway series against the Yankees. At the suggestion of Landis, the Series was returned to the best-of-seven basis.

The Giants won the Series in even more convincing fashion than the preceding year, with only a tie game to mar their record. Game No. 2 was called by umpire George Hildebrand because of darkness after 10 innings with the teams tied, 3-3. The outcry at the umpire's action, the general feeling being that enough daylight remained for play to continue, led Judge Landis to split the receipts of more than $120,000 between disabled veterans and New York charities.

Scott, repaying McGraw for the confidence expressed in him several months earlier, pitched the most impressive game, blanking the Yankees, 3-0, on four hits in the third contest.

1923

In a surprise decision, March 8, Commissioner Landis ruled that pitcher Rube Benton, then of the Giants, had not acted dishonestly in 1919.

Benton, who testified in the Black Sox investigation that he had been offered a bribe before the last game of the 1919 season, and had known of the crooked Series, played under a cloud for several years because of his "guilty knowledge." He was pitching well for St. Paul (American Association) when the Reds attempted to purchase his contract.

Heydler expressed the hope the deal would not be completed, but league direc-

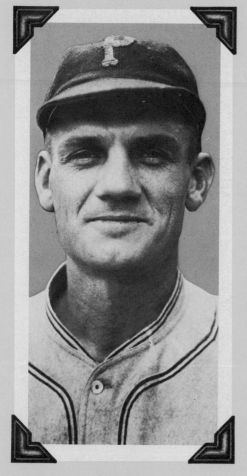

Max Carey

tors tossed the matter into the lap of Landis, who ruled that if punishment had been warranted, it should have been meted out two years earlier.

Benton pitched three years with the Reds, then drifted down to the minors, where he pitched until a motorcycle accident snuffed out his life in 1937.

The Braves underwent a change of ownership on February 20 when George Washington Grant sold out to a New York syndicate headed by former Giant pitcher and Red Manager Christy Mathewson, who was installed as the new president.

The Giants, reflecting the confidence born of two consecutive world championships, informed Heydler that they would welcome conflicting Sunday dates with the Yankees, their former tenants, who had been evicted from the Polo Grounds and were living uptown in plush Yankee Stadium.

Jack Bentley, hard-hitting pitcher-first baseman-outfielder purchased by the Giants from Baltimore (International) for $65,000, created a spring-time furor by announcing he would not report unless he received $5,000 of his purchase price from either the Giants or Orioles. When Bentley eventually signed—without the $5,000—and reported to the Giant camp, he was about 20 pounds overweight. Bentley managed, however, to melt off the lard in time to win 13 games as the Giants made it three pennants in a row, edging the Reds by 4½ games.

The season produced an unassisted triple play by rookie shortstop Ernie Padgett of the Braves. The rarity occurred against the Phils at Boston on October 6, when Padgett caught a liner off the bat of Walter Holke, stepped on second to double up Cotton Tierney and then tagged Cliff Lee for the third out.

Outfielder Cliff Heathcote of the Cubs sat out the last three weeks of the season as a result of a penalty slapped on him by Heydler for grabbing umpire Charley Moran by the shoulder while protesting a decision.

In the World Series, the Giants bungled their bid for a record third consecutive world title by losing out to the Yankees, four games to two. Casey Stengel clouted two decisive homers for the Giants, hitting a ninth-inning, inside-the-park homer to win the first game at Yankee Stadium, 5-4, and ripping one into the right field stands in the seventh inning of the third game, to give Art Nehf a 1-0 victory over Sam Jones.

Nehf also started the final game and held the Yanks to one run for seven innings, but five runs in the eighth, due mainly to Nehf's wildness, produced a 6-4 win and the world championship for the Yanks.

Rogers Hornsby . . . A .424 average, but no MVP plaque.

1924

Another scandal flared up in the 49th campaign and again the Giants were involved.

Jimmy O'Connell, young and talented outfielder, was the guilty party. As he passed shortstop Heinie Sand of the Phillies before the September 27 game, O'Connell remarked: "I'll give you $500 if you don't bear down too hard."

"Nothing doing," replied Sand, who notified his manager, Art Fletcher, who, in turn, apprised Heydler.

Summoned to a hearing before Landis, O'Connell said he thought all the Giants were aware of the bribe offer and approached Sand only because he had been told to do so by Cozy Dolan, a coach.

"They picked me," said O'Connell, "because they knew I had sort of a friendship with Sand. I never would have done it if they hadn't told me to do it."

When he was called on the carpet, Dolan had a sudden lapse of memory, insisting he couldn't·remember a thing.

Landis also quizzed three other New York

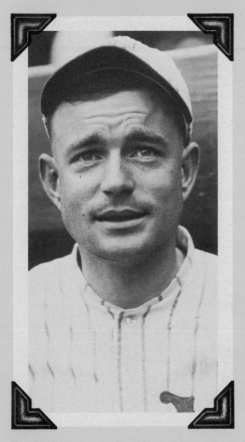

Jimmy O'Connell

players who were said by O'Connell to have knowledge of the incident, but all were acquitted, while the player and coach were suspended for life.

It was not all bad news for McGraw, however, as the Giants became the first National League team to win four consecutive pennants, beating out the Dodgers by 1½ games. Except for a week in April, the Giants enjoyed every weekend in first place.

On September 16, first baseman Jim Bottomley of the Cardinals established a major league record by driving in 12 runs, with six hits, against the Dodgers.

The league inaugurated the Most Valuable Player Award with a committee of writers selecting Dazzy Vance, Brooklyn pitcher with a 28-6 record, over Rogers Hornsby, Cardinal second baseman who batted .424, the highest figure in modern history.

Sam Breadon, St. Louis owner, kicked up a storm of protest, inquiring, "What does a guy have to do to win the award in this league?"

The finger of guilt in the voting pointed to Jack Ryder, Cincinnati scribe, who did not list the Rajah among the 10 top players. Vance beat out Hornsby 74 points to 62.

Despite the furor, league directors at their December meeting voted to continue the award, with a $1,000 prize to the winner, and with the provision that a player could be eligible every year.

McGraw, hoping to follow up his tenth and last pennant with his fourth world title, saw his Giants lose to Washington through a series of bizarre plays in the seventh game. With the Giants ahead, 3-1 in the eighth inning, Bucky Harris' grounder struck a pebble and leaped over third baseman Fred Lindstrom's head, scoring two Washington runs.

In the 12th inning, catcher Hank Gowdy's foot caught in his mask as he tried to catch an easy pop foul, giving Muddy Ruel a chance to hit a double, only his second hit of the Series. When another grounder by Earl McNeely bounced erratically over Lindstrom's head, Ruel scored the deciding run in the 12-inning, 4-3 thriller.

The Giants and White Sox, as they had done in 1914, arranged a month-long tour of Europe, starting in October. The first overseas game, at Liverpool, drew 3,500 persons, whereas in 1914, their first game, at Stamford Bridge, attracted an estimated 37,000. At Dublin, paid attendance was only 20, so discouraging the promoters that the game was cancelled.

When three games in Paris did little, if any, better at the gate, apparently due to lack of understanding and appreciation of the game, Comiskey and McGraw called off

Dazzy Vance . . . 28 victories, earned him the top honor.

games scheduled for Brussels, Nice, Rome and Berlin.

1925

In observance of the league's 50th season, Golden Jubilee celebrations were held in each of the eight cities, starting with the May 8 game at Boston between the Braves and Cubs, both charter members.

On these occasions, a special Golden Jubilee pennant was flown, President Heydler made an address and old-time players were brought back to take bows.

When batters started compiling robust averages, the "lively" pellet became a popular topic of conversation among players and executives.

League directors grew so concerned over the matter that they invited the president of the A. G. Spalding Co. to their summer meeting in New York for an explanation.

With the help of a professor from Columbia University, it was demonstrated satisfactorily that the 1914 and 1925 baseballs were identical, except for a superior brand of yarn wound around the cork center of the newer ball.

The Brooklyn club experienced a double disaster in mid-season when President Charles Ebbets and Vice-President E. S. McKeever died within nine days. A power struggle between the Ebbets and McKeever heirs ensued immediately and the stalemate was dissolved only by a compromise in which Manager Wilbert Robinson was elected president.

To relieve Uncle Robbie of much of his managerial responsibilities, the directors approved the appointment of outfielder Zack Wheat as assistant manager. According to the Reach Guide: "Wheat failed signally . . . and Robinson was compelled to again don a uniform and direct the team from the dugout."

The Pirates, who finished third the previous season, terminated the Giants' four-year reign as league monarchs by beating out John McGraw's club by 8½ games.

The key to the Pirate victory was a pre-season trade in which Barney Dreyfuss sent pitcher Wilbur Cooper, first baseman Charley Grimm and shortstop Rabbit Maranville to the Cubs for infielder George Grantham, pitcher Vic Aldridge and minor league first baseman Al Niehaus.

Grantham batted .326 and Aldridge won 15 games for the Bucs, who, starting slowly, moved in front to stay on July 23.

Stuffy McInnis, signed as a free agent following his release by the Braves, batted .368 in 59 games. Kiki Cuyler, however, was the Pirates' biggest gun with a .357 average, 144 runs, 220 hits for 366 total bases and 41 stolen bases.

Glenn Wright, who batted .308, turned in the defensive highlight of the season with an unassisted triple play on May 7. The play halted a six-run Cardinal rally in the eighth inning. The shortstop grabbed Jim Bottomley's liner, tagged second base to retire Jimmy Cooney and then overtook Rogers Hornsby trying to scamper back to first base for the final out.

Hornsby again topped the .400 figure at bat, finishing with .403, and won the MVP Award over Cuyler, 71 points to 61.

The World Series opened on a note of sadness, coinciding on October 7 with the death of Christy Mathewson, former Giant mound great, from tuberculosis at Saranac Lake, N. Y.

For the second consecutive year, the Series went the full seven games before the Pirates, under Bill McKechnie, edged the Senators. Max Carey, batting .458, and Ray Kremer and Aldridge with two victories each, led the Pirates.

Cuyler's bases-loaded double in the rain and encircling gloom—the drive was at first called a home run—off Walter Johnson climaxed a three-run, eighth-inning rally and gave the Bucs a 9-7 win in the final game.

Glenn Wright

The Striding Years
1926-1950

⚔⚪⚔

The middle 1920s were an era in which evangelists Billy Sunday and Aimee Semple McPherson held down the far right; they were a time in which John Thomas Scopes was found guilty for teaching evolution in a Tennessee high school, and Margaret Sanger was convicted on charges of disseminating birth control information in New York.

They were days when anarchists Sacco and Vanzetti got the electric chair, when thrill killers Leopold and Loeb escaped it and the guilty persons in the Hall-Mills murders avoided detection.

They were undisciplined times when bathtub gin was all the vogue, when speed and more speed was the watchword on mushrooming highways, when F. Scott Fitzgerald wrote "The Great Gatsby," Ernest Hemingway "The Sun Also Rises" and Theodore Dreiser "An American Tragedy."

This was also an occasion for the National League to celebrate. On February 2, 1926, at the Hotel Astor in New York City, the eldest sports association observed its golden anniversary with a star-studded dinner attended by nearly 1,000 invited guests.

The list of notables was long and bulged with dignitaries. It included Governors Gifford Pinchot of Pennsylvania, Albert Ritchie of Maryland and A. Harry Moore of New Jersey. Mayor James J. Walker of New York City was on hand, as were Senators George Wharton Pepper of Pennsylvania and R. S. Copeland of New York. Humorist Irvin S. Cobb was present, as were brass and braid from the armed forces and baseball chieftains such as Commissioner K. M. Landis, N. L. President John A. Heydler and National Association President Michael Sexton.

Heydler opened the evening's festivities by proposing a toast to the two chief fans in the United States, President and Mrs. Coolidge. The President, in wiring his regrets at being unable to attend, said: "Your league is one of the leading exponents of the national game. Anything that tends to interest the youth of the country in participation in a wholesome athletic sport is to be encouraged."

Vice-President Charles Dawes, Speaker of the House Nicholas Longworth, son-in-law of former President Theodore Roosevelt, and New York Governor Al Smith all were required to wire 11th-hour regrets at their inability to be present because of the press of business.

Billy McLean, who umpired the first N. L. game in 1876, was present, as were Deacon Jim White, one of Boston's original "Big Four," and former league presidents A. G. Mills and John K. Tener.

Since leaving office in 1884, after two years of service, Col. Mills had been instrumental in the formation of the Amateur Athletic Union. In 1924, he had marched at the head of the American athletes in the grand parade at the Olympic Games in Paris.

Although past 80, the Civil War veteran still was active as senior vice-president of the Otis Elevator Company. His address to the assemblage, reprinted in part in the Spalding Guide, emphasized:

"The men who organized the National League in this city 50 years ago today were all men of experience in baseball and had no illusions of the magnitude of the task confronting them, which involved rescuing the game from the state of demoralization into which it had drifted. They were men of intelligence, of broad vision, of high ideals, and of undaunted courage, and they tackled the job in the spirit of crusaders and patriots. Their chief objects, as set forth in the constitution they adopted, were to encourage, foster and elevate the game and to make baseball playing respectable and honorable.

"In its very first year, the league sought to ally with it any other associations willing to join it in a campaign for decency and honesty, and despite some rebuffs and conflicts more or less bitter, it adhered to this policy until finally there was reared that splendid structure known as 'Organized Baseball,' with the principles avowed by the founders of the league as its sure foundation.

"I have said that the founders of the league were patriotic; and it is interesting to note the effects of their work upon the country at large. Here I think it may justly be claimed that baseball, as purified and promoted by the founders of the National League, their successors and their allies, has exerted, and is exerting, a powerful influence in promoting the moral and physical betterment of the youth of our country.

"I trust that we all favor all forms of wholesome recreative sports, but we may claim that baseball is the most democratic, the most popular and the most beneficial. Its implements are simple and within the reach of all. The small boy—and there are millions of him—not only finds pleasure and physical benefit from tossing the ball, but also each has his hero among the expert players and becomes fired with ambition to gain distinction for himself on the ball field, although few expect to win world fame, as did A. G. Spalding, or to gain the love and admiration of the whole country, as did Christy Mathewson."

Exhorted by tne tribute from Col. Mills, the league executives faced confidently their second half-century of recreational service to the American public.

1926

St. Louis, without a championship since Charley Comiskey's Browns won their last title in 1888, returned to the spotlight through the combined efforts of Branch Rickey and Rogers Hornsby.

Rickey, father of the farm system which was started in 1919 with the acquisition of part interest in the Houston club, was responsible for much of the young talent, and The Rajah maneuvered the club to a two-game margin over the Reds.

The Redbirds, as low as fifth in May, captured the lead on September 5 and retained it to the finish, while the Pirates, who led through August, finished third, following an "ABC Mutiny" that resulted in the disposal of three of the foremost players.

The Pittsburgh uprising centered around Fred Clarke, former manager who occupied a seat on the bench as a sort of aid to Manager Bill McKechnie. A bit tactless at times, Clarke incurred the wrath of Babe Adams, Carson Bigbee and Max Carey with his crude remarks.

When Carey, in a horrendous slump, learned from Bigbee that Clarke had suggested to McKechnie that the manager bench Max in favor of "anybody, even the batboy," Carey called a secret meeting in his room with an eye toward demanding the removal of Clarke.

A secret ballot favored Clarke, but word of the meeting reached management. Owner Barney Dreyfuss was in Europe at the time, but was believed to have cabled his son Sammy with instructions to remove the trio. Bigbee and Adams were released and Carey, drawing a $16,500 salary, was sold to the Dodgers for $4,000.

The trio asked Heydler to investigate charges of "insubordination" brought against them and the league president, on August 17, announced that it was only "mistaken zeal" that led the players to act as they did and added that all three left the club with good names.

Hornsby, saddled with the extra responsibilities of manager, batted only .317, a drop of 86 points from 1925, but another Cardinal, catcher Bob O'Farrell, won the MVP award, beating out Hughie Critz, Cincinnati infielder, 79 points to 60.

The World Series, one of the most dramatic of all time, matched the Cardinals against

Branch Rickey

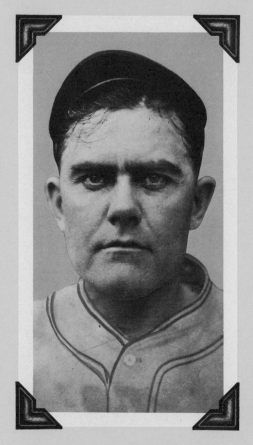

Babe Adams   **Carson Bigbee**

the powerful Yankees. Most of the histri-
onics were reserved for the seventh game
when Grover Cleveland Alexander, a 10-2
winner in game No. 6, emerged from the
bullpen with the bases loaded in the seventh inning to strike out Tony Lazzeri for
the third out. The game, and the Series,
ended when O'Farrell threw out Babe Ruth,
who was trying to steal second base with
two out in the ninth inning, preserving the
Cardinals' 3-2 margin.

After two months of celebration, St. Louis
fans learned in December that Hornsby,
their long-time idol, had been traded to New
York for Frank Frisch.

One explanation was that Owner Sam
Breadon and Hornsby were hopelessly deadlocked in a salary hassle, Breadon refusing
to grant a three-year contract at $50,000 an-
nually.

Another theory was that Breadon was still
seething over some purple prose that The
Rajah had used on him during the season
after learning that Breadon had scheduled
an exhibition game, without consulting the

pilot, at New Haven, Conn.

On December 16, Commissioner Landis
was given a new seven-year contract at an
increase in pay from $50,000 to $65,000.

1927

As the teams moved out of spring training
camps and toward the start of another season, a delicate situation developed unexpectedly on the Giants.

Rogers Hornsby, now the New York second baseman, still owned stock in the Cardinals and while this condition was not strictly
forbidden in the league constitution, nobody
questioned the fact that it was unethical and
would have to be corrected before the regular season.

Cardinal Owner Sam Breadon made the
Rajah an offer.

"I want $116 a share," announced Horns-
by.

"But you paid only $45 a share,"
screamed Breadon.

"That was before I won a world championship," shot back Hornsby. "I have had

the stock appraised and I want $116."

Heydler suggested that the Giants make up the difference between Breadon's offer and Hornsby's demand, a suggestion that was promptly refused. The league president then called a meeting of the club owners at which it was decided that since The Rajah was a big drawing card, it would be to their advantage to chip in equally to pay off the player, a precedent-setting move that, fortunately, never has had to be repeated in baseball.

Hornsby was in the Giants' opening-day lineup at Philadelphia on April 12, but Ross Youngs, the star outfielder, was missing. Youngs, suffering from Bright's disease, was bed-ridden in San Antonio, Tex., where he died on October 22.

The Pirates, under new Manager Donie Bush and starring the Waner brothers, Paul and Lloyd, squeaked through to the pennant, beating out the Cardinals by ½ game. The Buccos won despite the fact that Kiki

Cuyler, star of the 1925 championship club, spent much of the season on the bench as a result of frequent clashes with Bush. The manager wanted Cuyler to play left field and bat second, Cuyler preferred right field and the third spot in the order. When Cuyler was injured, Bush replaced him with Clyde Barnhart, who went on a hitting spree and Kiki continued on the bench following recovery.

Eventually, Cuyler returned to action as a right fielder, but incurred Bush's wrath by failing to slide in a play at second base. He was fined $50 and benched again. Cuyler played only 85 games and batted .309. After the season Owner Barney Dreyfuss traded him to the Cubs, for whom he starred in two pennant-winning seasons.

The Pirates were victims of an unassisted triple play on Decoration Day when shortstop Jimmy Cooney of the Cubs speared Paul Waner's liner, stepped on second to retire Lloyd Waner and tagged Barnhart off

Sam Breadon

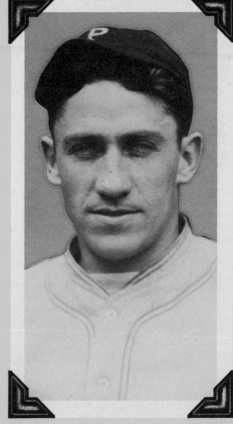

Kiki Cuyler

Lloyd and **Paul Waner** . . . Poison was their profession.

first. The play was instrumental in snapping an 11-game Buc winning streak.

The Pirates were forced to get along without catcher Earl Smith, as the result of the catcher being fined $500 and suspended 30 days by Heydler for assaulting Manager Dave Bancroft of the Braves at home plate in late June.

Paul Waner, in his second season as a Bucco, won the MVP award. Big Poison batted .380, 25 points higher than his brother, Lloyd, in his freshman major season.

In the World Series, playing without Cuyler, the Pirates were obliterated in four games by the Yankees, regarded by many as the No. 1 club of all time. The deciding run of the fourth contest scored on a ninth-inning wild pitch by Johnny Miljus, Pirate righthander.

1928

A new managerial concept was introduced by Judge Emil Fuchs, owner of the Braves, when he appointed Jack Slattery, Boston College coach, as pilot of the club. Slattery's only previous major league experience was as a catcher-first baseman, totalling 103 games, for several clubs, after which he served as a coach and scout for the Braves under George Stallings.

After the Braves finished in seventh place, Fuchs made another change, installing himself as the manager, with Johnny Evers, star of the 1914 Miracle Braves, as his assistant.

On the same date as Fuchs announced his self-promotion, Massachusetts, in a referendum, approved Sunday baseball.

John Heydler, who was given a new four-

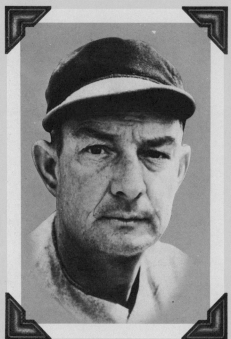

Judge Emil Fuchs

Bill McKechnie

year contract as league president, at an increase in salary, presented a suggestion at the winter meeting that was adopted 45 years later—by the American League.

According to the editor of the Reach Guide: "President Heydler made his famous suggestion to modify the playing rules so that the manager would be empowered to pick a tenth man for the lineup, if he so elects, to bat throughout the game for the pitcher.

"In other words, a pinch-hitter would bat in the place of the pitcher while the pitcher would be permitted to stay in the game. President Heydler pointed out that the majority of flingers were jokes with the stick and there was a slowdown in the tenseness of a keen game when an ill-hitting curver came to bat. President Heydler believes that the introduction of a tenth man in the order to hit for the pitcher will speed up the game and promote interest and avert any suggestion of an anti-climax."

Prior to the 1973 season, the American League adopted the Designated-Hitter rule along the lines proposed by Heydler.

After being edged out for the pennant in 1927, the Cardinals returned to the winner's circle, clinching the flag on the next-to-last day of the season. Except for three days in August, the Redbirds occupied the top spot from June 15 to the finish, under the guid-

ance of Bill McKechnie, who had won with the Pirates three years earlier.

Jim Bottomley batted .325 for the Cards, scored 123 runs and drove in 136 to win the MVP award, beating out Fred Lindstrom of New York, 76 points to 70. Rogers Hornsby, now with Boston, won his seventh and last batting title with a mark of .387.

In the World Series, the Cardinals fared no better than had the Pirates of a year earlier. With Babe Ruth hitting .625 and clouting three homers, all in one game, and Lou Gehrig batting .545 and poling four homers, the Yankees wiped out the Cardinals in four games.

After the season, Cardinal Owner Sam Breadon demoted McKechnie to the manager's job at Rochester of the International League and named Billy Southworth as his successor.

During the winter, the league named a vice-president for the first time, the honor going to Barney Dreyfuss, senior owner who had been a stockholder in the Pirates since 1902.

1929

Recapping the season at the league's meeting in December, President Heydler disclosed, among other things, that the eight teams had used 55,980 baseballs, an in-

Jim Bottomley . . . A most valuable fellow in 1928.

crease of 4,644 from the previous season. Part of the increase, noted Heydler, was due to the record number of home runs, 754, which was 144 more than in '28.

The number of baseballs used would have been even greater, indicated Heydler, if screens had not been erected on the walls of the St. Louis and Philadelphia parks.

Also, at mid-season umpires introduced the practice of rubbing the gloss from baseballs before the game and immediately the production of home runs fell off dramatically.

At the summer meeting, league directors voted to discontinue the Most Valuable Player Award after six years. Rogers Hornsby, Cub second baseman, won the award for the second time with a .380 batting average, 40 homers and 149 runs batted in.

Frank (Lefty) O'Doul set a league record with 254 hits and his Philly teammate, Chuck Klein, hit 43 homers, one more than Hornsby's league mark of seven years earlier.

But Grover Cleveland Alexander, beating Philadelphia, 11-9 on August 10, did not receive credit for the record he thought he had set. The Cardinal veteran chalked up his 373rd league victory, and was told that it was a new N. L. mark, surpassing the total of Christy Mathewson. However, when researchers discovered that Matty also had won 373 times, Alex was forced to settle for a tie, and he never won another game.

On July 23, Billy Southworth, who had succeeded Bill McKechnie as manager of the Cardinals after the Redbirds were humiliated in the 1928 World Series, was sent back to Rochester (International) and the canny Scot was promoted again to the St. Louis helm.

With daily broadcasts creating fan excitement and with Ladies Days attracting turnaway crowds, the Cubs, in their fourth season under Joe McCarthy, captured their first flag since 1918, beating out the Pirates by 10½ games.

The Cubs captured the title with virtually no help from their heavy-hitting catcher, Gabby Hartnett. A .302 hitter in '28, Gabby suffered from a sore arm and appeared in only 25 games, mostly as a pinch-hitter.

In the World Series, the Bruins fell victims in the opening game to Howard Ehmke, surprise Philadelphia starter, who struck out 13 Chicagoans to set a Series record.

At that, the Cubs were on the verge of deadlocking the Series at two victories apiece when the Athletics erupted for 10 runs in the seventh inning of the October 12 game to pull out a 10-8 victory.

After an off-day because of the Pennsylvania Sunday blue law, the A's finished off the Cubs on Monday and rubbed salt in the visitors' wounds by scoring three runs in the ninth inning, two of the runs scoring on Mule Haas' homer.

The Reds underwent a change in ownership when Sidney Weil, a druggist from Newport, Ky., increased his holdings in one week's time from 43 to 3,200 shares and gained control from Lou Widrig.

Joe McCarthy

1930

The jackrabbit baseball had more bounce to the ounce than ever before in the league's 55th season.

Six clubs, the Giants, Phillies, Cardinals,

Chuck Klein and **Lefty O'Doul** . . . Front-rank Phillies.

Bill Terry . . . A Sweet William with the stick.

Hack Wilson . . . At the top of the RBI heap.

Flint Rhem . . . Some believed, and some doubted.

Cubs, Dodgers and Pirates, compiled team averages of .300 or higher, with the Giants posting a .319 average. The Phillies batted .315, but their pitching staff yielded 1,199 runs, an average of 7.7 runs a game, and the club finished a dismal eighth, seven games behind the Reds, in seventh place.

Bill Terry, Giant first baseman, collected a record-tying total of 254 hits and batted .401, the last National Leaguer to reach the .400 level.

And Hack Wilson, sawed-off slugger of the Cubs, made it a year to remember by driving home 190 runs, a major league record, and clouting 56 homers, a National League record.

Eleven players who appeared in 100 or more games hit .350 or better and officials grew so weary of base-hit barrages that they secretly removed some of the juice from the baseball during the off-season and averages dropped dramatically the following season.

Another factor that helped inflate averages was the sacrifice-fly rule in effect since 1926 which exempted a batter from a time at-bat if he advanced any base-runner. The next season the rule was wiped off the books.

It also was the year of Flint Rhem, a talented and colorful St. Louis pitcher who was especially effective against the Dodgers. When the Cardinals, surging from 12 games off the pace, went into Brooklyn for a crucial three-game series on September 16, the South Carolina righthander was scheduled to pitch the opening game.

That morning, Rhem showed up at the hotel unkempt, red-eyed and reeking from an over-indulgence of Prohibition booze. He also had a bizarre story to tell.

On the previous evening, while standing outside his hotel, he was hailed by an unfamiliar voice in a nearby cab. When he approached the cab, he was suddenly shoved into the vehicle, where a gun was thrust into his ribs, explained Flint.

In short order he was transported into New Jersey where he was forced to quaff liquid grain throughout the night. It was, said Flint, a palpable effort to sabotage the Cardinals' pennant chances.

While some observers, acquainted with Rhem's propensity for intoxicants, nodded

Pepper Martin . . . A wild horse with winning ways.

knowingly, the St. Louis club requested an investigation by police authorities. Flint never was able to identify the house in which he was held captive and his tale, while never fully believed, also was never completely discounted.

Meanwhile, back at Ebbets Field, the Cardinals, one game behind the Dodgers in the standings, called on Bill Hallahan, suffering from a huge finger blister as a result of pinching the digit in a car door. Wild Bill was equal to the occasion and pitched a 10-inning, 1-0 victory.

When the Birds, under Rookie Manager Gabby Street, added two more victories, they left Flatbush with an advantage they protected until season's end. From the day they started their move, they won 39 of 49 games.

An all-time baseball oddity occurred at Cincinnati, July 27, when Ken Ash, called in to relieve Larry Benton with two Cubs on base and none out in the fifth inning, made one pitch, which Charley Grimm hit into a triple play. In the home half of the inning, Ash was lifted for a pinch-hitter, the Reds gained the lead and won the game, giving the young righthander the distinction of winning the game with only one pitch and accounting for three putouts.

In late September, Joe McCarthy resigned as manager of the Cubs. The move was not totally unpopular with Owner William Wrigley, who was still feeling the disappointment of the Cub collapse in the previous World Series. McCarthy later accepted the managership of the Yankees while the Cubs were placed under the control of Rogers Hornsby, who fractured an ankle sliding into third base, June 30, and played only 42 games.

In the World Series, the Cardinals split the first four games with the heavy-hitting Athletics, but then succumbed 2-0 and 7-1. George Earnshaw started both games for the A's. On October 6 in St. Louis he went seven innings before leaving for a pinch-hitter. Lefty Grove relieved and was the winner when the Mackmen scored the game's only runs in the ninth on Jimmie Foxx' home run with one on. After a day off for the trip back to Philadelphia, Earnshaw came back to close out the Series, stopping the Cardinals on five hits.

On December 4, William F. Baker, president of the Phillies, died suddenly in Montreal and Lewis Charles Ruch was elected to succeed him. One of the club's new directors was John K. Tener, former league president.

At the winter meeting, Heydler reported that the league had enjoyed its most prosperous season, with approximately 5.5 million paying customers, 500,000 more than in 1929, the previous best season. Brooklyn topped the million mark for the first time and the Cubs' home attendance of 1,463,264 was a league record.

1931

Christened Johnnie Leonard, but nicknamed Pepper (surname Martin), he joined the Cardinals from Rochester and forced the Birds to find a regular spot for him, which they did by trading center fielder Taylor Douthit to the Reds.

Martin batted .302 as a rookie and played the game with a zest that made watching him worth the price of admission. As the Cardinals breezed to the pennant, 13 games ahead of the Giants, the Wild Hoss of the Osage performed like a runaway truck, and in a uniform that usually was saturated with grime and grit from countless bellywhopper slides.

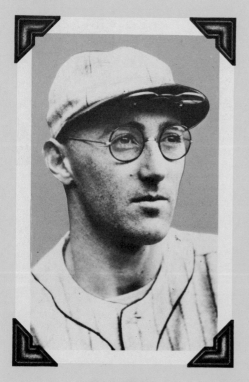

Chick Hafey

Pepper caught the fancy of the league and the nation in the World Series when he stole five bases, rapped 12 hits and batted .500 to lead Gabby Street's Birds to victory over the Athletics in seven games.

The restoration of offense-defense balance which the league fathers sought when they "de-juiced" the baseball paid off in the closest batting race in history. Chick Hafey and Jim Bottomley of the Cardinals and Bill Terry of the Giants finished "under a blanket," Hafey batting .3489, Terry .3486 and Bottomley .3482.

St. Louis provided the dateline for numerous headline stories during the season. On July 12, a doubleheader with the Cubs drew an overflow crowd of 45,770, about 13,000 more than capacity. The spectators rimmed the playing area, turning ordinary fly balls into ground-rule doubles. Nine doubles were credited in the opener, won by the Cubs, 7-5, and 23 in the nightcap, won by the Cards, 17-13.

One afternoon at Sportsman's Park, the visiting Boston Braves, far out of the race, sought to give the handful of spectators a few chuckles by huddling at the pitcher's mound. Then, with the inimitable Rabbit Maranville acting as quarterback, they ran off a series of football-type plays before the umpires intervened and bade the game go on.

Also in St. Louis, John McGraw unleashed what was perhaps the final tirade of his fiery career. In the heat of a July afternoon, McGraw was ejected from a game. The next day when he arrived at the park, he found a wire from league President Heydler informing him of a $150 fine.

As the Giants went through their pregame drills, McGraw spotted Heydler in the stands and unloosed a fusillade of oaths, berating the chief mainly for failing to obtain McGraw's version of the rhubarb, although in the same town.

The more Heydler tried to pacify McGraw, the louder Muggsy raged. Finally, after excoriating the fans who stopped to listen and delivering a final withering blast at Heydler, McGraw turned the club over to coach Dave Bancroft and went back to his hotel, where he regained his composure.

If there was a subsequent fine for McGraw's outburst, Frank Graham failed to mention it in his entertaining volume THE NEW YORK GIANTS.

McGraw and his partner, Charles Stoneham, also engaged in a courtroom battle against the third partner, Judge Francis McQuade. Contending that he had been voted out of office by a dummy board of directors in 1928, the Judge sought reinstatement plus $10,000 annual salary for three years.

Charlie Grimm . . . A pennant on his first try.

The case was heard in the Supreme Court of New York where Justice McCook rendered a split dicision, granting McQuade only his back salary. The club, however, took the case to the Court of Appeals, which ruled in the Giants' favor, removing McQuade from baseball completely.

At the end of the season, Brooklyn management, consisting of President Frank York and treasurer Steve McKeever, decided that Wilbert Robinson must go, canning the manager after a colorful 18-year career and naming Max Carey to replace him.

At the league's meeting in December, directors voted to reduce visiting teams' batting practice from 30 minutes to 20, and rejected a motion to reestablish the Most Valuable Player Award, which had been taken over by the Baseball Writers Association of America and voted to Frank Frisch, captain and second baseman of the champion Cardinals.

1932

The longest and most colorful managerial career in league history came to an end on June 3, and only one baseball writer was there to report it.

After a doubleheader with the Phillies had

been rained out, Tom Meany of the World-Telegram stopped by the clubhouse in search of a story and came away with the biggest scoop in many years. John McGraw, said a notice on the bulletin board, had resigned as manager of the Giants, after a 30-year reign that produced 10 pennants, and had been succeeded by Bill Terry.

The selection of Terry came as a surprise to most observers who felt that Fred Lindstrom was the hand-picked successor to the 59-year-old McGraw. Lindstrom shared that opinion and at the close of the season, after the Giants had finished in a sixth-place tie with the Cardinals, Lindstrom asked Terry to trade him because "the way I have been lied to, I don't want to stay with the ball club any longer."

Lindstrom got his wish and played the next season with the Pirates.

Two months after McGraw resigned, Rogers Hornsby stepped down as manager of the Cubs and was succeeded by first baseman Charlie Grimm. Immediately, the Cubs went on a winning streak that carried them to the pennant, four games ahead of the Pirates.

The defending world champion Cardinals never rose above fourth place and finished in a tie for sixth. There were, however, some redeeming features, such as the arrival of Dizzy Dean and Joe Medwick as Redbird regulars.

Compensating, in part, for the collapse of Pepper Martin, who batted .238 in 85 games, Dean led the league in strikeouts with 191

and won 18 games. Medwick, called up from Houston at the close of the Texas League season, batted .349 in 26 games.

Dean, known variously as Jay Hanna or Jerome Herman, with birthplaces like Holdenville, Okla., or Lucas, Ark., was frequently in disciplinary jams. On one occasion, when he was supposed to accompany a number of teammates to a small Pennsylvania town for an exhibition game, Diz reported that he awoke in the wrong Pullman car and found himself in Pittsburgh with the main group of Cardinals. He was fined $100, which he vowed not to pay.

On the club's return to St. Louis, Diz asked Manager Gabby Street if he would remove the fine in exchange for a shutout over Brooklyn. "I'll see," replied Street. When Dean blanked the Dodgers, Street lifted the fine.

Chuck Klein, Phils' outfielder, was voted the Most Valuable Player on the strength of a .348 batting average, 38 homers and 137 RBIs.

In the World Series, the Cubs were beaten by the Yankees in four straight.

Two club owners died during the year. On January 26, William Wrigley, Jr., owner of the Cubs, passed away in Phoenix, Ariz., from acute indigestion accompanied by a stroke of apoplexy. Control of the club passed to his son, Philip K. Wrigley.

On February 5, just two months after he had been reelected vice-president of the league, Barney Dreyfuss died at Mt. Sinai Hospital in New York of pneumonia a month

Gabby Street

Frank Frisch

Dizzy Dean . . . Color was his middle name.

after undergoing surgery for a glandular disorder. In February, 1931, Barney's son, Sammy, also had died of pneumonia. Control of the Pirates passed into the hands of Dreyfuss' son-in-law William Benswanger.

On April 25, Garry Herrmann, former president of the Reds and chairman of the National Commission, died in Cincinnati.

1933

As the nation started its recovery from "The Great Depression," the editor of the Spalding Guide considered it significant that President Franklin Roosevelt, in a radio address, should make a point with a baseball idiom:

"In an address which he delivered early in May . . . when the season had just begun and men were inclined to think more readily of things in a baseball way, he said, 'I have no expectation of making a hit every time I come to bat. What I seek is the highest possible batting average, not only for myself, but for the team.' "

A couple of important developments

Mel Ott

caught the public's fancy in July, one at Chicago, on July 6 when, as a sidelight of the World's Fair, American and National League players collided in the first All-Star Game.

Connie Mack, managing the junior circuit, scored a 4-2 victory over John McGraw, who came out of retirement to manage for the last time.

In the same month, Sam Breadon, convinced that Gabby Street was unable to produce another winner in St. Louis, fired the Old Sarge and appointed Frank Frisch, second baseman, as manager of the Cardinals.

Earlier, the Redbirds had acquired Leo Durocher from the Reds to plug the shortstop hole created when Charley Gelbert suffered serious injury to his left leg in a hunting accident the previous fall.

With Frisch, Durocher, Dean, Medwick and Martin rough-housing their way around the league, it soon became apparent that this was not an elegant club looking for an afternoon tea.

One day, at the Polo Grounds, Frank Graham of the New York Sun discussed the merits of the club with Durocher and Dean. When Diz offered the opinion that the Cards could win a pennant in any league, even the American, Durocher observed: "Oh they wouldn't let us play in the American League. They'd say we were a bunch of gashouse players."

Graham used the expression in his column the next day and the "Gashouse Gang" was born.

The Giants, in their first full season under Bill Terry, moved into first place on June 10 and led all the way. Two of their most memorable victories were achieved at the Polo Grounds on July 2, when they swept a doubleheader from the Cardinals, each game by 1-0. Carl Hubbell won the first game in 18 innings, gaining the decision over Jesse Haines, who pitched two innings in relief of Tex Carleton. Roy Parmelee edged Dean in the nightcap.

The shutout by Hubbell was one of 10 he registered during the season. From July 13 to August 1, the future Hall of Famer accumulated 46 consecutive innings of shutout pitching.

One of the key members of the Giant flag drive was shortstop Blondy Ryan, an inspirational player who was sidelined by a spike wound in the foot in the second game of the July 2 doubleheader. Left behind to receive treatments as the club headed westward, Ryan sent a telegram to his teammates: AM EN ROUTE, THEY CAN'T BEAT US. The wire became a battle cry for the Giants, who pulled clear of the threatening Pirates and won by five lengths.

Carl Hubbell . . . Giants lived well on Meal Ticket.

The Braves finished in the first division for the first time since 1921, clinching fourth place on the final day when Wally Berger hit a pinch grand-slam homer for a 4-1 win over the Phils.

Chuck Klein captured the league Triple Crown with a .368 batting average, 120 RBIs and 28 homers. On November 23, the Philadelphia outfielder was traded to the Cubs for three players and $65,000.

The Giants opposed the Senators in the World Series just as they had in their last previous Series appearance in 1924. This time they had better luck, disposing of Joe Cronin's Nats in five games. Hubbell won two games, one in 11 innings, as the Giant staff compiled a 1.53 earned-run average and Mel Ott batted .389, with a pair of homers.

Brooklyn, which finished sixth in the pennant race, and Cincinnati, which finished eighth, made post-season changes in their front offices. At Brooklyn, Bob Quinn, veteran minor league operator, replaced Dave Driscoll as general manager, and at Cincinnati, where Sidney Weil had resigned as president and director and turned the club over to the Central Trust Co., Larry Mac-Phail was brought in to make some changes, which he did, immediately and successfully.

At its winter meeting, the league voted to renew its service bureau. Engaged to operate the publicity department was Ford Frick, New York baseball writer and broadcaster.

1934

A flippant word in New York, the Gashouse Gang in St. Louis, a garbage shower in Detroit—they all made headlines during the whackiest of whacky years.

Bill Terry made a sizeable contribution to the magnificent zaniness during the spring meetings at the Hotel Roosevelt in New York. The Giant manager was giving his evaluation of the various National League clubs to a group of writers when Roscoe McGowen of the Times asked: "How about Brooklyn, Bill?"

Terry, who generally eschewed public wisecracks, replied: "Brooklyn, is Brooklyn still in the league?"

Indignant Dodger fans buried Bill under letters of protest. Anytime Terry stuck his head out of the dugout at Ebbets Field, catcalls cascaded from 30,000 throats. Matters might not have been so bad had the off-hand remark not come home to roost. To Bill's misfortune, the Giants' last two games of the season were against the Dodgers at the Polo Grounds, while the Cardinals were at home for two with the last-place Reds. The Giants and Cards were deadlocked for first place.

When Van Lingle Mungo beat the Giants in the Saturday game, 5-1, and the Dodgers followed with an 8-5 Sunday victory, while the Cardinals were winning twice, Terry's misery was complete.

Meanwhile, in the league's western outpost, the Dean brothers, Dizzy and Paul, (Me 'n' Paul) were etching their own brand of headlines, sometimes as heroes.

On August 12, after pitching and losing a doubleheader to Chicago, the Deans failed to show up for the train to Detroit, where the Cards were scheduled to play an exhibition game the next day. Fines of $100 for Dizzy and $50 for Paul were announced by Manager Frank Frisch, which Dizzy announced would not be paid. To emphasize their point, the Deans refused to take the field for the next regular game and Diz, accommodating a photographer, ripped up two uniforms to demonstrate his towering rage.

When they took their case to Commissioner K. M. Landis, however, the Deans learned they were out of line. Uncomplainingly, they accepted their punishment and went back to work.

On September 21, at Brooklyn, Dizzy blanked the Dodgers, 13-0, on three hits in the opener and Paul followed with a no-hit, 3-0 victory.

It was after the double triumph that Diz made one of his best-known cracks: "If I'da knowed Paul was gonna pitch a no-hitter, I'da pitched one, too."

For the season, the brother combination accounted for 49 victories, Dizzy posting 30 as the first National Leaguer since Grover Cleveland Alexander in 1917 to achieve that total, and rookie Paul adding 19.

After their hair-thin pennant triumph, the Cardinals opposed the Tigers in the World Series, which they won in seven games. The Cards received a big scare in the fourth game when Dean, running for Spud Davis, was knocked unconscious when he was struck on the head by a thrown ball while breaking up a double play. The Great One pitched the next day and lost, 3-1, but was at his peerless best for the finale, which the Cardinals won, 11-0.

The contest, at Navin Field in Detroit, was highlighted by the bleacherites' fusillade of over-ripe produce aimed at left fielder Joe Medwick, who had incurred their displeasure by what they considered an overly enthusiastic slide into third baseman Marv Owen.

When police and park attendants were unable to stem the flow, Commissioner Landis removed Medwick from the game as a safety precaution.

The second annual All-Star Game, played at the Polo Grounds, featured the masterful pitching of Carl Hubbell, Giant lefthander,

Frank Frisch, Joe Medwick and Judge Landis . . . Early curtain.

who, in the first two innings, struck out in succession Babe Ruth, Lou Gehrig, Jimmie Foxx, Al Simmons and Joe Cronin, although the A.L. won the game, 9-7.

The Phillies were no factor in the race, finishing an undistinguished seventh, although Baker Bowl provided a handsome bit of baseball lore. On a sultry afternoon, the Phils played the Dodgers, for whom Hack Wilson played right field. Through many innings, Hack chased baseballs that caromed off the near right field wall. When Brooklyn Manager Casey Stengel removed pitcher Walter Beck in a late inning, the disgruntled hurler fired the ball against the wall. Aroused from a doze, Wilson, thinking it was just another base-hit, retrieved the ball and fired it into second base, trying to nail a phantom runner. Ever after, the irate pitcher answered to the name of Boom Boom Beck.

The Reds finished last in the race, but the future was not so bleak, inasmuch as the Reds played under new ownership. Powel Crosley, Jr., successful radio manufacturer, purchased controlling interest in the club, paving the way for brighter days ahead under the front-office genius, Larry MacPhail.

On February 25, at New Rochelle, N.Y., John J. McGraw died of uremia, less than two years after retiring as manager of the Giants. And on December 11, John A. Heydler, who had sparred with McGraw on many occasions, stepped down as league president. He was succeeded by Ford Frick, who was promoted after one year as director of the league's service bureau.

1935

Anyone with less fortitude or determination would not have attempted to shatter baseball tradition, but Larry MacPhail was well-stocked in both qualities and so night baseball came to the National League in its 60th year.

While Clark Griffith, Washington owner, declared that "there is no chance of night baseball ever becoming popular in the bigger cities because high-class baseball cannot be played under artificial lights," the indefatigable redhead obtained permission to play seven night games, one against each opposing club, starting on May 24 against the Phillies.

President Franklin D. Roosevelt pushed a button in the White House that activated 632 lamps at Crosley Field and league President Ford Frick tossed out the first ball before 20,422, about 10 times more than an afternoon contest against the same club would have attracted.

To Paul Derringer went the honor of pitching the first arc game and the big right-hander responded with a 2-1 decision over Joe Bowman.

When other club officials evaluated the attendance benefits of after-dark baseball, they, too—Griffith included—installed lights. Within 13 years every major league club, the Cubs excepted, converted to arc lights.

In Boston, the Braves made big news with

Babe Ruth

a new player, vice-president and assistant manager, all in the person of Babe Ruth. The Bambino, miffed when the Yankees rejected his managerial demand, signed with the Braves for $25,000. Before leaving New York he was quoted: "I will take full charge of the Braves on the field next year (1936)."

The Babe opened the season in left field, and with 22,000 rooting him on, responded in grand style, clouting a homer and double to help the Braves beat Carl Hubbell and the Giants, 4-2.

Because of assorted ailments, Ruth played only 28 games for the Braves and batted .181. He bowed out in a blaze of fireworks at Pittsburgh, however, clouting three home runs on May 25, the 712th, 713th and 714th of his career. He never collected another hit. On his final at-bat, on Memorial Day in Philadelphia, he was retired by Jim Bivin.

On June 2, he called a press conference in Boston and announced he was going on the voluntarily retired list and was quitting the Braves. A series of disagreements with Judge Emil Fuchs, the owner, hastened The Babe's retirement at age 40.

The American League posted its third consecutive All-Star victory when Lefty Gomez won over Bill Walker before 69,831 at Cleveland.

On September 17, Len Koenecke, young Brooklyn outfielder, was killed during a fight in a private plane en route from Detroit to Buffalo. Koenecke, according to the two-man crew, grew obstreperous in mid-flight and, in an effort to subdue him, the co-pilot struck him on the head with a small fire extinguisher. The blow proved fatal.

The Dodgers also lost a front-office executive in December when Bob Quinn accepted the general manager's post with the Braves.

Casey Stengel, with his customary flair for humor in the midst of perversity, contributed an anecdote to the archives. After the Dodgers snapped a four-game winning streak by dropping a doubleheader to the Cubs in a classic display of ineptitude, Old Case stepped into a Chicago barber chair with the sage words:

"A shave please, but don't cut my throat. I may want to do it later myself."

Except for one day in July, the Giants led the pennant race continually from late April to late August when the Cardinals moved ahead. But the Gashouse Gang, after 18 days, slipped to second as the Cubs, on a historic 21-game winning streak, pulled ahead and held the lead until the finish.

When the Cubs arrived in St. Louis for the closing five-game series, the Cards still had a chance. That opportunity quickly evaporated, however, when Phil Cavarretta hit a home run to win the first game for the

When the lights went on in Cincinnati in 1935.

Bruins, 1-0, and Bill Lee, despite an early 2-0 St. Louis lead, beat Dizzy Dean in the opener of the next day's twin-bill, 6-2, to clinch the flag.

Lon Warneke won the first and fifth World Series games against the Tigers, but they were the only games Chicago captured. Detroit wrapped up its first world title when Goose Goslin singled to score Manager Mickey Cochrane in the ninth inning of game No. 6 for a 4-3 triumph.

1936

During the Democratic national convention at Houston in 1928, Dick Kinsella, a delegate from Illinois and also a scout for the Giants, took advantage of a lull in the proceedings by attending a Texas League game between Houston and Beaumont.

On the mound for the visiting club was a lean lefthander who caught Kinsella's eye. Once the property of Detroit, he had been released because Tiger officials predicted he would "throw his arm away" by his addiction to the screwball.

At Kinsella's suggestion, the Giants purchased the hurler and eight years later Carl Hubbell enjoyed his finest major league sea-

Larry MacPhail

son, winning 26 games while losing only six, as New York won the pennant by five games over the Cardinals and Cubs.

King Carl, affectionately referred to as Bill Terry's "Meal Ticket," closed out the season with 16 consecutive wins—he would win eight more before losing in 1937—and won the Most Valuable Player Award.

The Giant success occurred in Horace Stoneham's first year as president, the 33-year-old taking office following the death of his father on January 7.

The Cubs' failure to repeat as champions could have been attributed to their fatiguing spring exhibition schedule. Starting in Los Angeles on March 15, the Bruins, in three Pullman cars, traversed 12 states and played 10 teams, some of them more than once, in communities like San Antonio, Houston, New Orleans, Pensacola, Tallahassee, Lakeland, Tampa, St. Petersburg, Bradenton, Clearwater, Winter Haven, Sarasota, Selma, Dothan, Monticello, Montgomery, Gadsden, Thomasville, Atlanta, Birmingham and Nashville.

The Cardinals, who spent much of the season in first place, were hampered by the ineffectiveness of Paul Dean, who suffered from a sore arm and dropped from 19 vic-

Horace Stoneham

tories to five. And Bill DeLancey, the brilliant 24-year-old catcher, missed the entire season because of a lung infection that led to his death on his 35th birthday anniversary, November 28, 1946.

Chuck Klein, reacquired by the Phillies from the Cubs, enjoyed the most productive day of his career on July 10 when he tied a major league record by hitting four home runs in a 10-inning, 9-6 victory over the Pirates at Pittsburgh. Klein narrowly missed a fifth homer, backing Paul Waner against the right field fence in the second inning.

Bob Quinn, in his first year as chief executive of the Boston club, rechristened the team the Bees, changed the name of the home grounds from Braves Field to National League Park, or the Beehive or Aviary as the local fans called the park, and saw the club come home sixth.

On July 7, a disappointing turnout of 25,556 watched the N.L. win its first All-Star Game in four tries, 4-3, at Boston.

Cincinnati finished fifth in the race. Larry MacPhail had revitalized the franchise, fan interest was soaring and bank debts were declining when, on September 18, the Redhead announced that he would resign, effective November 1. His successor was Warren Giles, general manager of the Cardinals' farm club in Rochester.

During the season, MacPhail ran afoul of Commissioner Landis, who declared Lee

Bob Quinn

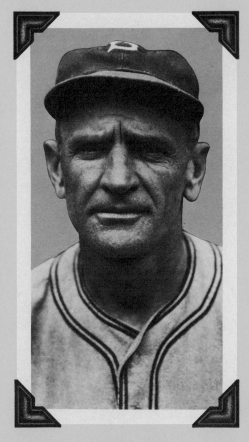

Casey Stengel   **Burleigh Grimes**

Handley a free agent due to optioning ir- regularities and the infielder signed with the Pirates for $20,000.

The Dodgers, who paid Max Carey not to manage in 1934, repeated their generous gesture after the season, canning Casey Stengel in favor of Burleigh Grimes, old Flatbush idol whose Louisville club had fin- ished eighth in the American Association.

At a dinner honoring Casey, Joe McCar- thy, fired in Chicago in 1930, reassured the victim: "Maybe you're getting a break. Maybe you're getting kicked upstairs, too."

In the World Series, Hubbell gave the Gi- ants a first-game edge with a 6-1 victory, but the Yankees won in six, as outfielder Jake Powell batted .455.

The first Hall of Fame election produced five members for the new shrine in Coopers- town, N. Y.—Ty Cobb, Babe Ruth, Honus Wagner, Christy Mathewson and Walter Johnson.

1937

In one way or another, Dizzy Dean suc- ceeded in avoiding obscurity.

During spring training, Diz engaged in a punching match with Jack Miley, New York Daily News columnist, in the lobby of the Tampa Terrace Hotel.

Early in the season, in a game at St. Louis, Dean and Jimmy Ripple of the Giants collided in a play at first base, touching off a free-for-all between the two clubs.

Later in the same game, umpire George Barr called a balk on Dean for failure to come to a complete stop in taking his "stretch" with a runner on base.

In his next start, Diz announced he would obey the new balk rule in all details. Three times in the second inning, he delayed so long in his delivery that umpire Beans Rear- don called a balk for delay of game.

A few nights later, Dean appeared at a dinner in nearby Belleville, Ill., during which he declared: "Ford Frick and Barr are a pair of crooks." He termed the league chief "our great little president—but a pain in the neck to me."

The Great One was suspended and called to New York, where he told Frick he had been misquoted. When Frick asked him to

Chuck Dressen

Hank Leiber

sign a retraction, Dean snorted: "I ain't signin' nuthin."

Three days later, he was reinstated at, said Owner Sam Breadon, no loss in pay.

When the All-Star Game was played in Washington, Dean started for the N. L. and pitched three innings. In the third, after Lou Gehrig had smacked a two-out, two-run homer, Earl Averill smote a line drive that struck Dean on the right foot, breaking a toe. On his return to action, Diz favored the still painful foot and placed an unnatural strain on his arm. A soreness developed in his arm and Dean faded quickly, washed up before he was 30 years old.

Gloomy as the season was for Dean, it was correspondingly bright for his teammate, Joe Medwick, who captured the Triple Crown with a .374 batting average, 154 RBIs and 31 homers.

A spring training mishap cast a pall over the Giants. In one of their numerous spring games with the Indians, Hank Leiber, their husky blond outfielder, took a Bob Feller fast ball to the head. Recuperating rapidly, Leiber played the next day and continued into the season when, one day, he collapsed in the clubhouse. A doctor warned that con-

tinual play could cause loss of sight and speech and Leiber took time out, playing in only 51 games.

In Boston, wily Bill McKechnie came up with two greybeard rookies, Lou Fette and Jim Turner, each of whom won 20 games as the Bees finished fifth. The achievement earned for McKechnie THE SPORTING NEWS accolade as Major League Manager of the Year "for his managerial skill and his ability in handling men, especially pitchers, enabling him to pilot a mediocre team to a fifth-place finish."

Charley Dressen, having been told by Warren Giles that he did not figure in the Reds' future plans, resigned on September 14, along with coaches George Kelly and Tom Sheehan, and Bobby Wallace, a scout, was placed in charge of the club which lost 20 of its last 25 games, including the last 14 in a row.

After the season Giles signed McKechnie to a two-year contract at $25,000 annually.

Carl Hubbell won his first eight decisions for the Giants, extending his two-year skein to 24 wins, before the Dodgers kayoed him on Memorial Day, but King Carl finished with 22 victories, his fifth consecutive year

Ford Frick . . . He squared off against Ol' Diz.

in the 20-win class, and the Giants repeated as league champions.

They were even less impressive in the World Series than a year earlier, however, bowing to the Yankees in five games. Hubbell posted the only Giant victory, beating Bump Hadley in the fourth contest, 7-3.

At the league's annual meeting, Frick was reelected president for three years at an increase in pay and the Reds again were granted permission to play seven night games.

1938

A lefthander with the speed of sound, Johnny Vander Meer for years was handicapped by control that smelled. Twice, as a farmhand of the Braves and Dodgers, his wildness cost him his job.

But under the patience of Bill McKechnie, Vandy altered his pitching style and found the control necessary to catapult him into national prominence in his first full major league campaign.

His record for the season would show only 15 wins and his lifetime total would be an undistinguished 119-121, but on the afternoon of June 11 and the night of June 15, the 23-year-old lefty performed a feat achieved neither before nor since.

On the first date, Vandy blanked the Braves, 3-0, without a hit, walking three and

George Barr

permitting no runner to reach second base.

Four days later, for the first night game in Brooklyn history, the Dodgers announced that the pitcher for the visiting Reds would be Johnny (No-Hit) Vander Meer. As the game developed, it appeared to the 38,748 spectators that Vandy was taking his no-hit reputation too seriously. The Dodgers were not hitting him, either.

With one out in the ninth, Vandy encountered a streak of wildness and walked Babe Phelps, Cookie Lavagetto and Dolf Camilli on 18 pitches. McKechnie called time and strolled leisurely to the mound where he calmed down the youngster, pitching before his parents and 500 neighbors from Midland Park, N. J.

Composed now, Vandy forced Ernie Koy to ground to third baseman Lew Riggs, who forced Goodie Rosen, running for Phelps, at the plate. He then retired Leo Durocher on a short fly to the outfield to wrap up his second no-hitter, 6-0.

Vandy's record no-hit streak ended at 21⅔ innings on June 19, when Debs Garms singled in the fourth inning at Boston.

The Ebbets Field spectacular occurred five months and two days after Larry MacPhail, returning after a year's absence from the game, signed as general manager of the financially-distressed Dodgers. In addition to the installation of lights, making the Dodgers the second nocturnal club in the league, MacPhail brought Babe Ruth back into uniform, hiring the big fellow as a coach in July. In the back of Larry's mind was the thought that The Babe might be a popular successor to Burleigh Grimes as manager, but, after learning of a near-fight between Ruth and Durocher in the clubhouse, MacPhail discarded the notion and released Babe at the end of the season.

Under the skillful manipulations of McKechnie and with the addition of pitcher Bucky Walters from the Phillies in June, the Reds jumped from eighth place to fourth, only six games out of first place and one game out of third.

The major drama in the pennant race took place in Wrigley Field, September 27-29, when the Cubs opposed the Pirates in a series to determine the championship.

The Pirates, who had constructed a new press box at Forbes Field and made other types of arrangements in anticipation of a World Series, enjoyed a 1½-game lead when they went into Chicago for a three-game series.

In the opener, Dizzy Dean, purchased from the Cardinals for three players and $185,000 in April, defeated the Buccos, 2-1. The next day, the teams battled to a 5-5 tie for 8½ innings. With darkness settling over Wrigley Field and a drawn game a distinct possibility, Gabby Hartnett, who had replaced Charlie Grimm as manager in July, tagged a Mace Brown fast ball for his historic "homer in the gloaming." The Cubs now led the Pirates by half a game and they completed the sweep the following day with a 10-1 rout.

The Phillies, having peddled Walters to Cincy and Camilli to Brooklyn, finished 24½ games behind the seventh-place Dodgers. The major development of the campaign for many fans was the club's midseason move from Baker Bowl to Shibe Park, home of the Athletics.

The N. L. registered its second All-Star victory, beating the A. L., 4-1, at Cincinnati, July 6.

The World Series was pure disaster for the Cubs, who were eliminated by the Yankees in four straight.

At its annual meeting in December, the league took two unprecedented steps, permitting Cincinnati to open its 1939 season a day ahead of the other clubs, and electing MacPhail to the league's board of directors. Previously, only club owners served as directors. Inasmuch as their landlords, the A's, had installed lights, the Phils were granted permission to become the third N. L. club with a night schedule.

1939

Salary negotiations between Bill Werber and Connie Mack reached an impasse in mid-March, so the Athletics' manager, in Lake Charles, La., wired his old friend Bill McKechnie in Tampa, Fla.: "Would you be interested in Werber?"

The Cincinnati manager lost no time in replying in the affirmative, Werber became a Red and the Reds became pennant-winners two years after they finished in the basement.

Werber, an honor graduate from Duke University who became a wealthy insurance executive in Washington, D. C., solidified the infield that helped Bucky Walters win 27 games, Paul Derringer win 25 and the club win its first pennant since 1919.

A 12-game winning streak in May, including two decisions over the Cardinals, their strongest competition, carried the Reds into first place, which they never abandoned.

Tempestuous Leo Durocher, in his first season as Dodger manager, battled early and often with his equally turbulent boss, Larry MacPhail, who was warming up for what one writer liked to call the "Reign of Terror."

Before the start of spring training, Leo visited Hot Springs, Ark., for rest and relaxation in his own fashion. When stories appeared in New York papers that Leo had won $750 in a bingo game and assaulted his

Johnny Vander Meer . . . A double diet of goose eggs.

caddy on a golf course, MacPhail reached for the telephone and fired his manager. It was the first of countless "dismissals" that, Leo was to learn, were rescinded as soon as Larry regained his composure.

The Lip was a constant thorn in the side of officialdom. He was booted out of two games in July and fined each time. In the second half of a July 2 doubleheader, Hal Schumacher, pitching for the Giants, fired a fast ball near Leo's skull. Leo, grounding the next pitch to shortstop Bill Jurges, spiked Zeke Bonura as he crossed first base and a free-for-all ensued. Durocher was fined $25, a sum collected by his fans and presented to Leo in the form of 2,500 pennies.

Two weeks later, Durocher and pitcher Whit Wyatt squawked so vociferously over a ball-and-strike decision against the Dodgers that both were chased. Leo was docked $50, Wyatt $25.

The Giants sank two more spots in the standing, to fifth place, but earned a spot in the record book on June 6, when five players connected for home runs in one inning in a 17-3 victory over the Reds. The record setters were Harry Danning, Frank Demaree, Burgess Whitehead, Manny Salvo and Joe Moore.

On June 12, league officials joined with an estimated 10,000 fans in celebrating the centennial of baseball at Cooperstown, N.Y., erroneously believed to be the birthplace of the game. Highlight of the day was the dedication of the Hall of Fame and Museum presided over by Commissioner Landis and which was attended by 10 of 11 living immortals elected to the shrine.

A crowd of 62,892, at Yankee Stadium on July 11, watched the N.L. All-Stars bow to the A.L., 3-1, although outhitting the winners, seven safeties to six.

The Reds succumbed meekly to the Yankees in the World Series, bowing in four consecutive games, although their catcher, Ernie Lombardi, was perhaps the best remembered participant because of his "snooze" at the plate in the 10th inning of the final contest.

A single by Joe DiMaggio drove in Frank Crosetti with the run that broke a 4-4 tie and when Charley Keller also crossed the plate, he collided with Lombardi, knocking out the big catcher only a few feet from the dish. With nobody covering the plate, DiMaggio completed his tour of the bases for a 7-4 Yankee victory.

At the winter meeting, the league appointed a committee to study a plan by MacPhail in which both majors would engage in a 16-team post-season series which would

Bucky Walters and Paul Derringer . . . Kings in Queen City.

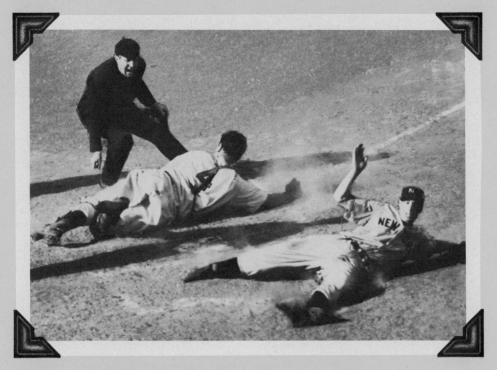

Ernie Lombardi snoozes as **Joe DiMaggio** scores.

figure in the standings of all the clubs. When the A.L. directors failed to display any interest, however, the proposal expired.

1940

The scene was an elevator in the Hotel New Yorker on June 19; the occupants were Bob Bowman, a Cardinal righthander; Joe Medwick, acquired by the Dodgers from St. Louis a week earlier in a deal that included $125,000 of Dodger money, and Leo Durocher, Brooklyn manager and, like Medwick, a resident of the hotel.

As might be expected, Durocher and Medwick unsheathed the oral needle and gave full measure to Bowman, scheduled to pitch that afternoon.

"I'll take care of both of you this afternoon," was Bowman's parting thrust as the players went their separate ways.

On his first trip to the plate, Medwick was rendered unconscious by a Bowman fast ball to the head. Recalling the elevator incident, the Dodgers grabbed bats and charged Bowman, accusing the pitcher of deliberately beaning Medwick.

Larry MacPhail rushed from his private box spouting epithets; then, assured that Medwick was removed to the hospital, he dashed to his office, where he phoned Ford Frick demanding that Bowman be barred from baseball for life, a request the league president rejected.

When order was restored, Manager Billy Southworth, who had replaced Ray Blades as Redbird manager a few weeks earlier, removed a visibly shaken Bowman. Medwick, suffering a concussion, rejoined the Dodgers after about a week's absence, but was never the offensive powerhouse he had been for the Cardinals.

Hysteria, which had been on a rapid crescendo in Flatbush, climaxed on a September afternoon at Ebbets Field in a game with the Reds. Durocher, badgering umpire George Magerkurth throughout the game, excited the fans to such a pitch that, as the arbiter was walking off the field, he was assaulted by a 200-pound fan, Frank Germano. Magerkurth, a hulk of a man himself, was no match for his surprise attacker and was knocked to the ground where the pair exchanged blows, until Bill Stewart, Magerkurth's partner, drove off the assailant. Later, it was revealed that Germano was a parole violator. He was recommitted and Durocher was fined $100 by Frick "for prolonged argument and conduct on the field tending to incite a riot."

While the Dodgers earned most of the headlines, the Reds, and particularly Deacon Bill McKechnie, scored heaviest on the field.

McKechnie managed an N. L. All-Star team to victory in a preseason exhibition for the Finnish Relief Fund in Florida; he directed the N. L. to a 4-0 victory in the annual All-Star Game at Sportsman's Park in St. Louis and, after winning the N. L. pennant, McKechnie added the world championship to his trophies with a seven-game decision over the Tigers.

The Cincinnati triumph was not without its note of sadness. On August 3, while the club was playing a double-header in Boston, second-string catcher Willard Hershberger committed suicide at the club's hotel by slashing his throat with a razor. Hershberger had been despondent for several days, accusing himself for "making a bad call" on a pitch that Harry Danning hit for a game-winning homer at the Polo Grounds.

Three clubs introduced night baseball during the season, the Giants on May 24 and the Pirates and Cardinals on June 4.

After a six-year managerial reign by Pie Traynor, the Pirates presented a new pilot at season's start, bringing Frank Frisch back to the diamond after a one-year stint as a baseball broadcaster in Boston. The Old Flash produced immediate results, lifting the Bucs from sixth place to fourth.

The Pirates also boasted the league batting champion, although the laurels may have been somewhat wilted. Debs Garms, obtained from Boston in March, batted .355, but played in only 103 games and had only 358 official times at bat. Despite some objections that Garms had not batted often enough to qualify for the crown, Frick awarded the outfielder-third baseman the title.

Frank McCormick, Cincinnati first baseman, won MVP honors, beating out Johnny Mize of the Cardinals, 274 votes to 209. At the league's December meeting, Frick was voted a four-year extension on his contract and Bill Klem was appointed chief of staff of umpires. New arbiters were Al Barlick and Jocko Conlan.

1941

War guns boomed ever louder in Europe and the nation, preparing for the inevitable clash of arms, implemented the Selective Service Act, which claimed, as its first baseball draftee, Hugh Mulcahy, Phillies' pitcher who had lost 22 games in 1940 while giving up a league-leading total of 283 hits.

The big noise on this side of the Atlantic was supplied by the big boomers of Brooklyn, Larry MacPhail and Leo Durocher. Never at a loss for words—or screams, shouts and shrieks—the general manager and manager battled each other and the opposition in the Dodgers' first pennant-winning season since 1920.

To shore up weak spots of 1940, MacPhail purchased Kirby Higbe from Philadelphia, Mickey Owen from St. Louis and, after the season began, Billy Herman from Chicago.

The club trained in Havana, ordinarily a poor spot for good discipline, but only one player, Van Mungo, strayed off the reservation.

When Durocher stationed Paul Waner, a pickup from Pittsburgh, in right field instead of Dixie Walker, the Peepul's Cherce, a wire containing signatures of 5,000 Flatbush fans, advised Leo: "Put Walker back in right field or we will boycott the Dodgers."

Predictably, Durocher, with MacPhail's blessing, continued to play Waner until Paul's average dropped below .200 and Walker took over to the great delight of the fans.

In a game at Pittsburgh, September 18, umpire George Magerkurth called a balk on Dodger righthander Hugh Casey. When Du-

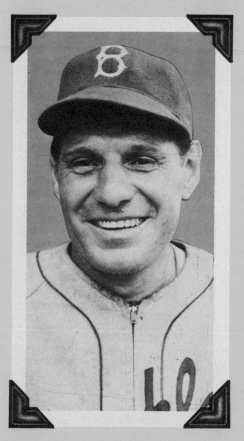

Leo Durocher

George Magerkurth . . . Blind-sided in Brooklyn.

rocher reacted violently, he was bounced from the game, which cost him $150 in a fine levied by Ford Frick.

The next morning, after arriving in Philadelphia, Durocher went for a stroll and encountered Ted Meier of the Associated Press, who inquired about the Pittsburgh rhubarb. The Lip took exception to the query and knocked Meier down. When the combatants were separated, they shook hands, Meier had his story and they parted as reasonably good friends.

After the Dodgers clinched the pennant in Boston, they boarded a train for New York where a gigantic celebration awaited them in Grand Central Station. Fearful that some players would sneak off the train if it made its scheduled stop at 125th street, Durocher ordered the engineer to continue on to its destination.

Unbeknownst to Leo, MacPhail had taken a cab to the 125th street station, hoping to

board the train and participate in the club's hour of glory.

Infuriated, MacPhail hailed a taxi and raced to Grand Central, where he greeted Durocher with "You're fired," a pronouncement that was withdrawn the next morning when Larry learned the reason for Leo's order.

The Dodgers' victory margin over the Cardinals was 2½ games, but the outcome might have been reversed had not a flood of injuries sidelined, at one time or another, such St. Louis players as Johnny Mize, with a broken finger; Jimmy Brown, with a hand injury; Walker Cooper, with a broken collarbone; Mort Cooper, with elbow surgery; Enos Slaughter, also with a fractured collarbone, and Terry Moore, with a head injury after being struck by a fast ball from Art Johnson of the Braves.

The Pirates finished fourth in the race, but ranked high in laughs, thanks to Frank

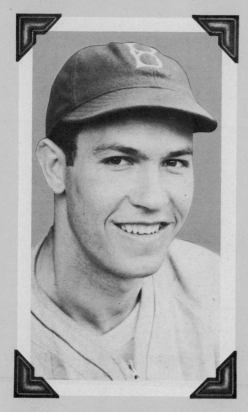

Pete Reiser

Dolf Camilli

Frisch. On one rainy afternoon, trying to convince the umpires that play should be suspended, Frisch appeared on the coaching lines wearing boots and carrying an umbrella, a little pantomime that won him quick banishment.

Another time, when Leo Durocher drew the thumb, Frisch, knowing that Leo had to exit through the Pirate dugout, ordered towels laid like paving blocks for The Lip's recessional. Leo not only kicked every towel individually, but, as he stormed to the clubhouse he smashed every light bulb on his route.

Pete Reiser won the batting championship with a mark of .343, gaining the distinction of becoming, at 22, the youngest swatting king in league history. Previously, Arky Vaughan of the Pirates held the distinction at 23.

In the Most Valuable Player balloting, Reiser finished second to teammate Dolf Camilli, 300 votes to 183, with still a third Dodger, pitcher Whitlow Wyatt, No. 3 with 151.

Vaughan clouted two home runs in the All-Star Game at Detroit, July 8, but was forced to yield hero honors to Ted Williams,

whose two-out, three-run homer climaxed a four-run ninth inning and gave the A. L. a 7-5 victory.

Two cruel breaks figured prominently in the Dodgers' World Series struggle with the Yankees. With the teams deadlocked at one victory apiece, Fred Fitzsimmons, pitching for the Dodgers, was struck on the leg by a line drive off the bat of Yankee pitcher Marius Russo in the seventh inning of the third game. At the time, neither team had scored, but Hugh Casey, replacing Fitzsimmons, yielded two runs in the eighth inning, and the Yankees won 2-1.

Even more merciless was the blow that crushed the Dodgers in game No. 4. With the Dodgers leading, 4-3, and two out in the ninth inning, Casey fanned Tom Henrich on a sharp curve ball—many insisted it was a spitball—and Mickey Owen was unable to hold onto the ball. Henrich reached first base safely, the Yankees poured four runs across the plate and won, 7-4. They finished off the Dodgers the next day, 3-1.

1942

They were hectic times, they were foreboding times . . . 191 National League

Strike 3 evades **Mickey Owen** in historic series misplay.

players were serving in the armed forces, and still, with it all, there developed one of the most dramatic seasons in the loop's 67-year history.

Slashing and snarling with the assurance of winners, the Dodgers built up a 10-game lead by late August. Every opponent had felt the fury of the Dodger beanballs, knuckles and flashing spikes. Joe Medwick brawled with Frank Crespi of St. Louis, Whit Wyatt and Manny Salvo engaged in a duster contest in Boston; Leo Durocher drew a $50 fine and three-day suspension as the result of a rhubarb with umpire Tom Dunn; Paul Erickson and Hi Bithorn of the Cubs took aim at Dodger scalps. It was all part of the Dodger game plan.

Despite the 10-game lead, Larry MacPhail was uneasy. He told his players they should be 20 games ahead. Dixie Walker offered to bet his boss $200 that the Bums would win, a wager that was declined.

With five weeks remaining, the Dodgers held a 7½ game edge as they started on their last swing of the West. First stop, St. Louis.

Max Lanier, Morton Cooper and Johnny Beazley won the first three games before Curt Davis salvaged the finale for Brooklyn. Recovering, the Dodgers split in Chicago, won three of four in Pittsburgh, took two in Cincinnati, but returned with only a two-game margin over the rampaging Cardinals, whom they were scheduled to meet in two games.

Mort Cooper won the first game, 3-0, on a three-hitter and Lanier followed with a 2-1 win, knotting the race.

While the Cardinals were dividing two in Philadelphia the next day, the Dodgers dropped two, to Bucky Walters and Ray Starr of the Reds, whose club batting average of .231 was the lowest in the N. L. since 1910.

The Cardinals were in front to stay and, winning 21 of 26 games in September, finished with 106 victories, two more than the Dodgers.

The Giants, in their first season under Mel

Ott, successor to Bill Terry, finished third. Their record might have been one game better except that on the last day of the season, 9,000 juvenile guests swarmed onto the field in the eighth inning and the Giants, leading by 5-2, were tagged with a 9-0 forfeit loss by umpire Ziggy Sears.

The Polo Grounds also was the scene of the 10th All-Star Game, which was won by the A. L., 3-1, before 34,178, July 6. The next night, in the second half of an All-Star presentation, the A. L. defeated a team of service all-stars, managed by Mickey Cochrane, 5-0, at Cleveland before 62,094, who contributed a net of $71,611.14 for the Ball and Bat Fund and Army-Navy relief.

The Braves, despite a fourth consecutive seventh-place finish, furnished batting headlines twice. On May 13, pitcher Jim Tobin, who had pinch-homered the preceding day, clouted three round-trippers in a 6-5 victory over the Cubs, and on June 19 Paul Waner, ex-Pirate and Dodger, became the seventh major leaguer to collect 3,000 hits, attaining that milestone with a single against Rip Sewell of the Pirates.

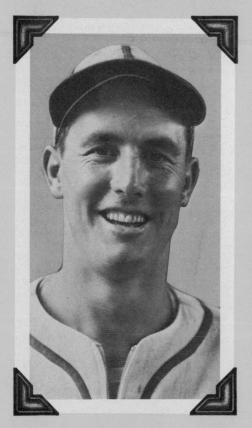

Mort Cooper

The World Series matched the Cardinals against the Yankees, who had won eight world titles and had not lost a World Series since the Cardinals defeated them in 1926. The Bombers started out as though to make short work of the Birds and led, 7-0, through eight innings of the first game. But the momentum generated by a four-run ninth inning in the opening game carried the Cards to four consecutive victories behind Johnny Beazley, Ernie White, Max Lanier and Beazley again. Whitey Kurowski's two-run homer in the ninth inning established the Cards as 4-2 winners in the last contest.

Mort Cooper, who won 22 games for the Cards, won MVP honors with 263 points out of a possible 300, beating out teammate Enos Slaughter.

With the World Series over, MacPhail had only a few weeks to clean up his desk and prepare for his departure from the Dodgers. The Redhead had announced on September 24, "There's a war going on, and I figure they can use me somewhere." He accepted a lieutenant colonel's commission in the Service of Supply.

On October 29, it was announced that Branch Rickey, father of the farm system and architect of the Cardinal powerhouse teams, had signed a five-year contract at undisclosed terms to succeed MacPhail.

1943

Wallingford, Conn., Bear Mountain, N. Y., Hershey, Pa., Cairo, Ill.—these were some of the unfamiliar datelines that preceded spring training stories in the second year of World War II.

Baseball, which had received the green light from President Franklin D. Roosevelt the previous year, now cooperated with Joseph Eastman, director of the Office of Defense Transportation, in reducing travel by training north of the Potomac River and east of the Mississippi.

More top-flight players swapped baseball uniforms for military garb, familiar names like Johnny Beazley and Terry Moore of the Cardinals, Pee Wee Reese and Pete Reiser of the Dodgers, but just as FDR had predicted, even diluted baseball served as a powerful morale booster for a populace gripped by wartime regulations while enjoying a new affluence.

Even the Phillies started the season with brightened prospects. Long burdened by financial "shorts," the Phils were operated for a while by the league, which eventually found a new owner. William D. Cox, heir to a lumber fortune, purchased the club from Gerry Nugent.

One of Cox' first moves was to hire Bucky Harris as a managerial successor to Hans

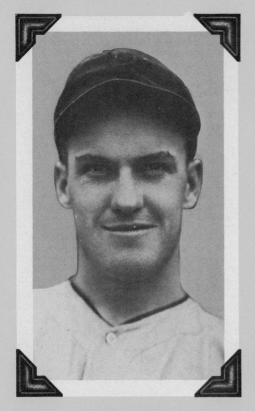

Arky Vaughan   **Dixie Walker**

Lobert, but neither Harris nor Cox survived the year.

Habitually, Harris confined his baseball activities to the ball park. Cox thought he should be a 24-hour-a-day manager. Because of that difference, the two drifted apart.

On July 28, when the Phils arrived in St. Louis, they—and Bucky—learned from newsmen that Cox had announced in Philadelphia four hours earlier that Harris had been succeeded by Fred Fitzsimmons, who had been released by Brooklyn in order to take the job.

Incensed over the shabby treatment of Harris, Phil players threatened to strike, but relented only after Bucky asked them to take the field as a favor to him.

Back in Philadelphia a day or two later, Harris told sportswriters: "He's a fine guy to fire me. He gambles on his own club's games."

Word of the accusation reached the ears of Commissioner Landis, who conducted an investigation and, on November 23, permanently barred Cox from baseball.

The Dodgers also threatened mutiny as the result of a row between Leo Durocher and reporter Tim Cohane, who had quoted The Lip as accusing pitcher Bobo Newsom of playing for individual records only, not for the team. The charge grew out of Newsom's refusal to admit that he had thrown an illegal spitter during a game.

In protest to what he considered a slap at Newsom, an angry Arky Vaughan tossed his uniform at Durocher's feet; Dixie Walker offered the manager his uniform as well.

In a showdown between Cohane and Durocher, the writer extracted from the manager an admission that the quotes were accurate. To many, Leo's job appeared in jeopardy, but he survived the crisis and shortly thereafter Newsom was traded to the St. Louis Browns.

With second-year star Stan Musial enjoying an MVP season, the Cardinals cakewalked to their second consecutive pennant, beating out the Reds by 18 games. The Man led the league in hitting, .357; hits, 220; doubles, 48; triples, 20 and total bases, 347, while scoring 108 runs, second best in the league.

In the All-Star Game at Philadelphia, the N. L. outhit the A. L., 10 to 8, and received a three-hit performance from Vince Di-

Maggio (homer, triple and single), but bowed, 5-3. One of the N. L. hurlers was Rip Sewell, who, en route to a 21-victory season for Pittsburgh, introduced a new word, the "ephus" pitch, to baseball's lexicon. The delivery, which approached the plate on a high arc, also was known as the blooper pitch and was an integral part of Rip's repertoire as a change-up.

Two days before the start of the season, Casey Stengel, strolling in Kenmore Square, Boston, was struck by a taxicab and suffered a badly broken leg that confined him to a hospital for two months.

With Casey providing only minimal assistance to his coaches, George Kelly and Bob Coleman, the Braves climbed one notch, to sixth place. After the season, Dave Egan, crusty columnist for the Boston Record, suggested editorially that the cab driver who ran down Stengel be cited as "the man who did the most for Boston baseball in 1943."

In the World Series, the Cardinals failed to match their performance of the previous October and bowed to the Yankees in five games. Mort Cooper accounted for the Redbirds' only victory, 4-3, in the second contest.

1944

With military demands draining more and more able-bodied players, clubs were hard-pressed to find replacements, but somehow they succeeded.

The Reds, for example, received a letter recommending a player, Jesus (Chucho) Ramos, a Venezuelan outfielder whom they signed without a scouting report. Ramos appeared in four games, batted .500 and then disappeared from the National League scene.

On June 10, the Reds unveiled a 15-year-old lefthanded pitcher from Hamilton, O. Joe Nuxhall, entering a game against the Cardinals with the Reds trailing, 13-0, thereby gained the distinction of being the youngest player ever to appear in a major league box score.

The youngster pitched two-thirds of an inning, issued five walks, uncorked a wild pitch and yielded two singles and five runs in the 18-0 Redbird rumble. Nuxhall disappeared from the N. L., also after that baptism, but returned eight years later to resume a major league career that produced 135 victories.

The manpower crunch also accounted for an iron-man catching performance by Ray Mueller of Cincinnati. Mueller, who had worked the final 62 games in 1943, was behind the plate in all of the Reds' 155 contests in 1944.

The Braves debuted under new ownership. Lou Perini, Guido Rugo and Joseph Maney, fondly referred to as "The Three Little Steamshovels," had been minority stockholders for several years, but grew weary of almost annual assessments and finally offered to buy out fellow owners for what they had paid for their stock.

The energetic trio retained Bob Quinn as general manager, but fired Casey Stengel as manager and promoted coach Bob Coleman to the position.

The Phillies also boasted new ownership, Robert R. M. Carpenter, Sr., an executive in the duPont empire, who bought the Bill Cox interests and installed his son, Bob, Jr., as president of the club.

Before entering the service a short time later, young Bob hired Herb Pennock, former Yankee mound great, from the Red Sox organization to be his general manager. Among Pennock's early moves was the hiring of Johnny Neun and Eddie Sawyer from the Yankee farm system. The pair of well-schooled talent hunters soon developed the young players that produced a Philadelphia pennant and made the Phils contenders for years.

After winning their first game of the season, a 3-0 decision over Bucky Walters and the Reds, the Cubs lost their next nine games and Jimmy Wilson resigned as manager.

Coach Roy Johnson managed the club for one day, in which the Bruins, not surprisingly, were beaten. The next day, he turned the reins over to Charlie Grimm, imported from Milwaukee, where he was vice-president and manager of the American Association club. Despite the horrendous record when he took control, Grimm brought the club home fourth and barely missed a .500 season.

Jim Tobin, who pitched a hitless inning in the N. L.'s 7-1 All-Star victory at Pittsburgh, July 11, accounted for the season's outstanding mound achievement. The Boston righthander hurled two no-hitters, blanking the Dodgers, 2-0, April 27, and the Phils, 7-0, June 22, in a five-inning gem called because of darkness.

Tobin figured in a third no-hitter on May 15, when he was on the losing end of Clyde Shoun's 1-0 masterpiece in Cincinnati. Tobin, drawing a base on balls, was the only batter to reach base against Shoun.

Although the military stripped the Cardinals of more front-line players—Harry Walker, Lou Klein, Al Brazle, Howard Krist, Ernie White—Billy Southworth had enough talent remaining to win his third consecutive pennant with a record of 105-49, a duplicate of his 1943 figures.

Mort Cooper won 22 games, his third consecutive 20-win season, Ted Wilks, released by the Army because of an ulcer, contributed a 17-4 record and George Munger, before his induction in July, won 11 of 14 decisions.

Even Pepper Martin, star of earlier Cardinal champions, made a contribution. Back in the majors after managing farm clubs for three seasons, the 40-year-old Wild Hoss appeared in 40 games and batted .279.

Stan Musial failed to repeat as batting champion, his .347 being overshadowed by Dixie Walker's .357 for Brooklyn.

The Cardinals did retain their MVP honors, however. Marty Marion, the "Mr. Shortstop" of 144 games, beat out Bill Nicholson of the Cubs, 190 points to 189.

The Redbirds regained their world championship laurels in the first World Series played exclusively west of the Mississippi River by defeating the Browns in six games. The batting leader of the Cardinals was second baseman Emil Verban, who batted .412, a figure that was due, reportedly, to Emil's anger at the Browns for placing his wife in a seat behind a post for the third, fourth and fifth games.

On November 25, Kenesaw M. Landis, first Commissioner of Baseball, died at St. Luke's Hospital in Chicago, five days after his 78th birthday. Pending the election of a successor, baseball was governed by Leslie O'Connor, long-time aid to Landis.

Hank Borowy

1945

One good turn delivered on May 6, 1941, deserved another in mid-season four years later, the result of which was Charlie Grimm's third pennant as manager of the Cubs.

On the first date, James Timothy Gallagher, business manager and chief operating executive of the Cubs, sold aging Billy Herman to Brooklyn, where the second baseman congealed the infield and transformed the Dodgers into pennant-winners.

Now, four years later, Gallagher is still the No. 1 man in the Cub front office. His old trading partner in Brooklyn, Larry MacPhail, has returned from military service and is part owner and general manager of the Yankees.

On July 27, Gallagher and Grimm took advantage of an off-day to go fishing. When he returned home, Gallagher was informed that a New York party had sought repeatedly during the day to contact him.

As he deliberated on whether to return the call at such a late hour, Gallagher's phone jangled. It was MacPhail, asking: "What will you give for Borowy?" Hank Borowy, a righthander out of Fordham University, had a 10-5 record for the Yankees.

"How will you get him through waivers?" Gallagher asked.

"I've already got waivers," MacPhail assured him, removing any lingering obstacles Gallagher may have entertained. The deal was completed whereby the Cubs handed over $97,000, and Borowy won 11 games while losing only two for the Bruins, an accomplishment that stamped him as the only pitcher to win a total of 20 games while dividing the season between two major leagues.

Borowy was the pitcher of record when the Cubs clinched the flag on September 29 with a 4-3 conquest of the Pirates. Their final margin over runner-up St. Louis, winner of the last three N.L. flags, was three games.

A week after the start of the season, on April 24, club owners of both major leagues elected Albert B. (Happy) Chandler, former Kentucky Governor and U.S. Senator, as the new Commissioner of Baseball. The 43-year-old Kentuckian was granted a seven-year contract at $50,000 annually.

In a bid to conserve transportation, the annual All-Star Game was cancelled. Instead, a series of inter-league games was arranged with all receipts donated to war relief agencies. The matchups for the games, on a Monday and Tuesday in early July, were: Cubs at White Sox; Yankees at Giants; Reds at Indians; Browns at Cardinals; Dodgers at Senators and Phillies at Athletics. An eighth game involving Pittsburgh and Detroit was cancelled at the request of the Office of Defense Transportation because of the amount of travel that would be required.

The season's foremost batting achievement was credited to Tommy Holmes, Braves' outfielder, who established a modern league record by hitting safely in 37 consecutive games, from June 6 through July 8. The streak, in which Holmes batted .423, was snapped by Hank Wyse in Chicago.

The record hitting was not enough to earn the MVP award for Tommy. Phil Cavarretta, who led the league in hitting with .355, three points higher than Holmes, compiled 279 votes, compared with Holmes' 175.

The Phillies pulled a managerial switch on June 30, canning Fred Fitzsimmons, under whom the Quakers had won only 17 times, in favor of Ben Chapman, the former speed merchant who was acquired from Brooklyn with a 3-3 pitching record. The Phils won only 29 games under Ben, finishing with a record of 46-108, and trailing seventh-place Cincinnati by 15 lengths.

The Cubs, in their last World Series of the league's first century, carried the Tigers to seven games before bowing out. Borowy worked in four games, including the finale, when, with only one day of rest, he failed to retire a batter in the Tigers' five-run first inning and was charged with the 9-3 loss.

During the Series, Boston President Lou Perini lured Billy Southworth away from the Cardinals with a contract that offered $35,000 yearly and a bonus arrangement that promised additional monies up to $20,000 for a pennant.

The season was over. The wars in Europe and in the Pacific had been brought to a successful conclusion. Players had already started to drift back into baseball uniform before the close of the pennant races and everybody knew that the big names would be on hand for the beginning of the next campaign.

In the midst of this auspicious baseball climate, on October 23, Branch Rickey, The Mahatma of Brooklyn's Montague Street, dropped his largest bombshell. Baseball's unwritten, but long observed (since 1880s) color line had been broken. B. R. had signed two Negroes, Jackie Robinson, a shortstop who had played with the Kansas City Monarchs, and John Wright, a pitcher with the Newark Eagles, for the Dodgers' International League farm club at Montreal.

1946

One century after United States forces marched on Mexico, five Mexican brothers, armed with a bulging bankroll, returned the compliment in the first post-war season.

At a time when the nation was trying to adjust to a peace-time economy, the Pasquel brothers—Bernardo, Jorge, Gerardo, Alfonso and Mario, but mostly Jorge—spread discontent among major league players by offering princely salaries to play in their outlaw Mexican League.

Danny Gardella, Sal Maglie, Ace Adams, Harry Feldman, Adrian Zabala, Roy Zimmerman and George Hausmann of the Giants succumbed to the blandishments; so did Luis Olmo and Mickey Owen of the Dodgers. Max Lanier, who had a 6-0 record, and his Cardinal teammates, Fred Martin and Lou Klein, jumped across the border. Stan Musial, back from a year in the Navy, looked hungrily at a $65,000 advance and a five-year offer of $130,000, but turned it down to remain with the Cardinals.

Curious about the methods of Pasquel,

A. B. (Happy) Chandler

Owner Sam Breadon of the Redbirds made a secret flight to Mexico City. Unfortunately for Sam, he was recognized on the streets of the city by Gordon Cobbledick, a Cleveland newspaperman, who broke the story.

As a result of his meeting with Breadon, Pasquel announced he would no longer attempt to entice Cardinal players.

On his return to St. Louis, Breadon was summoned before Commissioner Chandler to explain his mission. When Breadon refused, he was fined $5,000.

Sam explained that he had visited Mexico as a private citizen, interested only in protecting his own investments. This he had explained to Pasquel. If he had gone before Chandler, Breadon said, Pasquel would have thought him guilty of representing baseball. Satisfied, Chandler revoked the fine.

No more players jumped. Those who had broken their major league contracts, or reserve clauses, were suspended for five years, a term that was softened to three years in 1949.

The Braves, in their first game under new Manager Billy Southworth, drew 18,261 to Braves Field, but at least 5,000 of the fans went home sore and soiled. Green paint, applied to the seats a short time before the opener, had failed to dry and found its way onto all manner of costly garments during the afternoon.

The next day this ad appeared in Boston dailies: "An Apology to Braves Fans: The management will reimburse any of its patrons for any expense to which they may be put for necessary cleansing of clothing as a result of paint damage."

Not unexpectedly, more than 13,000 claims were filed, some from California, Nebraska and Florida. Two lawyers labored through the summer screening claims, and the club opened a "Paint Account" at a local bank for this purpose. Eventually, 5,000 claims were honored, the smallest for $1.50, the largest for $50. Altogether, it cost the club $6,000, but the Three Steamshovels considered that the free advertising and goodwill made it money well spent.

The Braves became the seventh N.L. club to install arc lights, making their home debut at night on May 11, when they lost to the Giants, 5-1.

A new influence was felt in the league in mid-season when Robert Murphy, a Harvard-educated lawyer experienced in labor relations, organized the American Baseball Guild. He directed his initial efforts toward the Pirates, representing an industrial community. On the evening of June 5, the matter came to a head in the form of a strike vote among the Pirates.

President Bill Benswanger visited the

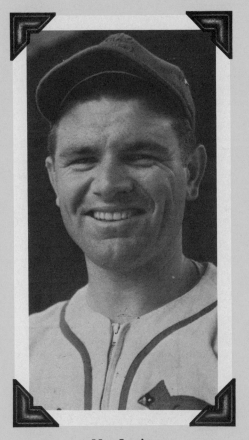

Max Lanier

clubhouse for the first time in 12 years to speak to the players. Murphy recommended a strike, but the players, by a vote of hands, voted to play the game with the Dodgers.

Two nights later, before a game with the Giants, Murphy requested a secret ballot in the clubhouse barred to everyone but playing personnel.

This time the vote was 20-16 in favor of a strike, short of the required 75 percent.

Lee Handley, speaking for the anti-strike faction, said: "We didn't strike because we hold President Bill Benswanger in high regard. His record in dealing with the players is so fine, we fellows thought twice before we did anything so drastic."

As a consequence of labor agitation, owners, meeting in New York, September 16, granted a number of concessions to the players, including a $5,000 minimum salary, a maximum 25 percent slash in salary from one season to the next, and a $25 weekly allowance for incidentals in spring training. In tribute to the lawyer whose work helped bring on these concessions, the players referred to the $25 as "Murphy Money."

On August 8, the Dreyfuss family, which had been prominent on the Pittsburgh sports scene for nearly half a century, sold the Pirates to a syndicate consisting of Frank McKinney, Indianapolis banker; John W. Galbreath, Columbus realtor and contractor; Thomas Johnson, vice-president of the Standard Steel Spring Co., and Harry Lillis (Bing) Crosby, stage, screen and radio entertainer. One of the first moves of the new owners was to install Roy Hamey, president of the American Association and Yankee-trained executive, as general manager. On September 30, Billy Herman was obtained from the Braves and appointed manager, succeeding Frank Frisch, who was released.

Eight days earlier, on September 22, Bill McKechnie announced his retirement as manager of the Reds. He was replaced by Johnny Neun, who was finishing the season as interim pilot of the Yankees.

The All-Star Game series was resumed at Fenway Park, July 9, and proved to be a rout for the A.L. who outhit their opponents, 14 to 3, and coasted to a 12-0 victory as Ted Williams hit two homers and two singles, in addition to scoring four runs and driving in five.

For the first time in National League history, a pennant race finished in a tie, the Cardinals and Dodgers posting records of 96-58, necessitating a best two-out-of-three playoff.

Leo Durocher, who had coined his famous expression "Nice guys finish last" during a pre-game dugout chat at the Polo Grounds, July 5, won the flip of the coin to determine which club received the third-game advantage at home. The Lip chose to play the first contest at St. Louis, where the Cardinals won, 4-2, behind Howard Pollet.

Two days later, on October 3 at Ebbets Field, the Redbirds built up an 8-1 lead before the Dodgers scored three times in the ninth inning of an 8-4 defeat.

In the World Series, the Cardinals defeated the Red Sox, four games to three, with Enos Slaughter scoring the deciding run of the final game on an historic dash from first base on a short double to left-center field by Harry Walker, who led the Cards with a .412 batting average.

Stan Musial won his second MVP award, polling 319 of a possible 336 points and earning 22 of 24 first-place votes.

1947

On the long-range projection, the foremost development of the season was expected to be the readmittance of the Negro to major league baseball as represented by Jackie Robinson of the Dodgers.

Robinson came through as programmed, but the impact of his arrival was overshadowed by the unscheduled departure of Leo Durocher.

Never one to avert headlines, good or bad, the Dodger manager had accumulated some unsalutary pals along the way, for which he received an official reprimand from Commissioner Chandler.

After Laraine Day obtained a United States divorce, in which she was ordered not to remarry for one year, Leo accompanied the actress to Mexico, where she obtained a second divorce, and then flew to El Paso, Tex., where, in January, she and The Lip were married, incurring further public censure.

During spring training, the Dodgers headquartered at the Hotel Nacionale in Havana where the gambling casino was operated by, according to official dictum, an undesirable figure. Trying his best to walk a circumspect path, Leo spent most of his idle time in his hotel room.

When the Dodgers and Yankees opened an exhibition series, March 8, Connie Immerman, major domo at the casino in the Hotel Nacionale, and Memphis Engelberg, a well-known bookmaker, occupied a box seat behind the Yankee dugout, apparently the guests of Yankee President Larry MacPhail.

Spotting the pair, Durocher wondered aloud: "Are there two sets of rules, one for managers, and one for owners?"

When newspapers gave the story the prominence it deserved, MacPhail insisted that Immerman and Engelberg did not occupy the Yankee box, but an adjoining box as guests of the Dodgers.

A column in the Brooklyn Eagle reported that Larry had offered the Yankee managerial job to Leo, a disclosure that MacPhail ridiculed, saying it was just the reverse, that Durocher had sought the Yankee position.

In the welter of charges and counter charges, MacPhail filed a bill of particulars with Chandler, accusing Durocher of "conduct detrimental to baseball."

Chandler conducted two hearings, one at Sarasota, the other at St. Petersburg, and on April 9, announced his bombshell decision:

Durocher was suspended from baseball for one year, the Yankees and Dodgers were fined $2,000 apiece and Harold Parrott, Dodger road secretary who ghosted the Brooklyn Eagle column, was fined $500.

At the height of the furor, the Dodgers announced the acquisition of Robinson's contract from Montreal and a short time later Branch Rickey revealed that Burt Shotton,

Jackie Robinson and **Branch Rickey** . . . A barrier fell.

a Dodger scout who had served as The Mahatma's "Sunday manager" in the days when the devout Rickey abstained from Sabbath piloting with the St. Louis Browns, would serve as Durocher's replacement.

Robinson's rookie season overflowed with racial incidents. Abuse struck from all sides and when the Cardinals threatened to strike, league President Ford Frick took immediate steps, announcing: "I do not care if half the league strikes. Those who do it will encounter quick retribution. All will be suspended and I do not care if it wrecks the National League for five years. This is the United States of America and one citizen has as much right to play as another."

Despite his harsh reception, Robinson batted .297 and stole 29 bases, two statistics that weighed heavily in the Dodgers' flag-winning performance.

Although the Reds finished fifth and the Pirates in a tie for seventh, the two clubs produced plenty of individual headlines.

Ewell Blackwell, nicknamed "The Whip" for his pitching style, won 16 consecutive games for the Reds. Included among the triumphs was a no-hitter against the Braves, June 18, and a two-hitter against Brooklyn four days later. In the second game, Blackwell was only two outs away from matching Johnny Vander Meer's double no-hit effort when Eddie Stanky broke the spell with a single.

The Pirates, having acquired Hank Greenberg from the Tigers, sought to cash in on the slugger's power by building a double bullpen in left field that sliced 30 feet off the home-run distance at Forbes Field. While Hank failed to make capital of the inviting target, christened "Greenberg Gardens," his young teammate, Ralph Kiner, made the most of the new hitter's aid to the degree that he clouted 51 homers to tie John Mize of the Giants for the league leadership.

Kiner's emergence as premier power hitter of the game could not save Billy Herman's managerial career and on September 25 the Pirates announced that the veteran second baseman would not be retained as skipper, although the second half of his two-year contract, calling for $25,000, would be honored.

In the All-Star Game, at Wrigley Field in Chicago, the N. L. suffered a 2-1 defeat before 41,123, who contributed $105,314.90 to the players' pension fund.

The World Series, matching the Dodgers and Yankees, produced two memorable moments. In the fourth game, Cookie Lavagetto's pinch-double with two out in the ninth inning snapped Bill Bevens' bid for a no-hitter and drove in two runs, enabling the Dodgers to win the game, 3-2, and deadlock the Series at two wins apiece.

In the sixth game, Al Gionfriddo of the Dodgers made an implausible catch of Joe DiMaggio's bid for a homer near the left field exit gate at Yankee Stadium, 415 feet from the plate, that snuffed out a Yankee threat and enabled the Dodgers to win, 8-6. However, the Dodgers lost the deciding game, 5-2, the next day.

Most Valuable Player honors went to Bob Elliott, who, in his first season with Boston following his acquisition from the Pirates, batted .317, hit 22 homers and drove in 113 runs to help the Braves finish third.

Following the season, a syndicate headed by Bob Hannegan, retiring as United States Postmaster General, purchased the Cardinals from Sam Breadon for approximately $4,000,000, a record price for a major league franchise.

1948

When Horace Stoneham reached the unalterable conclusion in midseason that Melvin Thomas Ott had outlived his usefulness as Giant manager, the first person he thought of as a possible successor was Burt Shotton, Leo Durocher's stand-in at Brooklyn a year earlier.

Before he could discuss terms with Shotton, however, the Giant owner was required to obtain permission from Branch Rickey, Shotton's employer.

Accordingly, Stoneham arranged a meeting with Rickey in the office of league President Ford Frick.

Relating developments in his entertaining book, THE NEW YORK GIANTS, Frank Graham wrote:

"Rickey, having heard Horace's request, began to talk. Since Branch, when it pleases him to apply it, has a gift for talking around a given point for minutes on end without actually getting to it, it was some time before Horace realized Branch was offering him, not Shotton, but Durocher. Once that was made clear, Horace moved in and an agreement was reached subject, of course, to Durocher's approval. This Leo gave at a meeting in his apartment that night."

The switch of pilots occurred on July 16. After the announcement, Leo flew to Pittsburgh to join the Giants who were already there awaiting the start of a Pirate series.

Ott accepted a front-office position as assistant to farm director Carl Hubbell; and Durocher's successor at the Dodger helm was, once again, the fatherly Shotton.

On the same day, July 16, the Phillies dismissed Ben Chapman as manager and, after a few days under an interim skipper, Dusty Cooke, promoted Eddie Sawyer from Toronto, where he was managing the International League farm.

The Sawyer-for-Chapman switch was the second of the year in the Phils' top command. On January 30, while in New York for major league meetings, General Manager Herb Pennock had died suddenly. The position remained vacant until midseason when, concurrent with the managerial turnover, club President Bob Carpenter announced he would assume the general manager's responsibilites.

The fourth club to undergo a managerial change, the Reds, on August 6, accepted the resignation of Johnny Neun and replaced him with veteran pitcher Bucky Walters.

A few weeks earlier, Cincinnati catcher Dewey Williams was handed one of baseball's most unusual penalties as the result of laying his hands on umpire Frank Dascoli during a rhubarb. Frick fined Williams $100 and suspended him five days, then tempered the punishment with mercy. Because Ray Mueller, another Red catcher, was out of action with a fractured leg, Frick ordered Williams to remain in the Cincinnati clubhouse, in full regalia, during the five-game period, with permission to move into action in the event some disabling injury struck Ray Lamanno, the club's only other able-bodied catcher. For every game that Williams played, a day would be added to his suspension.

Although the Reds finished seventh, their lefthander, Ken Raffensberger, accounted for two of the better pitching performances of the season. Twice the southpaw held the Cardinals to one hit. On May 31, he allowed only a leadoff single by Nippy Jones in the eighth inning in a 7-0 victory at Cincinnati, and on July 11, at St. Louis, Raffensberger permitted only a fourth-inning single to

Eddie Sawyer   **Robert R. M. Carpenter, Jr.**

Marty Marion while winning, 1-0.

Senior circuit representatives collected more hits in the All-Star Game at St. Louis, July 13, but the A. L. scored its 11th victory in 15 tries, 5-2.

After a 34-year wait, the Braves returned to the winner's circle, crossing the finish line 6½ lengths ahead of the Cardinals.

Righthander Johnny Sain won 24 games and lefthander Warren Spahn added 15, inspiring a popular local couplet:

Spahn and Sain

Then pray for rain.

Stan Musial enjoyed another landmark season for the Cardinals. The Man, who won MVP honors, led the league in eight offensive departments and fell only one shy of the home-run championship, which again was shared by Johnny Mize and Ralph Kiner, this time with 40.

Kiner's long-range hitting helped lift the Pirates, in their first season under Bill Meyer as manager, from a tie for seventh to fourth place.

,Sain got the Braves off to a winning start in the World Series, beating Bob Feller and the Indians, 1-0, but he lost his second start, 2-1, although allowing only five hits, and the Braves lost in six games. The only other victory was registered by Spahn with a superb relief job in the fifth contest.

When the major meetings were held in Chicago in December, Leo Durocher occupied a long familiar spot—on the carpet—before Commissioner Chandler.

The Lip was found guilty of tampering with Fred Fitzsimmons, whom the Giants signed as a coach in October, while the former pitcher was under contract to the Braves. The Giants were fined $2,000, Durocher $500 for conducting the negotiations, and Fitzsimmons $300, in addition to drawing a suspension extending from March 1 to April 1, 1949.

1949

Eddie Waitkus had played 54 games for the Phillies and was batting .306 when, at

12:40 a.m., June 15, he received a message at the club's base in Chicago, the Edgewater Beach Hotel.

"It's extremely urgent that I see you as soon as possible," read the hand-written message, signed by Ruth Ann Steinhagen, a guest in the hotel. For a few moments, the first baseman deliberated, then decided to answer the summons.

When he knocked on the girl's door, the 19-year-old bobby soxer greeted Waitkus with a .22-calibre rifle bullet in his chest.

While Waitkus was rushed to Illinois Masonic Hospital, where he spent many weeks in convalescence, interrogation revealed that Miss Steinhagen had a secret crush on the ballplayer and the previous winter, when Waitkus was traded by the Cubs to the Phillies, had threatened to move to Philadelphia to be near her idol.

The young lady had consulted a psychiatrist, it was learned, and was assured that her intense feelings toward Waitkus were not sufficiently serious to require treatment.

Later Miss Steinhagen was committed for psychiatric therapy, and Waitkus recovered from the shooting, although he played no more baseball the remainder of the season.

Even without their talented first baseman, the Phils finished in third place, the first time since 1932 that they had been out of the second division.

On the day after Waitkus was wounded, Lou Klein pinch-hit successfully for the Cardinals, marking the first time that one of the Mexican League jumpers of three years earlier returned to action in the league. Klein, who had drifted to the Quebec Provincial League, bought his release from the Sherbrooke club for $1500 in order to take advantage of the blanket amnesty extended by Commissioner Chandler to those who had abandoned Organized Baseball.

Concurrent with their return to good standing, Max Lanier and Fred Martin dropped their $2,500,000 damage suit and Danny Gardella withdrew his $500,000 suit against Organized Ball.

Once again Leo Durocher was the man in the middle of controversy, charged with slugging a fan following a game at the Polo Grounds.

The incident occurred on April 28 as the Giants were walking to their clubhouse in center field after absorbing a 13-2 shellacking by the Dodgers.

A spectator, identified as Fred Boysen, accused The Lip of flattening him with a left hook as Boysen was running after Jackie Robinson to congratulate the Dodger star on his performance in the game.

Pre-empting the authority of league President Ford Frick, Commissioner Chandler

conducted a hearing at which both Giant coaches, Fred Fitzsimmons and Frank Frisch, testified in Leo's defense, and the manager was absolved of all blame.

As a consequence of the episode, Giant Owner Horace Stoneham ordered all spectators kept off the field after a game until uniformed personnel of both the Giants and visitors had reached the clubhouses.

Because of the instant success of Jackie Robinson with the Dodgers, the Giants signed their first Negroes, Hank Thompson, who had received a trial with the St. Louis Browns in 1947, acquired from the Kansas City Monarchs, and Monte Irvin, purchased from the Newark Eagles. Both were assigned to Jersey City (International).

The N. L. suffered its fourth consecutive All-Star loss, and 12th in 16 tries, when A. L. representatives pounded out an 11-7 decision at Ebbets Field, Brooklyn, July 12.

The first death benefits of the player pension plan were paid to Mrs. Ernie Bonham, widow of the Pittsburgh pitcher who died suddenly on September 15. The 36-year-old hurler underwent an appendectomy and other abdominal surgery a week earlier. Benefits amounted to $90 monthly for 10 years.

Two managerial changes occurred during the campaign, On June 12, Charlie Grimm stepped from the Cubs' field leadership into a front-office position and was succeeded by Frank Frisch, who had been a coach with the Giants.

In the last week of the season, with the Reds trying desperately to escape the cellar, Bucky Walters was sacked in favor of Luke Sewell.

Fred Saigh, who acquired controlling interest in the Cardinals on January 27 when he purchased the interests of his partner, Bob Hannegan, narrowly missed a pennant in his first year of ownership.

On September 25, after winning their final home game, the Cards led the Dodgers by 1½ games. However, the Redbirds lost two games to the Pirates, including a 7-2 decision to Murry Dickson, who had been sold to the Bucs for $125,000 the previous winter, and two more to the Cubs before pulling out of their nosedive to capture the season's finale. By that time it was too late and the Dodgers, winning three of their last four games, slipped in by one game.

The Dodgers and Yankees exchanged 1-0 shutouts in the first two games of the World Series before the Bombers ran off three victories in a row to annex their 12th world championship.

Dodger second baseman Jackie Robinson, in his third year in the league, won Most Valuable Player honors, beating out Stan

Monte Irvin   Don Newcombe

Musial by a comfortable margin, and his teammate, Don Newcombe, gained the Baseball Writers' Association's rookie award by winning 17 games following his recall from Montreal on May 14.

1950

Christened the Whiz Kids because their average age was only 26 and they played the game with a youthful fire and determination, the Phillies ended a 35-year pennant drouth by clinching the flag in a dramatic last inning of the final game of the season.

Not since 1915 had the Phils known first-place glory and in 13 consecutive years during the interim they had finished in seventh or eighth place, earning the well-deserved nickname of "Phutile Phils."

On July 25, Bubba Church and Robin Roberts hurled a double shutout over the Cubs to usher in a home stand and the Phils took over first place, which they retained the rest of the way.

Thousands of pulses quickened, and tens of thousands of hearts skipped beats before the Phillies locked it up, making Pauline look like a piker in the process.

With 11 games remaining, the Phils enjoyed a 7½-game lead which all but vanished as the club lost eight of the next 10 games, forcing the race into the final day at Brooklyn with the Phillies clinging to a one-game lead.

Robin Roberts, pitching with only two days' rest, opposed Don Newcombe in the tell-all contest in which the Phils and Dodgers were tied, 1-1, entering the last of the ninth.

A walk to Cal Abrams and Pee Wee Reese's single put Roberts on the ropes. Another single by Duke Snider could have forced a playoff for the pennant, but center fielder Richie Ashburn tossed out Abrams at the plate as the other runners moved to third and second.

After an intentional pass to Jackie Robinson loaded the bases, Carl Furillo fouled out and Gil Hodges was retired on a fly ball.

In the 10th, Dick Sisler smashed a three-run homer to provide a dramatic climax to the league's 75th campaign.

In addition to Roberts, who won 20 games, and Curt Simmons, who won 17 before being summoned to military duty, the Phils boasted a third pitcher, rubber-armed Jim Konstanty, whose 16 wins in 74 relief appearances earned for him the Most Valuable Player honors, the first time a fireman had been so acclaimed.

The Giants, having acquired shortstop Alvin Dark and second baseman Eddie Stanky in a big winter trade with the Braves, finished only five games out of the lead and were the only club to win the season series from the Phils. Tempers flared on several occasions when the Phils and Giants met.

Robin Roberts . . . Foremost among the Whiz Kids.

Dick Sisler . . . His homer crowned Phils as champions.

The feud was born when Stanky, standing behind second base, waved his arms in a distracting manner while Andy Seminick, Phil catcher, was at bat. On orders from the umpires, Stanky desisted, but the next day, August 12, after Seminick slid hard into Hank Thompson, knocking the third baseman unconscious, Stanky resumed his gyrations and was ejected. Seminick later slid hard into shortstop Bill Rigney and a general melee ensued. Seminick and Rigney were fined $25 apiece by league President Ford Frick for precipitating the brawl.

On September 27, Monte Irvin crashed into Seminick in a play at the plate, inflicting a painful ankle injury that hobbled the catcher the remainder of the season.

The All-Star Game returned to its original site, Comiskey Park in Chicago, July 11, and the N. L. turned the tables on its long-time tormentors when Cardinal second basemen Red Schoendienst crashed a home run to account for a 4-3 victory in 14 innings, the first time the stellar classic went into extra innings.

The Pirates, who finished in eighth place, more than 30 games behind the Phils, made preseason headlines when they signed Paul Pettit, a California phenom, for $100,000, to be paid in 10 annual installments of $10,000 each.

The lefthanded pitcher had brief trials with the Pirates and, after an undistinguished minor league career, retired after more than a decade of riding the buses.

Gil Hodges, Dodger first baseman, joined

Gil Hodges . . . Into the four-homer society.

an exclusive society of sluggers on August 31, when he hit four home runs in a 19-3 victory over the Braves at Ebbets Field. Hodges was the fourth National Leaguer and sixth major leaguer to turn the trick.

On September 13, Sal Maglie, Giant right-hander, was only four putouts away from breaking Carl Hubbell's record of pitching $46\frac{1}{3}$ consecutive scoreless innings, when Gus Bell of the Pirates hit a 257-foot fly ball to right field that fell two feet fair and one foot above the brick wall for a home run at the Polo Grounds. The Giants won, 3-1.

In the World Series, the Phils expired in four games against the Yankees. Ace reliever Jim Konstanty started the first game and allowed only five hits, but the Phils collected only two safeties and bowed, 1-0. Roberts was beaten, 2-1, the next day on Joe Di-Maggio's 10th-inning homer and the Yanks wound things up in the next two outings, 3-2 and 5-2.

On October 24, Branch Rickey sold his interest in the Dodgers to Walter O'Malley and Mrs. John Smith for $1,050,000. He accepted the general managership of the Pirates.

One of the game's all-time tragi-heroic figures, Grover Cleveland Alexander, who had pitched the Phils to their first and only previous pennant in 1915, died in St. Paul, Neb., November 4, after a lengthy illness. Old Pete was 63 when death came in a room which he rented with part of his $150 monthly pension.

Ford Frick was awarded a four-year extension as league president, at an increase in salary to $55,000, during the winter meeting in Florida.

Commissioner A. B. Chandler did not fare as well. When only nine clubs, three short of the required 12, voted to extend his contract, Happy's number was up.

The Strutting Years
1951-1975

☒☉☒

The National League launched its fourth quarter-century of competition on April 16, 1951, amid a furor that extended from Washington, D. C., to Korea.

Three days after the first baseball was thrown in competitive anger, a distinguished septuagenarian stood before a joint meeting of Congress and proclaimed somberly:

"Old soldiers never die, they just fade away. I now close my military career and just fade away, an old soldier who tried to do his duty as God gave him the light to see that duty. Good-bye."

Douglas MacArthur, lionized for his role in World War II, closed an illustrious military career that was curtailed because of irreconcilable differences with President Harry Truman.

Elsewhere, attention was focused on McCarthyism, the doctrine of subversion preached by Senator Joseph McCarthy of Wisconsin; the 22nd Amendment was ratified, limiting the Presidency to two terms; James Jones wrote a best-seller, "From Here to Eternity," paperbacks and LP records were gaining popularity, American Telephone and Telegraph became the first corporation with more than one million stockholders and the employment of women attained a new high, 19,308,000.

On February 2, the National League declared a recess from spring training preparations to observe its 75th birthday.

Returning to the place of its birth, the Grand Central Hotel, at that time known as the Broadway Central, the National League celebrated its diamond jubilee with a monstrous party. Three thousand invitations were extended by President Ford Frick and 600 accepted. The tab, it was said, came to $20,000.

From Ty Cobb, the first Hall of Famer, to Jimmie Foxx and Mel Ott, the newest shrine members, honored guests came from all corners of the country. Former President John Heydler arrived from San Diego,

Mickey Cochrane came from Billings, Mont., Cy Young from Newcomerstown, O., and Fred Clarke from Winfield, Kan.

Arlie Latham, a remnant from the early years of baseball, was the party's elder citizen at 91.

The celebration commenced at 1 p.m. and continued without interruption until "Lullaby of Broadway" was more than a song title.

At the star-spangled dinner, emceed by Frick, a telegram was read from President Truman, in which the Chief Executive said:

"Baseball is our national sport and through the years it has increased its hold upon the public through those who play it in boyhood and later enjoy it as spectators. Today millions of us enjoy major and minor league games, not only from grandstands and bleachers, but over the air and on screens.

"The founders of the National League and the fans of that era never dreamed the game would achieve such popularity or there would be such inventions as radio and television to carry it to millions of Americans all over the world.

"Baseball has made great contributions in peace and in war it has asked for no special favors, nor will it in our present preparedness program.

"My message to all who attend the diamond jubilee dinner, 'May the sun never set on American baseball.' "

As the banquet drew to a close and as guests gathered in small huddles to cut up old touches or listen to the harmonizing of Commissioner A. B. Chandler and Branch Rickey, two familiar Broadway figures were seen to nod in agreement at one corner of the second-floor ballroom.

Eddie Brannick, long-time traveling secretary of the Giants, and Ward Morehouse, drama critic and playwright by profession but a deep-rooted baseball fan by avocation, were remarking about the splendor of the occasion.

Writing in the February 14, 1951, issue of THE SPORTING NEWS, Morehouse revealed: "I have a date with Eddie Brannick to attend the 100th anniversary party . . . a quarter century from now."

Unfortunately for the National League and its Centennial celebration, they were not able to keep the appointment. Morehouse died on December 7, 1966, and Brannick, aged 82, on July 18, 1975.

1951

A straggling few got up to go in deep despair. The rest cling to the hope which springs eternal in the human breast.

The couplet, immortalized by Ernest Thayer in "Casey at The Bat," must have occurred to more than a few on the afternoon of October 3 as some among the 34,320 payees at the Polo Grounds took one lingering look at the scoreboard and shuffled toward the exits.

The scoreboard legend was plain and pitiful to Giant aficionados. The home club, after eight innings of the third and decisive playoff game for the league championship, had only four hits off Don Newcombe and was trailing the Dodgers, 4-1, with only three outs remaining.

Indeed, things looked extremely rocky for the New York nine that day. The Dodgers, who had been denied the pennant on the final day of the preceding season, were not about to be deprived of another. Or so it seemed until . . .

Alvin Dark and Don Mueller singled, Monte Irvin popped out and Whitey Lockman doubled, scoring Dark and sending Mueller to third. Sliding into the base, Mueller injured his ankle and was replaced by Clint Hartung.

Ralph Branca was rushed to the pitching mound, replacing Newcombe. The reliever's first pitch was a called strike. On the next delivery,—"It was a high curve ball," said Branca—Bobby Thomson swung and arched a home run into the left field seats, bringing to a crashing, hysterical climax, not only the league's second playoff, but also an incredible season in which the Giants trailed at one point in August by 13½ games.

Somebody called the Giant victory "The Little Miracle of Coogan's Bluff," and it was nothing less, although Chuck Dressen, concluding his first season as Dodger skipper following the dismissal of Burt Shotton, had less elegant expressions.

The Dodgers grabbed the lead on May 13 and built up a cushion that, to pursuing clubs, appeared insurmountable by mid-August. Then the chinks began to appear.

Starting August 12, the Giants won 16 consecutive games, including three from the Dodgers and six from the Phillies. In the same period, the Dodgers were splitting even in 18 games. On the morning of September 9, Brooklyn led by 5½ games. Nine victories in their last 20 games were not enough. The Giants won 16 of their final 20 and forced the race into a playoff for a decision.

Jim Hearn won the opening game, 3-1, for the Giants, but Clem Labine tied the series with a 10-0 laffer the next afternoon. In game No. 3, the Dodgers cuffed Sal Maglie for eight hits and four runs before The Barber was lifted for a pinch-hitter and Larry Jansen finished up.

Oddly, Thomson, who collected three Giant hits, stood to be the goat of the game before his historic homer. In the second inning, the Staten Island Scot singled and ran head down toward second base, where Lockman was standing. Thomson was retired in a rundown, taking the Giants out of what might have been a productive inning.

Dave Koslo and Hearn accounted for Giant victories in two of the first three World Series games with the Yankees. The fourth game was postponed one day by rain providing Yankee pitching ace Allie Reynolds, first-game loser, with an extra day of rest. Reynolds won the fourth contest and the Giants failed to recover, losing the last two games as well.

En route to their classic collapse, the Dodgers engaged in one serious rhubarb. On September 27, at Boston, catcher Roy Campanella, second baseman Jackie Robinson and pitcher Preacher Roe led a demonstration against umpire Frank Dascoli, who had ruled Bob Addis safe in a play at the plate. Campy and Robinson were fined $100 apiece and Roe $50 by league President Ford Frick.

The decision was one of the last rendered by Frick as league president. On September 20, at a meeting of the 16 club owners in Chicago, Frick was elected Commissioner of Baseball, succeeding Albert B. Chandler.

One week later, on September 27, Warren Giles, general manager of the Reds, was elected 11th president of the league. The promotion entailed a minimum of physical change for Giles. He simply moved from the Reds' headquarters to Chandler's old quarters one block away and converted them into the league offices, while in New York Frick converted N.L. offices into the Commissioner's headquarters.

Gabe Paul succeeded his long-time boss as G.M. of the Reds.

With Stan Musial, Ralph Kiner, Bob Elliott and Gil Hodges clouting home runs, the

Bobby Thomson climaxes a miracle drive with a home-run shot
heard 'round the baseball world.

N.L. won the All-Star Game, 8-3, before 52,075 at Briggs Stadium, Detroit, on July 10.

The victory marked the heaviest offense by the N.L. in midsummer competition, and the first time the senior loop had won two consecutive games.

Two managerial switches occurred during the season, Billy Southworth resigning his Boston post on June 19 and being succeeded by Tommy Holmes, and Frank Frisch being dismissed by the Cubs on July 21 in favor of Phil Cavarretta.

After the season, the Cardinals released Marty Marion after one year as manager and hired Eddie Stanky.

Roy Campanella of the Dodgers was acclaimed MVP by the baseball writers, compiling 243 points to 191 by Musial. Rookie

honors went to Willie Mays, the Giants' spectacular center fielder.

1952

The season was barely five weeks old and the Giants, in first place with a 26-8 record, were leading the Dodgers by 2½ lengths.

Seven consecutive victories, including three over Brooklyn, had made life beautiful for Leo Durocher. Sal Maglie had won his first nine decisions, Jim Hearn was 4-1, Hoyt Wilhelm 4-0.

There was only one serpent in Leo's Eden. Irrepressible Willie Mays was scheduled for induction into the Armed Forces the next day, May 29, and with the Say-Hey Kid gone, things could not possibly be the same. The

Giants were not long in feeling the effect of Willie's departure. They lost eight of their next 10 games, Maglie losing two of them, and they drifted out of first place. By late August they were 10½ games behind the Dodgers and, although they later climbed to within three games of the top, Brooklyn was not about to crack again, winning seven of its last 11 games.

Two events of monumental importance occurred during the Dodger march to the pennant. On May 21, they set a modern major league record by scoring 15 runs in the first inning of a 19-1 rout of the Reds. Twenty-one Dodgers went to the plate, including 19 in a row who reached base safely. Of the 15 runs, 12 scored after two were out. Ten hits rattled off Dodger bats, which were combined with seven walks and two hit batsmen to produce the outburst. Duke Snider hit the only home run of the inning, although Bobby Morgan later smashed a pair of two-run homers.

On June 19, Carl Erskine barely missed becoming the first pitcher in 30 years to pitch a perfect game in the regular season. The righthander held the Cubs hitless in winning, 5-0, but issued a third-inning pass to his mound opponent, Willard Ramsdell, on four consecutive balls.

Four managers fell from favor during the season. On May 31, with the Braves in seventh place, Tommy Holmes was replaced by Charlie Grimm, who had been managing the club's American Association farm at Milwaukee.

On July 28, the Reds fired Luke Sewell and hired Rogers Hornsby, who had been axed less than two months earlier by the Browns.

Eddie Sawyer, heralded less than two years earlier for delivering a pennant in Philadelphia, was canned on June 27 and succeeded by Steve O'Neill, who had managed the Red Sox in 1951.

Prior to the next to last game of the season, Bill Meyer revealed that he would terminate a five-year term with the Pirates. The position was taken by Fred Haney, promoted from the Hollywood (Pacific Coast) Stars.

In his first season as league president, Warren Giles suspended Durocher three times for clashes with umpires. On June 29, The Lip kicked dirt on home plate and also booted umpire Bill Stewart in the shins, for which he drew a four-day suspension.

On August 17, Leo got into a hassle with Augie Donatelli and cocked his arm as if to strike the arbiter before players intervened. He was handed a five-day suspension for this offense.

An exchange of beanballs with the Dodgers on September 8 earned Leo a two-day recess from managing and a $100 fine.

On April 22, freshman Cardinal Manager Eddie Stanky protested vehemently Scotty Robb's ejection of Solly Hemus for flipping his bat in protest of a called third strike. Stanky was fined $50 and Hemus $25. Giles announced that Robb had been assessed considerably more than the combined fines against the players. Robb resigned on May 5, and two days later joined the American League staff.

All-Star accolades went to the N.L. for the third consecutive year as the result of a 3-2 victory, limited to five innings because of rain, at Shibe Park, Philadelphia, July 8.

Three players accumulated more than 200 points in the MVP balloting, with outfielder Hank Sauer of the Cubs edging Robin Roberts of the Phils, 226 points to 211. Joe Black, Dodger pitcher who was named Rookie of the Year, totaled 208 MVP points.

Black won the first World Series game, outdueling Allie Reynolds of the Yankees, 4-2. Preacher Roe won the third game, 5-3, and Erskine went 11 innings to a 6-5 victory in the fifth game, but then the Yanks ran off two consecutive victories, 3-2 and 4-2, frustrating the Dodgers' world championship ambitions for the sixth time in as many tries.

The sorriest member of the Dodger cast was Gil Hodges, who, after batting .254 with 32 homers and 102 RBIs during the regular season, went hitless in 21 Series at-bats.

1953

For 53 years—or since dropping four clubs in 1900—the National League had functioned as an eight-club entity, embracing Chicago, the only charter member with an uninterrupted membership, Pittsburgh, Cincinnati and St. Louis in the West, and Boston, New York, Brooklyn and Philadelphia in the East.

As recently as 1948, Boston had fared extremely well, attracting a season attendance of 1,455,439 in a championship season.

From that date, however, the gates clicked more slowly by the day, as season figures slipped to 1,081,795, then to 844,391, 487,475 and 281,278.

Lou Perini, who had bought out the two other Steamshovels, Joseph Maney and Guido Rugo, lost a reported $600,000 in 1952, when the Braves finished seventh, and soured on the Athens of America as a baseball mecca.

On March 13—Black Friday in Boston— N. L. owners, meeting at the Vinoy Park Hotel in St. Petersburg, granted Perini permission to transfer the Braves to Milwaukee, where the Braves already owned the

Warren Giles . . . Put a silencer on The Lip.

local American Association franchise and where spanking new County Stadium awaited a tenant with 44,091 open seats.

Success was instantaneous. From seventh place, the Braves soared to second, and played before 1,826,397 as not only Milwaukee, but all Wisconsin, lavished affection upon the players.

From the moment that Bill Bruton hit a 10th-inning home run, his only homer of the year, in the home opener to give Warren Spahn a 3-2 victory over the Cardinals, the Braves were the talk of baseball. From May 13, they were either first or second. Only a superior Brooklyn club, perhaps the most powerful in the history of that franchise, overshadowed the performance of the Braves, who finished 13 games out of first place.

One of the brightest spots of the season for Milwaukee fans occurred on May 25 when righthander Max Surkont established a

modern record by fanning eight consecutive batters during the second half of a double-header against Cincinnati, won by the Braves, 10-3.

The Cardinals, who had been sold twice in the five preceding years, underwent another change of ownership. On the eve of the season opener, Anheuser-Busch, Inc., purchased the club for $3,750,000 from Fred Saigh, who had been sentenced to 15 months in federal prison for income tax evasion. The brewery, under President August A. Busch, Jr., arranged to purchase the club to assure its remaining in St. Louis.

One of the Cardinals' first moves under the new ownership was to purchase Sportsman's Park from the landlord Browns for $800,000 and institute a giant renovating program costing $400,000. Initial plans also called for renaming the park Budweiser Stadium, but it was finally decided to rechristen it Busch Stadium.

Although he did not play the final three weeks of the season, Carl Furillo rebounded from a .247 batting average in 1952 to win the league batting championship with a mark of .344.

On September 6, the Brooklyn outfielder was struck by a pitch from Ruben Gomez of the Giants. Believing that Leo Durocher had ordered the knockdown pitch, Furillo trotted to first base, then wheeled and ran toward the Giant dugout, challenging the New York manager, who responded to the gesture. The two touched off a melee, during which Furillo suffered a bone fracture in his left hand. He recovered in time to play in the World Series.

A bizarre mishap on June 4 deprived the Phillies of what might have been a more successful season. Lefthander Curt Simmons, mowing the lawn at his suburban home, lost half an inch off his left big toe and suffered numerous lacerations as well

Walter Alston

as the result of being cut by the power mower. He was sidelined for a month.

On the same day, June 4, the Pirates engineered the biggest deal of the season, sending home-run king Ralph Kiner and three other players to the Cubs for six players and an estimated $100,000.

Matching the best record of the A. L., the N. L. won its fourth consecutive All-Star Game, posting a 5-1 decision at Cincinnati, July 14. The A. L. collected only two hits off Robin Roberts, Warren Spahn and Curt Simmons before combining three singles for their only run off Murry Dickson in the ninth. For the first time since 1944, the game failed to produce a home run.

The only managerial change in the majors during the season involved Rogers Hornsby and the Reds. On September 15, The Rajah inquired of General Manager Gabe Paul if he figured in the club's plans for 1954, and two days later was handed his walking papers. Coach Buster Mills directed the club through its last eight games, after which George (Birdie) Tebbetts, former American League catcher, was promoted from Indianapolis of the American Association.

Although Carl Erskine set a record by fanning 14 Yankees in the third World Series game, the Dodgers lost six out in six contests. Gil Hodges, goat of the '52 Series with an "0 for 21" record, bounced back to hit .364.

Less than a week after the Series, Charlie Dressen announced he would not return as Dodger manager in 1954 because the club had refused his request for a three-year contract.

Rather than settle for a one-year pact at a substantial increase in pay, Dressen accepted an offer to manage the Oakland (Pacific Coast) club, while Walter Alston, who had produced two first-place and as many second-place finishes at Montreal (International), was signed to the first of 23 one-year contracts.

The Dodgers swept player honors, catcher Roy Campanella winning the MVP award, and second baseman Jim Gilliam being named the top rookie.

1954

Stan Musial of the Cardinals established a major league record on May 2 by hitting five home runs in a doubleheader against the Giants in St. Louis.

And Joe Adcock, Milwaukee first baseman, equalled a major mark on July 31 by clouting four homers in a 15-7 victory at Brooklyn.

And on April 23, a Milwaukee rookie tagged Vic Raschi of the Cardinals for a home run that was to propel him on the path

Roy Campanella . . . A Dodger with MVP credentials.

to the all-time home-run championship, a youngster named Henry Aaron.

But the year belonged to Willie Mays, still young, and exuberant and inspirational after 21 months in the Army.

Twice the Say-Hey Kid had tried unsuccessfully to obtain an Army discharge because of dependency. But it wasn't until he showed a "cyclic employment contract" to officers at Fort Eustis, Va., that the league's No. 1 rookie of 1951 was separated from the service.

Willie appeared in all but three of the Giants' 154 games, batted .345, hit 41 homers and drove in 110 runs, an MVP performance, and led the Giants to a five-length victory over the Dodgers in the flag race.

Bobby Thomson, hero of the Giants' pulsating pennant-clincher of three years earlier, was not a member of the '54 cast, having been traded on February 1 to the Braves for Johnny Antonelli, the $75,000 bonus baby of several years earlier.

Thomson was of little value to the Braves, suffering a triple fracture of his right ankle in a spring training sliding accident, and appearing in only 43 games, during which he batted .232.

Antonelli, however, blossomed as a mound star, winning 21 games and losing seven and leading in earned-run average.

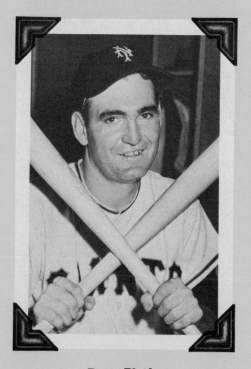

Dusty Rhodes

The season's most violent rhubarb took place in St. Louis, July 18, and involved the Phillies, managed by former Cardinal great Terry Moore, who had replaced Steve O'Neill only a few days earlier.

Because of a one-hour rain delay in the first game of a doubleheader, won by the Phils, 11-10, the nightcap did not get underway until 6:48. By the fifth inning the Phils led, 8-1, and the Cards started to stall, trying to take advantage of approaching darkness in the mistaken impression that the lights could not be turned on to complete the Sunday game.

Pitcher Cot Deal grew suddenly wild, an argument between St. Louis catcher Sal Yvars and Phil first baseman Earl Torgeson precipitated a free-for-all, causing umpire Babe Pinelli to award a forfeit to the Phils.

The next day St. Louis Manager Eddie Stanky offered a public apology to the fans, many of whom had cheered the forfeit. League President Warren Giles conducted a hearing and handed a five-day suspension to Stanky, commencing at that point, and fined him $100. Yvars was suspended three days and Torgeson two.

In addition to the Phils' managerial switch, the Cubs acquired a new skipper on March 29, when Phil Cavarretta was bounced in favor of Stan Hack.

While Moore survived the season in Philadelphia, he, too, was soon gone, replaced by Mayo Smith, who was promoted from Birmingham (Southern).

Front-office changes during the year featured H. Roy Hamey, assistant general manager of the Yankees, becoming G. M. of the Phils; Arthur (Red) Patterson, switching from the Yankees to the assistant G. M. chair with the Dodgers, and Clarence (Pants) Rowland, after 11 years as president of the Pacific Coast League, resigning on November 28, to become, at 75, executive vice-president of the Cubs.

In the All-Star Game at Cleveland, won by the A. L., 11-9, on July 13, a decision by umpire Bill Stewart engendered sharp repercussions later in the season.

Stewart, working behind the plate, rejected an N. L. charge that Dean Stone, pitching for the A. L., balked when Red Schoendienst of the Cardinals was thrown out while trying to steal home.

One month later, on August 13, Stewart was embroiled in a dispute with Manager Birdie Tebbetts of the Reds. Tebbetts, endowed with a good memory and a way with words, told the arbiter: "You're a lousy ump. You blew it in the World Series (a call favoring the Braves against the Indians in 1948), you blew it in the All-Star Game and you blew it tonight. Why don't you quit?" Tebbetts, fined $50 for his outburst, thought

Stan Musial . . . He made THE MAN household words.

he was engaging in private conversation with Stewart. He was overheard, however, by a field photographer, who reported the exchange to newsmen.

At the winter meetings, the league voted to bar photographers from the playing area, and Stewart, turned down in his request to be named supervisor of umpires, tendered his resignation to Giles after a 22-year career.

The World Series paired the Indians, who had established an A. L. record with 111 wins, against the Giants, who matched the Boston Braves' precedent-setting achievement of winning in four games.

Willie Mays highlighted the first game with a catch that many regard as the most spectacular in World Series competition. The Giant center fielder roamed to dead center field at the Polo Grounds to make an over-the-shoulder catch of Vic Wertz' 440-foot drive. Dusty Rhodes smashed a three-run pinch-homer in the 10th inning to give the Giants a 5-2 victory.

Bill Stewart

The part-time outfielder clouted a single and homer, driving in two runs, in the second game, a 3-1 New York victory; rapped a two-run pinch-single in the third, and then sat out the finale. For the Series, colorful Dusty collected four hits in six tries for 10 total bases.

Rookie honors for the year went to Wally Moon, .304-hitting Cardinal outfielder whose rapid development forced the Birds to trade long-time favorite Enos Slaughter to the Yankees two days before the start of the season.

1955

In the land of plenty, Walter O'Malley sounded the alarm—the Dodgers would transfer seven home games to Jersey City in 1956 and would abandon Ebbets Field for a new stadium after the completion of the 1957 season.

The O'Malley pronouncement, made in mid-August while the Dodgers were enjoying a 10-game lead in the pennant race and were attracting fans at a rate that would exceed 1,000,000 for the season, was regarded initially as only a power play, aimed at applying pressure on the city fathers for a new, spacious municipally-owned stadium to replace ancient Ebbets Field, with its 31,902 seats.

Whatever the motives, the city fathers would have done well to have heeded the words of the Dodger boss. Some serious thought and some well-apportioned funds might have spared National League fans in greater New York loads of grief—and the ignominy of being without an N. L. franchise two years later.

But the opulence of the moment permitted no fears of the morrow. Camelot was indestructible. The Dodgers had won 22 of their first 24 games and opened up a 9½ game lead within the first month.

The Brooks were never out of first place. They coasted from start to finish and clinched the flag on September 8, the earliest date in league history to sew up a pennant. This mark stood until Cincinnati topped it by one day in 1975.

While the Dodgers had all things their way, Ernie Banks, Cub shortstop, established a record by clouting five grand-slam homers. The senior circuit captured the All-Star Game at Milwaukee before 45,314 on July 12. Stan Musial's 12th-inning home run accounted for a 6-5 triumph.

One managerial head rolled during the season, Eddie Stanky being dismissed at St. Louis on May 28 in favor of Harry Walker, brought up from Rochester (International). After the season, Frank Lane, newly signed to a three-year contract as Redbird general

Ernie Banks . . . He made the Cubs respectable.

manager, announced the release of Walker and the hiring of Fred Hutchinson, one-time Detroit skipper who piloted Seattle (Pacific Coast) in '54.

At season's end, Leo Durocher resigned as manager of the Giants to accept an executive position with the National Broadcasting Co. and Fred Haney was informed in Pittsburgh that he would not be invited to return.

Durocher's career as Giant pilot ended dramatically, the Phillies executing a triple play to wrap up the second game of a twin-bill, 3-1.

Several weeks after taking charge of the Cardinals, Walker, on July 5, was principal in the year's foremost rhubarb. In the ninth inning of a game at Cincinnati, The Hat rushed to home plate to defend his battery-men who were being accused of stalling by Manager Birdie Tebbetts of the Reds.

Words led to fisticuffs between the two managers and the row led to $100 fines from League President Warren Giles, who witnessed the scrap. Cardinal catcher Bill Sarni also was docked $25 for his refusal to obey umpire Jocko Conlan's order to speed up play.

In addition to Lane's installation as the Cardinals' front-office chief, the Pirates made a change, naming Branch Rickey to an advisory role and appointing Joe L. Brown as general manager.

The Dodgers, in their eighth World Series and opposing the Yankees for the third time in four years, won the championship for the first time in a seven-game struggle.

After losing the first two games in Yankee Stadium, Brooklyn captured four of the last five decisions, behind Johnny Podres, 8-3; Clem Labine, in relief, 8-5; Roger Craig, 5-3, and Podres again, 2-0.

Feature of the deciding game came in the last half of the sixth inning when, with Billy Martin and Gil McDougald on base, Yogi Berra sliced a pitch down the left field foul line. Racing from left-center field, Sandy Amoros gloved the ball, then fired to short-stop Pee Wee Reese, whose relay to first baseman Gil Hodges doubled up McDougald to snuff out the threat.

Roy Campanella won MVP distinction from his teammate, Duke Snider, 226 points to 221, thereby joining Jimmie Foxx, Joe Di-Maggio, Stan Musial and Yogi Berra as the only players ever to win the honor three times. Mickey Mantle would join this elite group in later years.

Bill Virdon, acquired by the Cardinals in the deal for Enos Slaughter a year earlier, won Rookie of the Year honors.

At their annual winter meeting, league directors voted 6 to 2 to make compulsory the wearing of protective helmets by all players when batting.

1956

Indelibly engraved on the memory pads of millions of fans are the final scenes from a thrill-jammed game at Yankee Stadium on October 8.

Dale Mitchell, pinch-hitting with two out and the bases empty in the top of the ninth inning, takes ball one outside . . . then a called strike . . . then a swinging strike . . . then a sliced foul into the stands.

On the next pitch, a bit high, maybe a bit outside, Mitchell stands motionless. From behind the plate, a right arm jerks convulsively upward, umpire Babe Pinelli bellows "Strike three!" and Yankee Stadium turns into instant pandemonium.

In the most remarkable pitching performance of baseball's first hundred years, the Dodgers have fallen no-hit victims in a World Series, beaten by Don Larsen, 2-0, before 64,519 in the fifth contest of the 53rd World Series.

Heightening the drama is the fact that this was Pinelli's last game as a plate umpire. A few days before his 61st birthday, Pinelli participated in baseball's most unforgettable pitching masterpiece.

For nine interminable innings, the Dodgers tried to solve the big righthander and, amid ever-mounting tension, they walked away from the plate, an unbroken streak of frustration, 27 batters in a row. Thirteen were retired on fly balls, seven on grounders and seven on strikeouts.

Sal Maglie, who had hurled a 5-0 no-hitter against the Phillies, September 25, was on the losing end of Larsen's masterpiece. He allowed only five hits, but one of the safeties was Mickey Mantle's fourth-inning homer, and two other hits, combined with a sacrifice, produced the second run in the sixth inning.

Carl Erskine, Maglie's stablemate, also pitched a no-hitter, his second in the majors, on May 12, when he beat the Giants, 3-0, while allowing only two base-runners, both on walks.

Larsen's perfect game gave the Yankees, who dropped the first two contests of the Series, a 3 to 2 lead in games. Although Clem Labine spun a 10-inning, 1-0 victory the next day, Don Newcombe yielded five runs before being kayoed in the fourth inning of the seventh game and the Dodgers were wiped out, 9-0.

Newcombe, 27-game winner in the regular season, was voted the first Cy Young Award, inaugurated at the suggestion of Commissioner Ford Frick, to recognize pitching excellence in the major leagues.

Newk also earned MVP distinction, drawing 223 points to 183 for Maglie, who compiled a 13-5 record, and won a number of crucial games after his acquisition from Cleveland, May 15.

Frank Robinson of the Reds won Rookie of the Year honors. The slugging outfielder, who hit 38 homers, was a unanimous selection, the first time that a player received every vote since the award was begun in 1947.

A few weeks after the Series, Walter O'Malley announced he had sold Ebbets Field to Marvin Kratter, a real estate developer, for $3,000,000. The Dodgers then negotiated a three-year lease on the old ballpark for an annual "five-figure" rental.

The only managerial change of the year involved Charlie Grimm, who, on June 16, resigned the helm of the Braves, and was replaced by Fred Haney, the former Pittsburgh manager who had joined the Braves as a coach.

The Braves and Giants, in their first season under Bill Rigney, were parties in one of the most bizarre events in baseball history, July 17 in Milwaukee. In the second inning, New York pitcher Ruben Gomez hit Brave first baseman Joe Adcock on the wrist with a pitch. Adcock walked about 10 feet toward first base, then charged Gomez, who threw the baseball at Adcock, striking him on the thigh, and then took to his heels, racing through the Giant dugout and into the safety of the clubhouse.

Gomez was fined $250 by league President Giles and suspended for three days. Adcock drew a $100 plaster.

One of the season's most notable hitting feats was achieved by Dale Long, Pittsburgh first baseman, who homered in eight consecutive games, a record streak, before he was stopped on May 29 by Newcombe.

The annual All-Star Game, played at Griffith Stadium in Washington, July 10, was a 7-3 cakewalk for the N. L.

The Major League Baseball Players' Association was formally organized on October 1 in the New York offices of their attorney, J. Norman Lewis. Bob Feller (Cleveland) was elected president, Stan Musial (St. Louis) vice-president and Jerry Coleman (Yankees) secretary.

1957

Rumors had swirled for months that all was not well with the Giants, but few, if any, gave much credence to the likelihood that the club, a member of the league since 1883, would play anywhere except in New York.

When the announcement came on August

Johnny Podres . . . He turned the Yankees into losers.

19 that directors had voted 8 to 1 to move to San Francisco for the 1958 season, a reporter asked President Horace Stoneham:

"How do you feel about the kids in New York from whom you are taking the Giants?"

"I feel bad about the kids," replied Stoneham, "but I haven't seen many of their fathers lately."

Without citing statistics, Stoneham had to be thinking about attendance figures that showed a decline from 1,155,067 in the championship season of 1954 to 629,179 in 1956.

The lone dissenter to the Giants' transcontinental caper was a minority stockholder, M. Donald Grant, who, in later years, would serve as board chairman for the Mets, the Giants' N. L. successors in New York.

With the Giants having revealed their plans, there was less wailing when, on October 8, the Dodgers confirmed enduring reports that they would move to Los Angeles.

Walter O'Malley

The Dodger official family regarded the announcement of such minimal significance that President Walter O'Malley failed to attend the news conference announcing the shift.

The end for the Dodgers as a Brooklyn-based entity occurred the night of September 24, when Danny McDevitt, young lefthander, blanked the Pirates, 2-0, before 6,702.

For the Giants, the curtain fell on September 29. The previous night, Stoneham hosted a dinner party attended by many old Giant favorites, dating back to the 1895 manager, Jack Doyle. All of the old-timers were introduced to the 11,606 before the funereal finale, in which the Giants lost to the Pirates and Bob Friend, 9-1.

While fans in the nation's No. 1 metropolis mourned the passing of two franchises, those in the league's newest member city, Milwaukee, exulted to the achievements of the Braves. Beaten out by one game in '56, the Braves clinched their first pennant on September 23, with an 11-inning, 4-2 victory over the runner-up Cardinals. Hank Aaron's homer was decisive before more than 40,000 spectators. The Braves' home attendance for the season was a whopping 2,215,404.

In addition to producing the home-run champion in Aaron, with 44, the Braves also boasted the league's top winner, Warren Spahn, with 21, and the top percentage hurler, Bob Buhl, .720, on an 18-7 record. Spahn also won the Cy Young Award, and Jack Sanford, Phil righthander with a 19-8 record, was named Rookie of the Year.

The 24th All-Star Game, played at St. Louis, July 9, resulted in a 6-5 A. L. victory.

The Pirates, en route to a seventh-place tie with Chicago, changed managers on August 3. Bobby Bragan, who had engendered a few grins on July 31 when, having been ejected from a game at Milwaukee, he walked onto the field and offered the umpires a swig of the orange juice he was drinking, was replaced by coach Danny Murtaugh.

Bragan did not remain unemployed long. He was hired to manage Cleveland at the close of the season.

In a front-office turnover, Frank Lane, who had produced a second-place club in the second year of a three-year contract as Cardinal general manager, accepted a post-season offer to fill a similar position at Cleveland.

Lane's place was taken by Vaughan P. (Bing) Devine, an 18-year executive in the Cardinal system who had served as Lane's assistant.

Jackie Robinson, who broke the major's color line 10 years earlier when he started his brilliant career with the Dodgers, an-

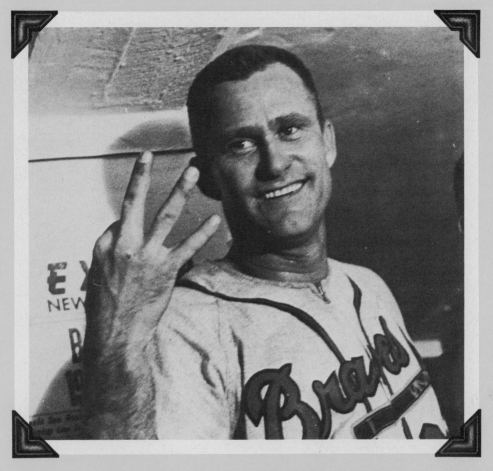

Lew Burdette . . . Toast of the Tepee three times over.

nounced his retirement from baseball before the start of the season, rather than report to the Giants, to whom he had been traded for pitcher Dick Littlefield and $35,000.

For the third consecutive year, the World Series went the limit. With Hank Aaron, the league's Most Valuable Player, batting .393, and Lew Burdette winning three games, two of them shutouts, the Braves completed their storybook season with a world championship.

Burdette blanked the Yankees, 1-0, on a seven-hitter in the fifth game and returned to the mound three days later to hurl another seven-hitter in a 5-0 decision that featured Del Crandall's home run.

When the Braves returned to Milwaukee that night, an estimated 750,000 wild-eyed fanatics lined the route of a 30-mile caravan, causing police authorities all manner of headaches, but bringing a fitting climax to Joe Cairnes' first year as club president. In January, Cairnes had succeeded Lou Perini, who became chairman of the board of the Braves.

1958

Visions of boundless wealth that lured the Dodgers and Giants from their Eastern birthplaces to the opposite side of the continent turned into instant reality in Los Angeles and San Francisco.

Memorial Coliseum, which had been converted into a baseball facility at the cost of approximately $300,000, was the site of a league regular-season record crowd on opening day, April 18, when 78,672 sat in unprotected seats to watch the Dodgers defeat the Giants, 6-5. The failure of Giant rookie Jim Davenport to touch third base in a ninth-inning rally contributed to the defeat.

From that auspicious start, the Dodgers

went on to draw a season total of 1,845,556 for a new club record.

In tiny Seals Stadium, the Giants opened before 23,448. For the season, they played to 1,272,625, nearly double their gate of 653,923 for the previous season in New York.

While the Dodgers were playing to large and enthusiastic crowds, a legal hassle between dissident taxpayers and the city boiled up to the State Supreme Court. Center of the wrangle was the city's awarding of a Chavez Ravine tract to the ball club in exchange for Wrigley Field, formerly the home of the Pacific Coast League club, plus other considerations. When the State Supreme Court, by a vote of 7 to 0, held that the contract between the city and Dodgers was valid, Walter O'Malley was ready to start construction on a new home for his club.

On the field, the Dodgers did not fare so auspiciously, falling to seventh place, just two games out of the cellar. One of the chief factors in the collapse was the absence of Roy Campanella. On January 28, the three-time MVP catcher suffered a broken neck in an automobile accident at Glen Cove, N. Y., and was paralyzed permanently below his waist.

Despite a rash of injuries that sidelined Bob Buhl with an arm ailment, Wes Covington with bad knees and Red Schoendienst with incipient tuberculosis, the Braves captured their second consecutive flag, beating out the Pirates by eight games.

After games of July 4, only seven lengths separated the first-place Braves from the last-place Dodgers, the smallest gap on that holiday in modern N. L. history. Previously, an 8½-game difference in 1915 was the smallest.

In the silver jubilee All-Star Game at Baltimore July 8, the A. L. scored a 4-3 victory, which was made noteworthy by the fact that there was not a single extra-base hit among the 13 safeties.

Three clubs changed managers during the year. On July 22, the Phils dismissed Mayo Smith and restored to command Eddie Sawyer, manager of the Whiz Kid champions of 1950 who had been divorced from baseball since 1952.

Birdie Tebbetts, Manager of the Year in 1956, resigned the Reds' managerial post on August 14, a day after the club lost a double-header to Milwaukee. Coach Jimmie Dykes handled the club the remainder of the season and, on September 29, Mayo Smith signed to pilot the club in 1959.

On September 17, the Cardinals fired Fred Hutchinson and his entire coaching staff of Stan Hack, Terry Moore and Al Hollingsworth. Hack agreed to handle the club the remainder of the season and, on September 29, Solly Hemus, acquired from Philadel-

phia, was appointed to the post.

Changes in the front office involved Tebbetts, who was named executive vice-president of the Braves, assuming the duties formerly performed by club President Joe Cairnes.

The Phillies underwent a change in general managers, Roy Hamey resigning after five years to rejoin the Yankees and being replaced by John Quinn, formerly of the Braves. In addition Jim Gallagher, ex-business manager of the Cubs, joined the Phils as director of scouting. And John McHale left the Tigers to join Milwaukee as general manager to replace Quinn.

The Braves, after building up a 3 to 1 lead in games, were beaten by the Yankees in the seven-game World Series. Warren Spahn dropped a 10-inning, 4-3 decision in game No. 6 and the Yankees then scored four runs in the eighth inning to defeat Lew Burdette, 6-2, in the finale.

Cub shortstop Ernie Banks earned 16 first-place votes to win MVP honors easily and Giant first baseman Orlando Cepeda, a .312 hitter, was hailed as the top rookie.

1959

In street clothes, Harvey Haddix and Roy Face never would be mistaken for "44 longs." But, in the uniforms of the Pittsburgh Pirates, Haddix, at 5-9, and Face, at 5-7½, were representative of the small packages in which valuable items frequently arrive.

Lefthanded Haddix and righthanded Face inscribed 24-karat achievements on the pitching tablets during the 1959 season, Haddix in one game and Face throughout the campaign.

On May 26, Haddix pitched 12 perfect innings against the Braves, only to lose in the 13th. The manner in which "The Kitten" was defeated was hardly a run-of-the-mill occurrence.

After establishing a major league record by retiring the first 36 batters, 33-year-old Haddix faced Felix Mantilla to open the fourth overtime stanza. Mantilla grounded to third baseman Don Hoak, whose low throw eluded first baseman Rocky Nelson. A sacrifice by Eddie Mathews and an intentional pass to Henry Aaron followed before Joe Adcock, twice a strikeout victim, lofted a long fly that barely made it over the right-center field fence.

Mantilla scored easily, but Aaron, believing that the ball dropped at the base of the fence, inside the playing field, touched second base and then headed for the Braves' clubhouse. Running blindly, Adcock passed

Harvey Haddix . . . A dozen perfect innings.

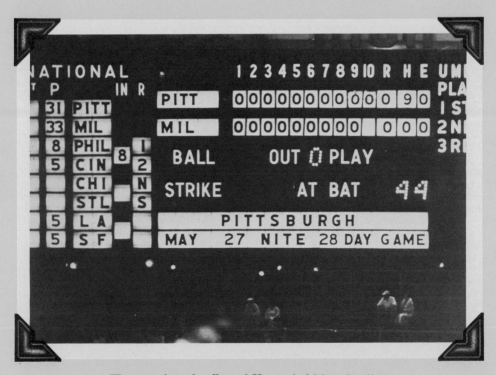

The scoreboard reflected Harvey's hitless hurling.

Danny Murtaugh and **Roy Face** . . . Relief was his business.

Aaron on the baselines and was retired automatically.

The game was over and the Braves had won, but what was the score? Manager Fred Haney and his Milwaukee coaches coaxed Aaron back to the basepaths and Hank preceded Adcock on his jog around the sacks. The umpires, ruling Adcock out, determined that Mantilla and Aaron scored legally and that the Braves had won, 2-0.

The next day, however, league President Warren Giles ruled that the game ended as soon as Mantilla touched the plate and that Adcock, for his base-running boner, was entitled to only a double. The score went into the books as a 1-0 Milwaukee victory.

Face, 31-year-old fireman, won 17 consecutive games and compiled an 18-1 record for the season. Eleven of his wins, and the last eight, were registered in overtime. With five consecutive victories at the end of the '58 season, Face boasted an unbeaten streak of 22 games, just two short of Carl Hubbell's major league record. Face's string was shattered by the Dodgers, who defeated the reliever, 5-4, in the first half of a twi-night doubleheader, September 11.

For the third time in league history, a playoff was necessary to determine a champion. On the final Tuesday of the season, Milwaukee held a one-game edge over the Dodgers, but three days later the standing was reversed. When the Cubs walloped the Dodgers, 12-2, on Saturday and Warren Spahn beat the Phillies, 3-2, the clubs again were deadlocked. Both clubs won on Sunday, requiring a best-of-three series to settle the issue.

Larry Sherry's 7⅔ innings of shutout relief and John Roseboro's home run featured the Dodgers' 3-2 triumph at Milwaukee, September 28, and the Dodgers clinched the pennant the next day in Los Angeles by scoring three runs in the ninth inning to knot the score and one in the 12th on a two-out walk to Gil Hodges, a single by Joe Pignatano and Carl Furillo's high bounder on which shortstop Felix Mantilla made a hurried and wild throw past first base, permitting Hodges to score the deciding run.

In order to raise additional funds for the players' pension fund, two All-Star Games were played, the N. L. winning the first, 5-4, at Pittsburgh, July 7, and the A. L. taking the second, 5-3, at Los Angeles, August 3.

Mayo Smith was fired as manager of the

Fred Hutchinson   **Solly Hemus**

Reds on July 8 and was replaced by Fred Hutchinson, who had been managing Seattle (Pacific Coast).

On September 28, the day after the close of the season, Bob Scheffing was dismissed as pilot of the Cubs, being replaced by the club's old standby, 61-year-old Charlie Grimm.

Several days later, Fred Haney, also 61, stepped down as skipper of the Braves, and was succeeded by Charley Dressen, acquired from the Dodgers, whom he had served as coach.

Solly Hemus, in his freshman season as Cardinal manager, was thumbed out of eight games and assessed a total of $650 in fines, including a $250 plaster, and a five-day suspension, for a rhubarb with umpire Shag Crawford on July 2.

With each of three games at Los Angeles drawing more than 92,000 spectators and an equal number of contests at Comiskey Park attracting more than 47,000 apiece, the World Series set a record with a total attendance of 420,784.

The Dodgers, each of whom received $11,231.18, captured the world championship in six games from the White Sox, each of

whom was rewarded with $7,275.17.

Ernie Banks, with 10 first-place votes, retained his MVP honors, the first player ever to repeat as the league's No. 1 player. Willie McCovey, who batted .354 for the Giants, was acclaimed the top rookie.

1960

In the long and sometimes spectacular competition for the world championship of baseball, no engagement can match the World Series of 1960 for erratic tempo and colossal climax.

The Pirates, excluded from the Series since 1927, when they lost four in a row to the Yankees, ended a 33-year drouth by finishing seven games ahead of Milwaukee. Their opponents once again were the Yankees.

In 1927, the Yankees outhit the Pirates, .279 to .223 and outscored the Bucs 23 to 10. In 1960, the Yanks outhit their rivals, .338 to .256 and outscored them, 55 to 27. Three New York victories were by scores of 16-3, 10-0 and 12-0.

By every line of logic, the Yankees should have captured the world championship, but by some inexplicable chemistry it was the Pirates who did the celebrating. For when the Pirates were not losing by football-type scores they were winning, 6-4, 3-2, 5-2 and 10-9.

Vernon Law and Harvey Haddix won two games apiece for the Buccos and Roy Face made three excellent relief appearances before fatigue took its toll and he gave up six hits and four runs in three innings of the final contest.

For unabridged drama, game No. 7 stands alone. With 36,683 alternately screaming and sighing in Forbes Field, the Pirates gained an early 4-0 lead, then fell behind 5-4, due mainly to Yogi Berra's three-run homer.

Two more Yankee runs in the eighth made the score 7-4 with only six more outs to go for another New York world title. Retiring those half-dozen batters was one thing, but retiring them without damage was a different matter.

In the Pittsburgh half of the eighth, Gino Cimoli pinch-singled and Bill Virdon grounded to Tony Kubek for what might have been a double play. The Yankees, however, retired no one. The ball took a weird bounce and struck the shortstop on the throat. Kubek was removed from the game and Virdon was credited with a single.

Dick Groat's single produced one run and Bob Skinner's sacrifice moved the runners into scoring position. Rocky Nelson's fly ball

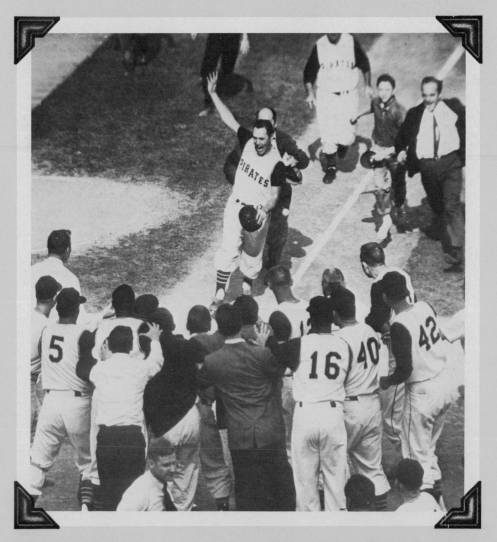

Bill Mazeroski . . . One swing, and pandemonium in Pittsburgh.

P. K. Wrigley

Bill Rigney

was insufficient to drive in Virdon. Roberto Clemente's infield single netted one run before reserve catcher Hal Smith tagged Jim Coates for a three-run homer, giving Pittsburgh a 9-7 lead and turning the historic ball park into instant madness. Only three outs remained for the Pirates to claim a world title.

Three singles and an infield out manufactured two Yankee runs in the ninth and again the teams were deadlocked 9-9.

The end came with dramatic suddenness a few moments later when Bill Mazeroski, whose homer had won the first game, clouted the second pitch from Ralph Terry for a home run, sending all of Pittsburgh into transports of merriment.

The season was only 36 hours old when the first managerial fatality occurred. After watching the Phillies drop a 9-4 decision to to the Reds, Eddie Sawyer decided that he had seen enough and turned in his portfolio. Coach Andy Cohen directed the club in the second game, a victory, and then turned the reins over to Gene Mauch, obtained from Minneapolis (American Association).

On May 4, with the Cubs in eighth place, Owner P. K. Wrigley fired Charlie Grimm and appointed Lou Boudreau, who had been

broadcasting Bruin games. Grimm took over Boudreau's air spot. It was a shift of managers, or broadcasters, however you look at it.

On June 18, scarcely two months after the dedication of the Giants' new home, Candlestick Park, Bill Rigney was deposed as skipper of the San Francisco club. Rigney was succeeded by Tom Sheehan, the Giants' 66-year-old super scout.

Gabe Paul, general manager of the Reds for nine years, announced his resignation on October 25, in order to accept a three-year contract for a corresponding position with the Houston club, scheduled to commence operations in 1962. Paul was succeeded by Bill DeWitt.

N. L. representatives won both All-Star Games, triumphing 5-3 at Kansas City, July 11, and 6-0 at New York, July 13.

To recognize the growing emphasis on relief pitching, The Sporting News introduced a new award, the Fireman Trophy, to be presented annually to the outstanding reliever in each league. The first N. L. winner was Lindy McDaniel, who won 12 games and saved 22 for the Cardinals.

MVP honors went to Pirate shortstop Dick Groat, while Frank Howard, a .268 hit-

Dick Groat . . . A Pirate edged in MVP gold.

ter with the Dodgers, was named the No. 1 rookie. Vern Law, with a mark of 20-9 for the world champion Pirates, was the winner of the Cy Young Award.

1961

Warren Spahn was five days late in celebrating his 40th birthday anniversary, but when the Milwaukee lefthander observed the milestone at which life is said to begin, he did it with a flourish befitting only one of his extraordinary talents.

Facing the Giants, ranked second in the league in total bases, on April 28, Spahn hurled the second no-hitter of his career, winning, 1-0, against Sam Jones.

Spahn's record at the All-Star break was a mediocre 8-11, but he won 13 and lost only two thereafter to finish with a 21-13 record.

One of the southpaw's victories, a 2-1 decision over the Cubs, August 11, was the 300th of his major league career. At age 40, he led the league in earned-run average, 3.01, and tied for the league lead in victories, 21, and shutouts, four.

Two days after Spahn's hitless performance, on April 30, Willie Mays enjoyed what he referred to as "the greatest day of my career" when he hit a record-tying four home runs at County Stadium in Milwaukee to feature a 14-4 Giant victory. Willie's four homers represented 50 percent of the total hit by the Giants who, having clouted five the preceding day, established a two-game league record of 13 round-trippers.

On August 23, the San Francisco siege guns fired a 12-run broadside against the Reds in the ninth inning to set a modern major league mark for the last inning. Five home runs, equalling a major mark, boomed off Giant bats in the explosive frame. The final score: 14-0.

P. K. Wrigley, seeking a way to shake the second-division miseries, abandoned the traditional managerial system and placed his Cubs in the hands of a "College of Coaches" at the start of the season. Returning Lou Boudreau to the radio booth, the chewing gum magnate appointed Vedie Himsl, Harry Craft, Elvin Tappe and Lou Klein to

Warren Spahn . . . Nothing but 20 wins a season.

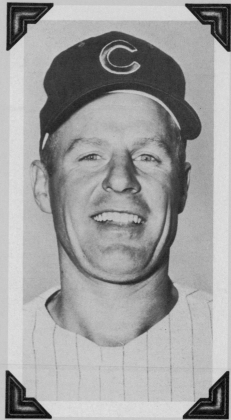

Vedie Himsl   **Elvin Tappe**

the rotating supervisory position. The arrangement fell short of the mark and the Bruins were superior only to the eighth-place Phillies.

Milwaukee, which finished fourth, and St. Louis, which came in fifth, played under two managers. Charley Dressen was fired by the Braves on September 2, and Birdie Tebbetts, the executive vice-president since 1958, moved into field command.

On July 6, with the Cardinals in sixth place, Solly Hemus was replaced by coach Johnny Keane.

The Phillies barely escaped an unenviable major league record on August 20, when they defeated the Braves, 7-4, in the second game of the doubleheader. The victory snapped a 23-game losing streak, one short of the major mark.

The N. L. won the first All-Star Game at Candlestick Park July 11, scoring two runs in the 10th inning for a 5-4 decision, and then played a 1-1 tie at Boston, July 31, the game being terminated by rain after nine innings.

With Frank Robinson gaining Most Valua-

ble Player honors, the Reds won their first pennant in 21 years by edging out the Dodgers by four games. The Reds were no match for the Yankees in the World Series, however, bowing in five games as Joey Jay, a 21-game winner, accounted for the only Cincinnati victory, 6-2 in the second game.

Cub outfielder Billy Williams, who hit .278 in 146 games, was named Rookie of the Year, and Stu Miller, Giants, won the Fireman accolade on the strength of 14 wins and 12 saves.

New York and Houston, preparing for the start of competition in 1962, shaped up their administrative personnel during the year. George Weiss, who had resigned as Yankee general manager, assumed a similar post with the Mets. Appointed manager of the new club was Casey Stengel, also an ex-Yankee, who named as his coaches Cookie Lavagetto and Solly Hemus, both experienced as major league managers.

In a surprise move, on April 27, Gabe Paul submitted his resignation as G.M. of the Houston Colts to accept the top executive

Frank Robinson . . . Called cadence on Red flag march.

Casey Stengel   **George Weiss**

position with Cleveland. The Houston general manager chores were shared by other executives until September 1, when Paul Richards resigned his post at Baltimore to accept a three-year Houston contract.

1962

For nearly nine seasons, Maurice Morning Wills languished in the minor leagues, waiting for Pee Wee Reese to retire so that he might receive a full-fledged opportunity with the Dodgers.

Reese retired following the 1958 season and Wills received his summons midway through the following campaign. He was a World Series shortstop in 1959 and an All-Star selection in 1961 before he exploded into super star status as a whirlwind base runner in 1962.

Wills did no running in the Dodgers' opener, a defeat by the Reds in the first game at new Dodger Stadium. Nor did he display any tendencies to steal in the second and third contests. However, starting on April 13, Mercurial Maury was a "Wills o' the wisp," sweeping base lines like a prairie fire. At the end of the 165-game season, which included three playoff games, he had accounted for 104 stolen bases, eight more than Ty Cobb swiped in 1915 when he established a modern major league record of 96 steals in 156 games.

In his first two complete major league seasons, Maury stole 50 and 35 bases, respectively, both league-leading totals.

Superlative as he was, MVP Wills was forced to share the spotlight with Stan Musial, Sandy Koufax and Jack Sanford during the league's first 162-game schedule as a 10-club circuit.

Musial, 41-year-old Cardinal star, broke Honus Wagner's N. L. record on May 19 when he collected his 3,431st hit, a single off Ron Perranoski of the Dodgers.

On June 22, Musial passed Ty Cobb as baseball's all-time total base champion by hiking his figure to 5,864, and on July 25, he eclipsed Mel Ott's league RBI record by raising his total to 1,862.

Koufax, the Dodger lefthander who had fanned 18 Giants in a 1959 game, duplicated the performance against the Cubs on April 24, matching Bob Feller's major league mark for the second time and setting an N. L. daytime record.

On July 19, by which time Koufax had won 14 games, it was announced that the lefthander would be sidelined for two weeks as a result of "the diminution of blood flowing to the index finger of his left hand." The projected two-week absence stretched to two months and Sandy did not return to action until September 21, losing his only two decisions the remainder of the season.

Maury Wills . . . A streak of light, and a record for robbery.

Sanford, San Francisco righthander, won only six of his first 12 decisions, but on June 17 he defeated the Cardinals, 6-3, and did not stop winning until he had posted 16 victories in a row. He was stopped by the Pirates, 5-1, September 15, then won his next two games for an overall season record of 24-7. Only Don Drysdale of the Dodgers won more, 25, an accomplishment that gained Cy Young Award laurels for the big righthander.

Ken Hubbs of the Cubs broke Bobby Doerr's major league record by handling flawlessly 418 chances (78 games) before he made a wild throw in Cincinnati September 5. Hubbs was a near unanimous choice for Rookie of the Year.

The Cubs continued to function under the coaching system pioneered by Owner P. K. Wrigley, although the number was reduced from four to three, Elvin Tappe, Lou Klein and Charley Metro. The club achieved its best record under Metro, leading to speculation that Metro might reign alone in 1963. However, on November 8, Metro was canned and, four days later, signed as chief scout for the White Sox.

The Bruins again finished one notch out of the basement, but, in the first year of a 10-club operation, they were ninth, below the expansion Houston Colt .45s and ahead of the expansion Mets.

After being in and out of first place for most of the season, the Dodgers took over the lead on July 8 and, as late as September 22 led by four games. By losing six of their last seven games, however, while the Giants were winning five of seven, Los Angeles was forced into their—and the league's—

Jack Sanford . . . Giant on the San Francisco mound.

Don Drysdale . . . Big D was Dodger dreadnaught.

Bill DeWitt . . . He surfaced in Cincinnati.

fourth pennant playoff.

In the final game of the regular season, the Dodgers bowed to Curt Simmons and the Cardinals, 1-0, on Gene Oliver's home run, while at San Francisco Willie Mays clouted an eighth-inning homer to give the Giants a 2-1 decision over Dick Farrell and the Colt .45s.

Billy Pierce hurled the Giants to an 8-0 victory in the opening playoff contest at Candlestick Park, but the Dodgers scored once in the ninth to win the second, 8-7, as the scene shifted to Dodger Stadium.

The Dodgers were only three outs away from the championship in the third game, but the Giants exploded for four runs in the final frame to pull out a 6-4 victory.

The Giants carried the Yankees to the limit in the World Series before bowing to Ralph Terry, 1-0, in the seventh contest.

Two All-Star games were played for the last time, the N. L. winning at Washington, 3-1, July 10, and the A. L. at Wrigley Field, Chicago, 9-4, July 30.

All managers survived the season, al-

though Birdie Tebbetts, on October 5, resigned as manager of the Braves to accept a three-year pact as field boss of the Indians. He was succeeded by Bobby Bragan, who had been a coach of the Houston club.

Prior to the opening of the season, ownership of the Reds changed hands, Bill DeWitt buying 98½ percent stock interest from the Crosley Foundation. In a post-season transaction, John McHale, general manager of the Braves, and six partners purchased the Milwaukee club from the Perini Corp., headed by Lou Perini.

1963

Companions on the climb up heartbreak hill the previous year, Sandy Koufax and the Dodgers found sublime, storybook happiness in each other's company in 1963.

Cured of the mysterious finger ailment that reduced his effectiveness and sidelined him for much of the '62 campaign, Koufax rebounded with a 25-5 season that included his second major league no-hitter, May 11,

Sandy Koufax . . . Incomparable and inimitable.

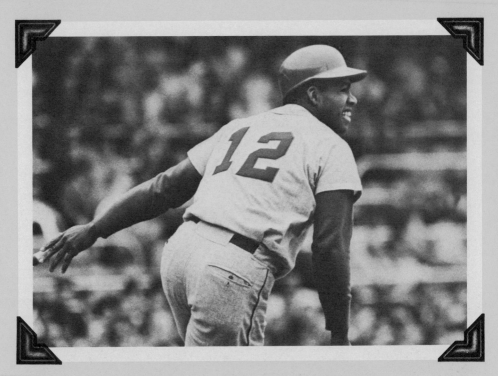

Tommy Davis . . . Two-time batting champion.

Ron Perranoski . . . First-rate Dodger fire extinguisher.

Willie Mays . . . "Spectacular" was his middle name.

Jerry Lynch

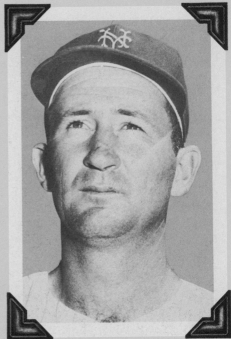

Roger Craig

when he blanked the Giants, 8-0, while allowing only two base-runners via walks to Ed Bailey in the eighth inning and Willie McCovey in the ninth.

The shutout was one of 11 registered by Koufax, a modern major league record for a lefthander.

Sandy's superlative season made him a unanimous choice for the Cy Young Award and a runaway winner in the MVP balloting, in which he earned 14 first-place votes to four for Cardinal shortstop Dick Groat.

Two other Dodgers also enjoyed extraordinary seasons. Outfielder Tommy Davis repeated as league batting champion with an average of .326 and lefthanded reliever Ron Perranoski posted the best winning percentage, .842, compiled on 16 wins and three losses.

While Koufax was arriving as a full-blown super star, Stan Musial was departing as one of the same. The long-time Cardinal great, approaching his forty-third birthday, batted .255 to close his 22-year career with an average of .331.

One of Stan's most poignant moments occurred on September 10 when, having just been notified that he had become a grandfather for the first time, he clouted a home run on his first at-bat against Glen Hobbie of the Cubs.

In his final game, against the Reds, September 29, The Man singled in the fourth and sixth innings against Jim Maloney of the Reds, then retired to a standing ovation from more than 27,000 fans.

On July 9, at Cleveland, Musial appeared in his 24th All-Star Game, lining out to right field as a pinch-hitter in the fifth inning of the N. L.'s 5-3 victory.

In recognition of Musial's contributions to baseball, the Cardinals retired his uniform number "6" and appointed him a vice-president of the club.

The season was downhill almost all the way for Roger Craig of the Mets. After winning two of his first four decisions, the righthander dropped 18 games in a row and was one short of the major league record when, on August 9, he defeated the Cubs, 7-3, with the help of Jim Hickman's two-out, grand-slam homer in the ninth inning.

Later in the month, Jerry Lynch of the Pirates broke the major league record for pinch-hit home runs when he hit for the circuit in the ninth inning of the Pirates' 7-6 victory over the Cubs, August 21. The blow was No. 15 of Lynch's career, one more than the total credited to George Crowe.

Warren Spahn, at 42, enjoyed his last big season as a winner. The Milwaukee lefthander etched a 23-7 record, numbering among his victories a 1-0 decision over the

Lindy McDaniel . . . At the top of the firemen's ladder.

Bobby Bragan

Bob Kennedy

Dodgers at Los Angeles, June 28. It marked Spahn's first victory in the home of the Dodgers, including Brooklyn, since August 21, 1948. In the interim, he had been defeated 14 times.

The Cubs, who introduced the "College of Coaches" two years earlier, abandoned the experiment in 1963 and appointed a one-man board of control, Bob Kennedy, under whom the Bruins finished seventh.

The Cubs were not without an innovation, however. Before the start of the campaign, Owner P. K. Wrigley created the position of athletic director and filled it with Col. Robert V. Whitlow, a retired Air Force officer who traveled with the club most of the season and filled many of the responsibilities ordinarily performed by a general manager or business manager.

No managerial heads rolled during the season and two pilots were rewarded with extensions on current contracts. On May 14, the Braves gave Bobby Bragan an extension through 1964 and, on August 6, the Phillies gave Gene Mauch security through 1965.

In the pennant race, the Dodgers took over first place on July 2 and held fast to the finish. Their most serious threat came from the Cardinals who, winning 19 of 20 games, climbed to within one game by mid-September.

In a three-game series at St. Louis, however, the Dodgers repulsed their pursuers, 3-1 behind Johnny Podres, 4-0 on a four-hitter by Koufax and 6-5 on a 13th-inning homer by Dick Nen, just up from Spokane (Coast).

The Dodgers made short work of the World Series, beating the Yankees 5-2 and 4-1 at Yankee Stadium, and 1-0 on Don Drysdale's three-hitter and 2-1 at Los Angeles. Koufax won the first and last games, both at the expense of Whitey Ford.

Pete Rose, Cincinnati second baseman, was named the league's No. 1 rookie, and Lindy McDaniel, Cubs, won his second Fireman Award, beating out Ron Perranoski of the Dodgers, 34 points to 32.

1964

The Cardinals were in fifth place, nine

Pete Rose . . . His spirit infected a ball club.

August A. Busch, Jr.

Bing Devine

games off the pace and apparently going no-where, when August A. Busch, Jr., dropped a bombshell on August 17 of St. Louis' Bicentennial Year.

"I want a pennant for St. Louis," declared the brewer-sportsman when he revealed that Bing Devine and Art Routzong had been asked to resign as general manager and business manager, respectively, and that Robert L. Howsam, longtime head of the Denver (American Association) club, had been named G. M. of the Cardinals.

The departure of Devine, a 25-year veteran of the Cardinal organization, was only one of several bizarre twists in the Redbird season.

Weeks later, reports circulated that Leo Durocher had been offered the managerial position, replacing Johnny Keane, but when the Cardinals raced out of the pack into first place with only two days to go, Keane was offered a new contract at a substantial increase in pay. Keane declined the offer, explaining he preferred to wait until after the season, but when that time arrived, and the Cardinals were world champions, the pilot detonated a bombshell of his own, resigning his position to accept a similar job with the Yankees.

Only a total collapse by the Phillies in the last two weeks of the season made the Cardinal championship possible. Leading by 6½ games on September 20, the Phils lost their

next 10 games to fall to third place, 2½ games behind the Cards, who had won eight in a row, and one behind the Reds, who had won nine straight.

On the last Friday of the season, the Cards were beaten by the Mets, 1-0, and lost again the next day, 15-5. Meanwhile, the Phils won one game from the Reds, forcing the race into the last day for a decision. While the Phils again defeated the Reds, 10-0, the Redbirds beat the Mets, 11-5, to win the title by one game.

The Mets, in their third season, figured prominently in the season's progress. On April 17, the New York club opened William A. Shea Stadium in Flushing and attracted 50,312 for the inaugural, which went to the Pirates, 4-3.

On June 21, the new park was the scene of one of the majors' rarest events, a perfect game. Jim Bunning, who had pitched a no-hitter for the Tigers, became the first hurler to account for a hitless game in each major, when he pitched the Phillies to a 6-0 conquest of the Mets in a none-reach-base spectacular.

On May 31, a crowd of 57,037 jammed into the 55,300-seat arena for a doubleheader with the Giants. When play ceased at 11:25 p.m., only about 15,000 fans remained. They had witnessed a 5-3 Giant win in the opener, and a 23-inning, 8-6 San Francisco victory in the nightcap. The nine hours and 52 minutes

Jim Bunning . . . A no-hitter in each major league.

Harry Walker   **Luman Harris**

of playing time established a major league record.

A third major event of the season at Shea Stadium was the 35th annual All-Star Game, which was won by the N. L., 7-4, on the strength of a four-run ninth inning that featured Johnny Callison's three-run homer. The victory enabled the N. L., which once trailed in the series, 12 games to 4, to deadlock at 17 victories each.

In addition to Bunning's perfecto, Sandy Koufax hurled his third hitless gem, tying Bob Feller's major league record, when he blanked the Phils, 3-0, June 4. In a third such performance, Ken Johnson of Houston humiliated the Reds April 23, but the right-hander lost the game, 1-0, as the result of two errors, one by Johnson himself, in the ninth inning.

Harry Craft was the only manager to be fired during the season. He was released by Houston September 19, and replaced by coach Luman Harris, who was given a two-year contract.

After the season, Danny Murtaugh, citing ill health, stepped down as Pirate skipper and was succeeded by Harry Walker, who had managed Jacksonville (International). Alvin Dark's four-year term as San Francisco pilot ended on the last day of the season

and Herman Franks, a coach, was appointed successor.

Fred Hutchinson, who had left the Reds on August 13 to enter a hospital for cancer treatment, tendered his resignation after the close of the season and Dick Sisler, who managed in Hutch's absence, was named to the position. On November 12, the Big Bear, age 45, died at Bradenton, Fla.

Other deaths during the year included Ken Hubbs, Cub second baseman and the league's top rookie of 1962, who perished in a private plane crash near Provo, Utah, February 15. On April 8, Houston pitcher Jim Umbricht died of cancer at 33.

After their pulsating pennant victory, the Cardinals kept right on going and defeated the Yankees in the World Series. Bob Gibson won the seventh game, 7-5, helped along by home runs off the bats of Ken Boyer and Lou Brock.

Boyer was an easy MVP winner with 14 first-place votes, while Richie Allen of Philadelphia took rookie honors and Al McBean, Pittsburgh, beat out Hal Woodeshick, Houston, for the Fireman Award, 26 points to 24.

1965

The Eighth Wonder of the World, it was called, and as such, the Houston Astrodome,

Ken Boyer . . . King Cardinal in a title year.

all enclosed and seating 44,500, fully deserved all the attention it received in the league's 90th season.

Constructed at a cost of $31,600,000 and featuring luxury boxes that sold for as much as $34,000 apiece, the air-conditioned palace opened officially on April 9, when a crowd of 47,876, including President Lyndon B. Johnson, jammed the architectural triumph for an exhibition game between the Houston club, newly christened the Astros, and the Yankees. The game lasted 12 innings before Nellie Fox pinch-singled to drive in the deciding run of a 2-1 victory. Mickey Mantle

earned the distinction of hitting the Dome's first homer to account for the losers' only run.

Judge Roy Hofheinz, guiding genius behind the Astros, gained controlling interest in the club in August when he purchased all but 10 percent of the 63 percent holdings of his partner, R. E. (Bob) Smith.

After the season, in which the Astros finished ninth while drawing a home attendance of 2,151,470, Hofheinz shook up the club's front office. He fired General Manager Paul Richards, farm director Eddie Robinson and Manager Luman Harris. Named

Jim Maloney . . . Two masterpieces in overtime.

to replace the trio were Tal Smith, appointed director of player personnel, and Grady Hatton, former manager at Oklahoma City (American Association), who was handed the dual role of vice-president and manager.

Two of the season's finest pitching performances were credited to Jim Maloney of the Reds. On June 14, the 25-year-old right-hander pitched 10 hitless innings against the Mets, only to be tagged for a leadoff homer by Johnny Lewis in the 11th inning and winding up with a two-hit, 1-0 defeat.

On August 19, Maloney again hurled 10 hitless innings, but this time defeated the Cubs, 1-0, while fanning 12 and walking 10.

Sandy Koufax recorded the season's most brilliant pitching effort on September 9, when he defeated the Cubs, 1-0, in a perfect game. The Dodgers scored their only run without benefit of a hit in the fifth inning off

Bob Hendley, who allowed only one hit, a seventh-inning double by Lou Johnson. The no-hitter was the fourth of Koufax' career, one more than the number registered by Bob Feller and Cy Young.

Koufax struck out a record total of 382 batters during the season, and also led the N.L. pitchers in earned-run average, victories and winning percentage. Koufax was on the hill August 22, facing the Giants, when the season's most serious rhubarb erupted. When Dodger catcher John Roseboro returned the baseball to Koufax, he exchanged a few words with the batter, Juan Marichal. With little warning, Marichal struck Roseboro on the head with the bat and touched off a free-for-all that lasted 14 minutes. Roseboro suffered a cut over his left eyebrow. Marichal was ejected. Later he was fined $1,750 by League President

The Astrodome . . . Another wonder of the modern world.

An interior view of the Astros' pad.

Warren Giles and suspended eight playing days.

Three managers were deposed during the season, one voluntarily. On August 30, Casey Stengel announced his resignation as field general of the Mets. The Old Professor had suffered a wrist fracture while the club was at West Point to play the United States Military Academy team on May 10 and, on July 24, suffered a hip fracture while getting out of a car. He was succeeded by Wes Westrum, a Met coach.

Bob Kennedy was released as head coach of the Cubs on June 14, and replaced by an assistant, Lou Klein.

The Cubs had undergone a change in front-office structure in January when Col. Bob Whitlow resigned as athletic director, ending a two-year experiment.

The day after the close of the season, October 4, Dick Sisler was dismissed as Cincinnati manager. Don Heffner, a Met coach, received a two-year contract as his successor.

For the first time since the inception of the All-Star Game, the N.L. moved ahead in the standings by winning at Minnesota, 6-5, July 13. Ron Santo's infield single in the seventh inning was the decisive hit in giving the N.L. an 18-17 lead in the series.

Metropolitan Stadium also was the scene of the seventh game of the World Series in which Koufax, spacing three hits, blanked the Twins, 2-0. The Twins, who won the first two games, had the satisfaction of defeating Koufax in game No. 2, but the Dodgers swept the three games in Los Angeles, with Koufax winning a 7-0 four-hitter in the fifth contest and then clinching the world championship after Mudcat Grant defeated Claude Osteen in the sixth contest.

Koufax was the unanimous choice for the Cy Young Award, while Willie Mays walked off with the MVP honors. Jim Lefebvre of the Dodgers was named No. 1 rookie and Ted Abernathy of the Cubs the top Fireman with 28 points, one more than Billy McCool of the Reds.

The search for a new commissioner to replace Ford Frick, who had announced he would not accept reelection, ended on November 17, when the owners, climaxing a screening process that started with 156 nominees, introduced the game's new chief executive, retired Air Force General William D. Eckert, at a press conference in Chicago.

1966

The most heavily patronized stadium in the league only a decade earlier, when it

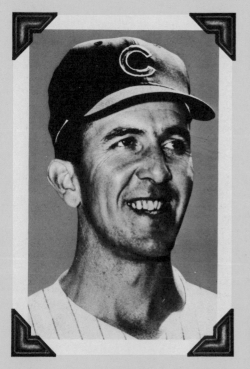

Ted Abernathy

Jim LeFebvre

Atlanta Stadium . . . Peach of a playing palace in Georgia.

Busch Memorial Stadium . . . Showcase in St. Louis.

was drawing more than 2,000,000 fans annually, County Stadium in Milwaukee resembled a depressed area in 1966 following the departure of the Braves to Atlanta.

Wisconsin's largest metropolis made a determined fight to retain the Braves and sought legal redress up to the United States Supreme Court. On July 27, more than three months after the Braves had opened the season in Atlanta, the State Supreme Court overturned a Circuit Court decision that held the Braves in violation of antitrust legislation, and cleared all legal obstacles for the shift to Georgia. The United States Supreme Court, subsequently, declined to hear an appeal.

Meanwhile, the Braves were greeted with open arms in Atlanta. An opening night crowd of 50,671 watched the club drop a 13-inning, 3-2 decision to the Pirates, and four more times during the season, throngs of more than 45,000 turned out to see the Braves who, by a strong finish, managed to wind up in fifth place. For the campaign, the club attracted 1,539,801 and showed a profit of $991,885.

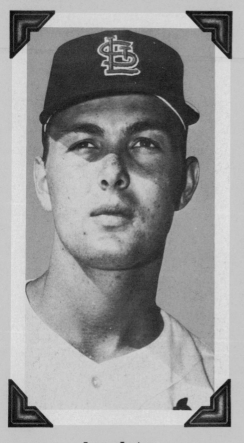

Larry Jaster

Atlanta Stadium was one of the two new parks in the league. On May 12, the Cardinals officially opened Busch Memorial Stadium, with a seating capacity of 49,450, by drawing 46,048 for a 12-inning, 4-3 win over the Braves.

Because of the inability to grow natural grass in the Astrodome, Houston officials came up with a new aspect to baseball playing facilities with the introduction of synthetic turf.

AstroTurf, the new surface, received its baptism in a two-game exhibition series with the Dodgers March 19-20 and was immediately pronounced satisfactory, although providing a much sharper and swifter bounce to ground balls.

Los Angeles pitching aces Sandy Koufax and Don Drysdale created preseason excitement by staging a joint holdout. The pair announced that neither would sign until both were satisfied with terms of their contracts.

It wasn't until March 30 that they accepted General Manager Buzzie Bavasi's offer, generally agreed to call for $120,000 for Koufax and $110,000 for Drysdale.

A wire service story on April 4 revealed that the Mets had won a drawing for the negotiation rights to a young University of Southern California pitcher, identified as "George" Seaver. The righthander, who was to gain fame under his middle name, Tom, was declared a free agent after the Braves were found guilty of signing him to a professional contract following the start of the Trojans' season.

Another pitcher who figured prominently in the news was Atlanta righthander Tony Cloninger, but it wasn't for his mound achievements. On July 3, Cloninger smashed two grand-slam homers in a 17-3 victory over the Giants, the first N.L. player ever to accomplish that feat in a single game.

One of the year's most remarkable performances was turned in by Larry Jaster, 22-year-old Cardinal lefthander. The rookie hurler shut out the Dodgers five consecutive times, the last time, 2-0 on September 28, four days before the close of the season.

The defeat cut the Dodgers' first-place margin to 1½ games. On the final day of the race, October 2, the Giants defeated Pittsburgh and the Dodgers lost the first game of a twin-bill to Philadelphia. If the Dodgers lost the finale, the Giants, one-half game back, would play a makeup game in Cincinnati, making possible a deadlock for the pennant.

But Koufax, pitching with only two days' rest for the first time during the season, beat the Phils, 6-3, in the nightcap in Philadelphia, to clinch the Dodgers' second consecutive pennant.

Roberto Clemente . . . Enormous cache of Pirate gold.

With a 27-9 record, a 1.73 earned-run average and 317 strikeouts in 323 innings, Koufax won his second successive unanimous Cy Young Award. In the MVP balloting, Koufax was beaten out by Roberto Clemente of Pittsburgh, 218 points to 208.

The All-Star Game, played in 105-degree temperature in St. Louis, was turned into a 2-1 N.L. victory when Maury Wills singled to score Tim McCarver in the 10th inning.

Tommy Helms, Cincinnati third baseman, won Rookie of the Year honors, and Phil Regan of the Dodgers captured the Fireman of the Year Award with 31 points.

One club changed ownership during the year. On December 5, Bill DeWitt sold the Reds for a reported $7,000,000 to a 13-man syndicate headed by Francis Dale, publisher of the Cincinnati Enquirer.

Front-office shifts included the appointment of Bing Devine as Met G.M. to replace George Weiss, who retired, and the appointment of Paul Richards as vice-president in charge of baseball operations by the Braves.

Don Heffner's term as manager of the Reds lasted until July 13, when he was fired by Bill DeWitt and replaced by coach Dave Bristol. Bobby Bragan received his walking papers at Atlanta August 9 and was succeeded by coach Billy Hitchcock.

1967

The year was only three weeks old when Bob Howsam notified the Cardinals that he was stepping out as general manager to accept a three-year contract to serve the Reds in a similar capacity at an estimated $50,000 annually.

With Howsam gone after only two complete years on the job, Owner August A. Busch, Jr., appointed Senior Vice-President Stan Musial the new general manager.

The Man, who set more than two score of records as a player, also established an administrative mark that may remain for all time by producing not only a pennant, but also a world championship, in his rookie season.

Musial's resignation in early December, occurring, he said, so he could attend to his many business interests, was followed shortly by another surprise development, the appointment of Bing Devine to the vacated spot. Devine, completing his first season as Mets' general manager, had been fired by Busch slightly more than three years earlier.

With Musial in the front office and his old roommate, Red Schoendienst, calling the shots on the field, El Birdos gained first place on June 18 when Dick Hughes defeated the Giants and pulled steadily away, finishing with a 10½-game cushion.

The Redbirds won convincingly despite the fact that on July 15, when their lead was only four games, they suffered the loss of their ace pitcher, Bob Gibson, with a fracture of the right fibula. Gibson was struck just above the ankle by a line drive off the bat of Roberto Clemente of the Pirates and was out of action for 52 days. During his absence, Nelson Briles shifted from the bullpen to the starting rotation and ran off nine straight victories until Gibby returned in September. Briles' 14-5 record topped the league in winning percentage.

Hughes was perhaps as big a surprise as Briles. The 29-year-old rookie compiled a 16-6 record.

Offensively, the Cardinals were led by Orlando Cepeda, whose .325 batting average, 25 homers and 111 runs batted in were sufficient credentials to beat out teammate Tim McCarver easily for MVP honors.

Gibson, who won 13 games for the Cardinals despite his extended layoff, won three games in the World Series against the Red Sox, including the seventh game in which he also socked a home run.

One of the season's most explosive batting displays was detonated by Adolfo Phillips of the Cubs on June 11. The outfielder hit one homer in the Cubs' 5-3 first-game win over the Mets, then followed with three homers

Red Schoendienst

Bob Gibson . . . A three-time winner in one Series.

Mike McCormick . . . Took home a Cy Young plaque.

and seven RBIs in the 18-10 nightcap victory that produced a National League record total of 11 round-trippers.

The N. L. set an All-Star Game record by scoring its fifth consecutive victory, a 15-inning, 2-1 marathon at Anaheim, July 11. Tony Perez' homer broke up the pitchers' battle in which 12 hurlers fanned 30 batters.

In addition to front-office turnovers at Cincinnati and St. Louis, H. B. (Spec) Richardson was promoted from business manager to general manager at Houston, ex-Yankee reliever Johnny Murphy, was named to fill Devine's position with the Mets, and John McHale resigned as president and general manager of the Braves to become administrative assistant to Commissioner William Eckert. McHale was replaced by Paul Richards.

Harry (The Hat) Walker was the first league manager to get the ax, being dismissed by the Pirates on July 18. Danny Murtaugh took over as interim pilot.

On September 19, Wes Westrum resigned as Met manager and, following the season, Gil Hodges resigned as the Washington skipper to accept the New York job.

Billy Hitchcock received the bad news at Atlanta September 30, seven days before Lum Harris was named to replace him.

Tom Seaver, 16-game winner for the cellar-dwelling Mets, was named Rookie of the Year, while Ted Abernathy of the Reds amassed 32 points to win his second Fireman of the Year trophy.

For the first time, dual Cy Young Awards were presented in the two majors. Mike McCormick, 22-game winner for San Francisco, polled 18 of 20 votes to capture the N. L. prize.

1968

If not completely forgotten, Howie Bedell's baseball career is remembered in only such villages as Pottstown, Pa., where he lived, and Milwaukee and Philadelphia, plus countless backwoods communities where he played and managed during a score of years.

In one memory, however, the name of Bedell will remain forever green. On the night of June 8, Don Drysdale, having already established a major league record for consecutive shutout innings, faced pinch-hitter Bedell in a game at Los Angeles.

In the fifth inning, with runners on first and third and one out, the Phils' part-time outfielder lifted a soft fly to left field, driving in Tony Taylor with the run that snapped the Dodger righthander's streak at 58⅔ shutout innings.

The RBI was the only one of the season for Bedell, who had only seven official times at bat in nine games.

Drysdale's streak surpassed the 56-inning

Gaylord Perry and **Ray Washburn** . . . No-hit twins.

string of Walter Johnson of the 1913 Washington Senators.

The season was distinguished by remarkable pitching performances. Bob Gibson shattered a league record by posting a season earned-run average of 1.12. The Cardinal righthander's mark shaved Grover Cleveland Alexander's record of 1.22 for the 1915 Phillies. Gibson hurled 13 shutouts during the campaign and won 15 consecutive games before the Pirates scored two unearned runs in the ninth inning to beat him, 6-4, August 24.

Gibson's teammate, Ray Washburn, participated in a rare pitching performance in September. After Gaylord Perry of the Giants hurled a 1-0 no-hitter at Candlestick Park, September 17, Washburn returned the compliment to the Giants the next day, winning 2-0.

The season was barely a week old when the Mets and Astros cracked the record book at Houston with a 24-inning, 1-0 Houston victory. The marathon set a major league record for the longest night game in innings and the 23 consecutive scoreless frames also set a mark. The six-hour, six-minute struggle ended at 1:37 a.m. CST.

Even the All-Star Game, at Houston, July 9, was a pitchers' showcase. The National League scored its sixth straight triumph, 1-0, with the help of an unearned first-inning run, a single by Willie Mays, an error on an attempted pickoff, a wild pitch and double play produced the only run. Only eight hits were made in the game.

Club owners, meeting in Chicago, May 27, awarded expansion franchises to Montreal and San Diego for $10,000,000 each. At the league meeting in Houston during the All-Star recess, N. L. owners joined A. L. magnates in adopting divisional play for 1969. Under the new arrangement, clubs in each division would play each other 18 times, while meeting clubs in the other division 12 times.

John McHale resigned as aid to Commissioner Eckert to accept the presidency of the Montreal Expos, while Jim Fanning was named general manager and Gene Mauch field manager. Mauch had been fired by the Phillies, June 15.

Buzzie Bavasi, who had resigned a vice-presidency with the Dodgers, assumed the presidency of the San Diego Padres and appointed Eddie Leishman as general manager and Preston Gomez as field manager.

Grady Hatton was bounced from the Astros' managerial chair June 18, to be succeeded by Harry Walker, and, following the season, Herman Franks resigned as pilot of the Giants. Franks, who finished second four consecutive seasons, was replaced by Clyde King, promoted from Phoenix (Pacific Coast).

The Cardinals won the pennant pretty

much as they pleased, piling up a 15-game margin by August 1 before tailing off to a nine-game edge at the finish.

Gibson was at his brilliant best in the World Series opener at St. Louis, fanning 17 Tigers to break Sandy Koufax' mark of 15 against the Yankees in 1963, and beating 31-game winner Denny McLain, 4-0.

After Mickey Lolich squared the Series in the second game, the Cardinals won the first two games in Detroit, before the Tigers snapped back to sweep the last three contests, Lolich winning his third decision in the finale, 4-1, with the help of Jim Northrup's liner that Curt Flood misplayed into a triple.

Gibson won both the MVP and Cy Young awards, while Cincinnati catcher Johnny Bench was acclaimed the foremost rookie and Phil Regan, traded by the Dodgers to the Cubs in early season, won the Fireman of the Year Award.

On December 6, Commissioner Eckert submitted his resignation and the two majors, after countless ballots and deadlocks, selected National League attorney Bowie Kuhn as his successor on February 4, 1969.

1969

In the years of their youth, when every movement was an exercise in futility, Casey Stengel called them "my amazin' Mets."

Five times in their first seven years they lost more than 100 games; only twice did they finish above .400.

Ineptitude was their birthright, laughs were their stock in trade, grim was their future.

The nondescripts who never finished higher than ninth, and that only twice, were permitted on the field, it was conceded, only to furnish comic relief.

Without particular warning, suddenly and mysteriously, the Mets were no longer the "ha, ha" fellows of the league. In the six-club East Division, they grew respectable and competitive; overnight they were contenders.

In third place, 9½ games behind the first-place Cubs on August 15, the Mets won 14 of their next 16 games and, just like that, were in second place, only two lengths back. As Chicago lost 11 of 12 games, the Mets spurted into first place in early September. At race's end, New York enjoyed an eight-game cushion with a record of 100-62.

Not the Miracle Braves of 1914, not the Giants of '51 could have created the unrestrained wave of incredulity that engulfed New York and their tatterdemalions-turned-titans.

In the first divisional playoff for a pennant, the Mets unhorsed the Braves in three straight games by scores of 9-5 and 11-6 at Atlanta, and 7-4 in New York.

But the best was still to come. After losing

John McHale

E. J. (Buzzie) Bavasi

the opening game of the World Series to the Orioles, the Mets were unbeatable. Brilliant defense, timely hitting, infallible strategy combined to provide an incredible climax to an impossible season.

Donn Clendenon, who hit three home runs and drove in four runs for the Mets in the Series, was the preseason storm center of a dispute that required the intervention of new Commissioner Bowie Kuhn.

Traded with Jay Alou by the Expos to the Astros for Rusty Staub, the first baseman initially announced his retirement, then revealed "the door is still open" for his playing with Montreal, although he emphasized he would not play for Houston.

Kuhn ruled that the deal would stand, that Clendenon did not have to report to Houston and that the two clubs should continue to negotiate terms of compensation for Clendenon.

While Houston officials seethed over what they considered a grave injustice, Clendenon rejoined the Expos and was hitting .240 on June 15, when he was swapped to the Mets. The Astros and Expos eventually settled on compensation for Clendenon, although Astro tempers were a long time cooling.

Another first baseman figured prominently in the news during the season. Richie Allen of the Phils, long unhappy with his situation, was fined $1,000 by Manager Bob Skinner in early May for reporting late for two games in St. Louis. On June 24, Allen failed to appear for a doubleheader in New York and was suspended until, said Skinner, Richie requested permission to rejoin the club. In the meantime, Allen would be fined $500 for each game he missed. Twenty-four games later and $12,000 poorer, Allen returned to the lineup, but was traded to St. Louis during the off-season.

The first postponement in All-Star Game history set the classic back from July 22 to 23, at which time the N. L. scored its seventh consecutive victory, defeating the A. L., 9-3, at Washington as Willie McCovey of the Giants socked two homers.

For the second time in major league history, no-hitters were hurled on successive days. On April 30, Jim Maloney pitched his third no-hitter as the Reds blanked the Astros, 10-0, at Cincinnati. The next day, Don Wilson of Houston retaliated with a 4-0 masterpiece. Other N. L. no-hitters were credited to Bill Stoneman of the Expos, 7-0 over Philadelphia, April 17; Ken Holtzman of the Cubs, 3-0, over the Braves, August 19, and Bob Moose of the Pirates, 4-0, over the Mets, September 20.

The Mets also were the victims of a record 19-strikeout performance by Steve Carlton on September 15. The Cardinal southpaw shattered the 18-strikeout mark shared by Sandy Koufax, Don Wilson and Bob Feller, although losing the game, 4-3, on a pair of two-run homers by Ron Swoboda.

Three managers were deposed during the year. On August 7, Bob Skinner was removed by the Phils. Coach George Myatt handled the club the remainder of the season and, in October, Frank Lucchesi was named skipper. In Pittsburgh, Larry Shepard was relieved of his duties on September 26. Alex Grammas finished the season after which Danny Murtaugh, for the third time, was handed the reins. In another post-season signing, Sparky Anderson took control of the Reds, replacing Dave Bristol, who was fired.

Annual awards were won by Willie McCovey, Giant slugger, as the MVP; Tom Seaver of the Mets as the Cy Young Award winner; Ted Sizemore, Dodger second baseman, Rookie of the Year, and Wayne Granger, Reds, No. 1 Fireman.

Ending an 18-year reign, Warren Giles resigned as league president during the winter meetings at Bal Harbour, Fla., and was succeeded by Charles (Chub) Feeney, Giant executive, who received a four-year contract.

1970

The huddle at home plate had a familiar appearance. Representatives of the two

Charles (Chub) Feeney

Tom Seaver . . . 19 Padres begged for mercy.

teams that would take the field shortly were discussing ground rules with the blue-clad figures, obviously the umpires assigned to handle the contest.

Closer scrutiny revealed one incongruity: the umpires, instead of talking, were listening intently as the rules were being explained to them.

The inverted tableau at Three Rivers Stadium in Pittsburgh, October 3, was the result of a strike by major league umpires, and the arbiters at home plate were minor leaguers, hired to work the game while N. L. umpires Nick Colosi, Bob Engel, Doug Harvey, Stan Landes, Paul Pryor and Harry Wendelstedt picketed the stadium carrying placards proclaiming: "Major League Umpires on Strike for Higher Wages."

A one-day demonstration was sufficient for the N. L. arbiters at Pittsburgh, and their A. L. brethren at the playoff in Minnesota to gain satisfaction. They returned to work the following day, having obtained pay increases as follows: Playoffs, $2,500 to $3,000; World Series, $6,500 to $7,500 in 1970 and '71, and to $8,000 in '72 and '73, and a flat $1,000 for the All-Star Game, a raise of $500.

To the Cincinnati Reds, the strike was the only disconcerting feature of the playoffs, for the West Division champions—by 14½ games over the Dodgers—swept aside the Pirates in three contests, 3-0 in 10 innings, 3-1 and 3-2.

Against the Orioles in the World Series, however, the Big Red Machine was less than terrifying and lost in five games. Lee May's three-run homer was the deciding blow in the Reds' only victory, 6-5, in the fourth game.

Although Tom Seaver failed to match his 25 wins of the preceding season, the Met righthander registered the most spectacular pitching performance April 22, when he fanned 19 San Diego batters, equalling Steve Carlton's one-year-old record, and set down the final 10 Padres on strikes to break the old modern mark of eight shared by Max Surkont, Johnny Podres, Jim Maloney and Don Wilson. Twelve times Seaver struck out 10 or more batters in a game and led the league in strikeouts (283) and earned-run average (2.81).

Bob Gibson established a major league record by fanning 200 or more batters for the eighth time, topping the marks of Walter Johnson and Rube Waddell. The Cardinal righthander also compiled a 23-7 record, a major factor in his winning the Cy Young Award for the second time.

Hoyt Wilhelm of the Braves became the first pitcher to work in 1,000 games when he relieved against the Cardinals, May 10. On August 11, Phil righthander Jim Bunning, by defeating Houston, 6-5, chalked up his 100th N. L. victory and thereby became the second hurler to reach the century mark in wins in both majors. Previously, Bunning had notched 118 A. L. victories with Detroit. Cy Young won 222 games in the American League and 289 games in the N. L.

Billy Williams' league endurance record ended at 1,117 consecutive games, September 3, when the Cub outfielder removed himself from the lineup, explaining, "I'm pooped."

Still another league record was etched by Vic Davalillo of the Cardinals, who collected 24 pinch-hits, two more than the former record held by Sam Leslie of the '32 Giants and Red Schoendienst of the '62 Cardinals.

Two new stadiums were ushered into the league's growing galaxy of ballparks, at Cincinnati and Pittsburgh. On June 30, with 51,050 in attendance, the Reds unveiled Riverfront Stadium, where, on July 14, the N. L. All-Stars, after scoring three runs in the ninth inning, posted a 12-inning, 5-4 victory, the eighth in a row for the senior loop.

The Pirates unveiled Three Rivers Stadium, July 16, and attracted 48,846, who saw the Bucs lose to the Reds, 3-2.

On the last day of the campaign, the league's oldest park, Connie Mack Stadium in Philadelphia, was consigned to the vandals' fury in a manner hardly dreamed of in 1909 when it was dedicated as Shibe Park.

The club had planned to conduct a drawing after the game through which it would award prizes to 62 fans among the 31,822 who represented the year's largest crowd.

The final out barely had been recorded, however, when the spectators started stripping the old lady of Lehigh Avenue of every conceivable item of souvenir value. One scavenger was spotted carrying away a toilet bowl, typical of the undisciplined mob that forced the Phils to call off the drawing.

The season's major award winners, in addition to Gibson, included Johnny Bench, Red catcher, the MVP; Carl Morton, Montreal pitcher, the N. L. Rookie, and Wayne Granger of Cincinnati, the top-ranked Fireman for the second straight season.

One manager was given the boot during the season. Clyde King, who managed the Giants to a second-place finish in '69, was sent packing by Owner Horace Stoneham on May 23, King's 46th birthday, after the club had dropped a 15-inning, 17-16 decision to the Padres. He was replaced by Charlie Fox, who had been managing the Phoenix (Pacific Coast) affiliate.

The year's executive changes included the promotion of Bob Scheffing to the general managership of the Mets, following the death of John Murphy, as well as the advancement of Peter O'Malley to the presidency of the Dodgers, replacing his father, Walter, who became chairman of the board, and of Dan Galbreath to the presidency of the Pirates, succeeding his father, John, who also was elected board chairman.

1971

The season for Steve Blass was, like Gaul, divided into three parts, all of them dissimilar.

During the East Division season, the Pirate righthander compiled a 15-8 record. In the pennant playoffs against the Giants, Steve was the least effective of all Pittsburgh pitchers, with an earned-run average of 11.57.

But, in the World Series, the 29-year-old from Connecticut was in a class unto himself. Blass started the third and seventh games and was overwhelmingly impressive, allowing only two earned runs and seven hits in two complete-game victories as he hurled the Pirates to the world championship over the Orioles.

In one two-month stretch, Blass failed to finish a game and for the season he went the route in only 12 of his 33 starts. His failure to last longer than five innings in the opening game of the Championship Series at San Francisco occasioned no surprise. The surprise was reserved for the Series.

After the Pirates were whipped, 5-3 and 11-3, at Baltimore, Blass drew the starting assignment in the opening contest at Pittsburgh. The result was a magnificent three-hit, 5-1 victory. The Pirates evened the Series the next night, October 13, in the first World Series game played under lights.

Four days later, with the Series deadlocked at three games apiece and the scene shifted back to Baltimore, Blass again received the nod from Manager Danny Murtaugh and this time responded with a glittering, four-hit 2-1 triumph.

Blass' Series co-star was Roberto Clemente, who batted .414 and hit two homers, including one in the seventh game.

Following the Series, Murtaugh, who had been hospitalized by chest pains five months earlier, resigned as manager of the Pirates because of ill health and was succeeded by Bill Virdon, a Pirate coach for four years.

All the managers who started the season were on the job at the finish, although Leo Durocher was rumored on the ropes several times in Chicago. The Lip was ridiculed publicly by several of his players and the clamor for Leo's scalp did not abate until Owner P. K. Wrigley bought a page advertisement in a Chicago daily in which he announced, among other things, that "Durocher is the Cub manager and the 'Dump Durocher Clique' might as well give up."

Three no-hitters spiced the 162-game schedule. Ken Holtzman of the Cubs handcuffed the Reds, 1-0, June 3, for his second major league masterpiece.

Rick Wise not only humiliated the Reds, June 23, but also clouted two home runs, driving in three tallies, in the Phillies' 4-0 victory.

Bob Gibson took the measure of the Pirates, August 14, when the Cardinals romped to an 11-0 win.

The Phillies opened the gates to new, 56,371-seat Veterans Stadium at season's start and set a club attendance record for the season with 1,511,223, an increase of 802,976 over the previous year.

One of the Phils' pitchers, 39-year-old Jim Bunning, struck out 58 batters in 29 games and moved into second place in the all-time strikeout list with 2,855 whiffs, second only to Walter Johnson's 3,508. After the season, Bunning announced his retirement.

Henry Aaron of Atlanta belted his 600th career home run on April 27 at the expense of Gaylord Perry, Giants, and wound up the season with 639, only 75 short of Babe Ruth's magical figure of 714.

And Willie Mays, on May 30, scored the 1,950th run of his career, on his 638th homer, to break Stan Musial's record for runs scored in a career.

After winning eight successive All-Star games, the N. L. suffered a 6-4 setback at Detroit, July 13, as A. L. sluggers unloaded three two-run homers.

Joe Torre of the Cardinals scored a convincing victory in MVP balloting, collecting 21 first-place votes to three for Willie Stargell, Pirate slugger who, among other things, established a major league record by clouting 11 home runs during April.

Dave Giusti, Pittsburgh, captured Fireman of the Year honors with 35 points on 30 saves and five victories. Earl Williams of Atlanta outdistanced all others for the Rookie award, and Ferguson Jenkins, winning 24 games and losing 13 for the Cubs, captured the Cy Young Award.

1972

Long a spectre in the baseball background, a player strike materialized suddenly while the clubs were in spring training and forced the cancellation of 86 regular-season major league games.

Source of the disagreement that led to the walkout was two-fold:

1—A player request for increased retirement benefits that would require about $800,000 and

2—A second request that the owners absorb an anticipated increase in annual premiums for medical and health care, amounting to about $400,000.

After extended negotiations availed nothing, player representatives, meeting in Dallas, voted 47-0 to authorize a strike. Wes Parker, Dodger delegate, abstained from voting, explaining that his teammates had ordered him to desist on the basis that they did not have sufficient information to take such action.

The strike began officially on April 1, the last Saturday of spring training.

For nearly two weeks, the owners, represented by John Gaherin, and the Major League Baseball Players Association, represented by Marvin Miller, attempted to hammer out a solution to their differences. Agreement was announced at 5:15 p.m. Eastern Time, on April 13. In exchange for the owners' consent to the player demands, the athletes agreed that none of the games would be made up and that they would accept salary deductions for the games that were missed.

Alphabetically, the clubs lost games as follows: Atlanta 8, Chicago 7, Cincinnati 8, Houston 9, Los Angeles 7, Montreal 6, New York 6, Philadelphia 7, Pittsburgh 7, St. Louis 6, San Diego 9 and San Francisco 7.

Each club was believed to have lost up to $200,000 in revenue, while a player earning $75,000 lost an estimated $1,670 after taxes.

The delay in the start of the season had no visible effect on the Pirates or Reds. Pittsburgh occupied first place in the East from June 19 to the end of the season, by which time it had built up an 11-game margin. Cincinnati took charge on June 25 and led by 10½ lengths at the finish.

On September 30, in a 5-0 win over the Mets, Roberto Clemente collected his 3,000th hit, the last of his illustrious career. On December 31, while flying provisions from his native Puerto Rico to earthquake victims in Nicaragua, Clemente perished in an off-shore crash of the DC-7.

Cincinnati's outstanding performers were Johnny Bench, whose 40 homers and 125 RBIs earned him MVP distinction, and Clay Carroll, the league's top Fireman with 43 points (37 saves and six victories).

Cub and Expo pitchers produced the majors' only no-hitters of the year, Burt Hooton blanking the Phils, 4-0, April 16; Milt Pappas duplicating his Cub mate's performance with an 8-0 masterpiece over the Padres, September 2, and Expo Bill Stoneman's 7-0 gem against the Mets, October 2.

Although the Phillies finished last in their division, they boasted the year's outstanding pitcher, Steve Carlton. Obtained from the Cardinals in a spring trade, the lefthander led the league in eight categories, including victories (27), earned-run average (1.98) and strikeouts (310) to sweep the boards in the Cy Young Award voting. Jon Matlack, Met southpaw, gained Rookie laurels.

Jim Barr, San Francisco righthander, established a major league record by retiring 41 consecutive batters in the course of hurling successive shutouts over the Pirates and Cardinals, August 23 and 29, while Nate Colbert, San Diego first baseman, equalled a Stan Musial record by clouting five home runs in a doubleheader at Atlanta, August 1.

The season was only 11 games old when Preston Gomez became the first managerial casualty. He was fired by San Diego and replaced by coach Don Zimmer on April 27.

On July 10, the Phils fired Frank Lucchesi, turning the reins over to General Manager Paul Owens, who finished the season and then stepped aside for Danny Ozark, ex-Dodger coach.

Leo Durocher tendered his resignation to the Cubs on July 24, paving the way for Whitey Lockman to be named to the position on the eve of his 46th birthday.

Durocher did not remain unemployed long. On August 26, he accepted the Houston helm, replacing Harry Walker, who was canned despite a 67-54 record.

In the Championship Series, the Pirates were on the verge of a second consecutive pennant, but two runs by the Reds in the last of the ninth inning in the final game, one on a home run by Bench and the other on a wild pitch by Bob Moose, produced a 4-3 Cincinnati victory that sent the Reds into the World Series, which they lost to Oakland in seven games.

1973

For most of the season, the Mets' clubhouse resembled a hospital ward. By actual count, eight players were on the disabled list simultaneously, believed to be a record.

John Milner, Rusty Staub, Jerry Grote, Willie Mays, Bud Harrelson and Cleon Jones—all front-liners—were sidelined at one time or another. With such a handicap, it was hardly surprising that the New York club languished in the East Division cellar for more than 70 days.

To intensify Yogi Berra's frustration, Tug

McGraw, mainstay of the bullpen, encountered a dry spell during June, July and August, in which he blew leads as well as games.

Fortunately for the Mets, the cripples recovered by late August and McGraw, exhorting his comrades with cries of "Ya gotta believe!" commenced to save games again. In the tight race, the club, which had been 13 games under .500 on July 31, started to move. By September 18, they were in fourth place, but trailing the Pirates, 4-1, entering the ninth inning. After they scored five runs, en route to a 6-5 victory, said Tom Seaver, "We began to believe in ourselves."

Three days later, they defeated the Pirates for the fourth consecutive time to move into first place, and they never were overtaken. They won nine of their last 11 games and were the only club in the division to finish over .500.

The Reds, who took charge of the West Division on September 3, never to be ousted, won the first game of the Championship Series, 2-1, on homers by Pete Rose and Johnny Bench before Jon Matlack won, 5-0, on a two-hitter, and Jerry Koosman chalked up a 9-2 win highlighted by a fight between Rose and Bud Harrelson at second base. When Rose returned to his left field position, he was greeted by a shower of missiles from the bleacherites at Shea Stadium that grew so intense Manager Yogi Berra and several Met players walked to the area and pleaded with the miscreants, who desisted and let the game go on.

After the Reds knotted the Series in 12 innings, 2-1, Tom Seaver, with ninth-inning help from McGraw, wrapped up the pennant for the Mets, 7-2.

The Mets carried the Athletics into seven games before being defeated in the World Series windup, 5-2. The Series marked Willie Mays' farewell to baseball. The one-time Say-Hey Kid batted .286 as a center fielder and pinch-hitter in the classic.

Three Atlanta players crashed 40 or more homers during the campaign. Henry Aaron, pursuing Babe Ruth's career record of 714, attained the 700 milestone on July 21 when he connected against Ken Brett of the Phillies and finished with 40. Darrell Evans clouted 41 and Dave Johnson 43, setting a record for second basemen.

Two managers were deposed during the year. On September 6, Bill Virdon was released by the Pirates, although the club was only three games out of the lead. It finished third under Danny Murtaugh.

After the close of the race, Don Zimmer was fired by the Padres and replaced by John McNamara, a San Francisco coach.

The Padres made more news off the field than they did on it during the year as a result of would-be buyers seeking to acquire the franchise from C. Arnholt Smith, who was charged by the Internal Revenue Service with $22.8 million in back taxes and interest.

Majorie Lindheimer Everett of the well-known racing family and Joseph Danzansky, a Washington grocery store chain magnate, bid for the franchise, but it wasn't until Ray Kroc, hamburger millionaire, entered the picture that the club was sold in early January, 1974.

Pete Rose, with 12 first-place votes to 10 for Willie Stargell, piled up 274 points to the Pirate's 250, to win Most Valuable Player laurels. Although falling short of the 20-win circle, Tom Seaver (19-10) won his second Cy Young Award, beating out Mike Marshall, Montreal reliever whose name was inexplicably left off 10 ballots. Marshall, however, breezed to the Fireman Award, amassing 45 points to 30 by Tug McGraw, and Gary Matthews, Giant outfielder, captured Rookie honors.

1974

Never before had American sports fans been caught up in such an emotional whirlwind. Not for Roger Maris' assault on Babe Ruth's one-season homer record, not for Joe DiMaggio's 56-game hitting streak, not for any other attack on a season or lifetime record.

Ever since the close of the 1973 season, the national sports pulse beat perceptibly faster in anticipation of Henry Aaron's pursuit of Babe Ruth's sacred mark of 714 career home runs.

For 20 years, the Atlanta super star had slugged baseballs out of ball parks, attaining yearly totals that ranged from 13 to 47. When Henry smacked a homer on the next-to-last day of the 1973 campaign, he climbed to one homer shy of the Bambino's total.

Through the interminable winter and into spring training, the tension mounted as media people speculated and predicted. With remarkable poise and detachment, Aaron rode the mounting tide.

When Braves' President Bill Bartholomay suggested that Aaron might be held out of the season's first series at Cincinnati in the hope that, for maximum publicity and benefits, he would tie and break the record at Atlanta, Commissioner Bowie Kuhn virtually ordered the club to play Henry at Cincinnati.

Henry dodged the controversy with an unembroidered statement: "He is the commissioner. I must abide by the rules."

Aaron wasted no time in hitting No. 714. On his first at-bat at Cincinnati, April 4, he tagged a Jack Billingham pitch for the 714th homer of his career. The next one would topple The Babe from his exalted perch. The world did not have long to wait.

Four days later, on April 8, against the Dodgers in Atlanta Stadium, the long wait ended. With millions watching on television, with one on base and none out in the fourth inning, Aaron met an Al Downing fast ball and drove it over the left-center field fence.

The time was 9:07 p.m. EDT; weather conditions: overcast, windy and cool, occasional drizzle, 62 degrees.

Moments after the historic accomplishment, Aaron received a phone call from Washington, D.C. The caller was kept waiting until Aaron returned to the dugout at which time he received congratulations from President Richard Nixon.

Aaron smashed 18 more home runs during the season, finishing with 733. In addition to his home-run achievement, he set two other major league marks, surpassing Ty Cobb's records for total games and at-bats.

Aaron was not alone in his record-setting performance. St. Louis outfielder Lou Brock established a new modern standard in base-stealing with 118 thefts, shattering the 104 mark set by Maury Wills of the Dodgers in 1962. It was the eighth time Brock led the league in stolen bases, and the 10th consecutive season in which he stole more than 50 bases.

Ray Kroc, new owner of the Padres, incurred the displeasure of his players on opening night in San Diego, when he took over the public address microphone and apologized to the fans "for the stupidest ballplaying I've ever seen." The Padres were losing to the Astros, 9-5.

When the athletes, backed by the Players' Association, expressed resentment at the public ridicule, Kroc offered another apology—this time to the athletes.

Mike Marshall, iron-man reliever of the Dodgers, broke his own record of 92 mound appearances in a season, pitching in 106 of his club's 162 games. Marshall won both the Fireman and Cy Young awards, while his teammate, Steve Garvey, walked off as the loop's MVP. Bake McBride, Cardinal outfielder, was named the N.L. Rookie of the Year.

Garvey, write-in winner of the first base position in the N. L. All-Star voting, captured most valuable distinction in the mid-summer classic by hitting a single and double, and driving in a run, to spark the senior circuit to a 7-2 victory at Pittsburgh's Three Rivers Stadium, July 23. It was the N.L.'s 11th win in 12 games and increased their series lead to eight games, 26 to 18.

The Dodgers eliminated the Pirates in a four-game Championship Series, the final

Henry Aaron . . . A new frontier in four-baggers.

The new king acknowledges plebeian plaudits.

game by the score of 12-1, but for the third consecutive year, the N. L. representative lost to the Athletics in the World Series, this time in a five-game set.

Three managers came to the end of the line during the year. On June 28, Charley Fox resigned as Giant pilot and was succeeded by Wes Westrum, the club's super scout. On July 24, Eddie Mathews was deposed at Atlanta and replaced by Clyde King, special assistant to General Manager Eddie Robinson.

Whitey Lockman stepped down as Cub skipper on July 24, and returned to his vice-presidential chair while Jim Marshall, third base coach, assumed control.

Chief among the executive changes was the resignation of Bob Scheffing as general manager of the Mets and the appointment of Joe McDonald.

1975

As if by dramatic design, the league's 100th season roared to a smashing climax in a World Series acclaimed by many as the most thrilling in the 72-year history of that event.

En route to the pennant, the Reds turned a close race into a cakewalk by winning 41 of 50 games between May 21 and July 13, and finished 20 games ahead of the Dodgers.

They won 64 games at home, a league rec-

ord; they played 15 straight errorless games, a major league mark; they stole 168 bases and their .8235 percentage of successes established another major record; their pitchers broke a major mark by yielding the fewest number of unearned runs in a season, 40.

When the Reds defeated the Giants, 8-4, September 7, they clinched the flag at the earliest date in league history.

Meanwhile, the fans poured into Riverfront Stadium to the tune of 2,315,603, for a club record.

Winners of their last five games and 10 of the final 11, the Reds rode the momentum into the Championship Series. They won the first two games from the Pirates, 8-3 and 6-1, before encountering John Candelaria in the third contest. The young lefthander held the Reds to one run, a homer by Dave Concepcion, and was leading, 2-1, with two out in the eighth inning when he walked Merv Rettenmund and served a home-run pitch to Pete Rose.

A walk with the bases full in the ninth enabled the Pirates to knot the score before the Reds, who stole 11 bases in the series, scored twice in the 10th for a 5-3 victory.

The Cincinnati juggernaut was brought up short in the opening game of the World Series when Luis Tiant, allowing only five hits, won for the Red Sox, 6-0.

The Reds were only one out away from defeat in the second game when Concepcion's

Steve Garvey . . . Twice an MVP in one season.

Joe Morgan

Boston grabbed an early 3-0 lead in the finale, but the clubs were tied, 3-3, at the end of eight innings and Morgan's single in the ninth produced a 4-3 win and a world championship for Cincinnati.

Morgan, with 21½ first-place votes, swept to the MVP award. Tom Seaver of the Mets, with a 22-9 pitching record, joined Sandy Koufax as a three-time Cy Young winner, while Al Hrabosky, Cardinals, was named Fireman of the Year and John Montefusco, Giants, the year's No. 1 Rookie.

Rennie Stennett of Pittsburgh joined Wilbert Robinson in the record book, September 16, when he collected seven hits in as many at-bats in the Pirates' 22-0 romp over the Cubs at Wrigley Field.

Managerial fatalities numbered four, starting with Yogi Berra on August 6. Yogi was succeeded by coach Roy McMillan who, after the season, was replaced by Joe Frazier.

On August 19, Preston Gomez was let go by the Astros, in favor of Bill Virdon, canned three weeks earlier by the Yankees.

Clyde King was tomahawked by the Braves, August 30. Connie Ryan, an aid to G. M. Eddie Robinson, served as interim pilot and, after the season, turned the job over to Dave Bristol.

Gene Mauch was fired by the Expos, October 1, being replaced by Karl Kuehl, and in late November, Horace Stoneham, in anticipation of his sale of the Giants, let Wes Westrum go.

That item would have been the final entry of the National League's 100th year except that on December 23 Peter Seitz, chairman of the game's three-man arbitration committee, ruled in favor of the Major League Baseball Players Association and granted free agency to pitcher Andy Messersmith of the Dodgers.

The ruling opened the forensic flood gates for management and labor alike. Dire warnings of management mingled with labor's exultant shouts that were unmatched since the Emancipation Proclamation.

Prospects arose for a new concept in player-owner relationships. Unquestionably, baseball's legal structure would undergo sharp revision. The entire climate of baseball, as it had existed for 100 years, was subject to drastic and immediate overhaul.

William A. Hulbert, Albert G. Spalding, Nicholas E. Young and all the others who had breathed life into the National League a century earlier could scarcely have foreseen such a cataclysmic upheaval in the solid old circuit.

Nor was it an inviting situation, or a propitious augury for the start of the second century.

single tied the score and Ken Griffey's double gave them a 3-2 triumph.

A record-tying six home runs sailed out of Riverfront Stadium in game No. 3, but a 10th-inning bunt created tons of controversy that helped stamp the Series one of the most memorable of all time.

After Dwight Evans' two-run homer enabled the Red Sox to tie the score, 5-5, in the ninth inning, Cesar Geronimo singled to open the 10th inning and Ed Armbrister, pinch-hitting, laid down a bunt on which he collided with catcher Carlton Fisk.

When Fisk disengaged himself from the batter and threw toward second base trying to retire Geronimo, the ball flew into center field, the runners winding up at second and third.

Despite vehement protests of interference from the Boston bench, A. L. umpire Larry Barnett, working behind the plate, permitted the play to stand. A walk to Rose loaded the bases and, with one out, Joe Morgan's single produced a 6-5 Cincinnati victory.

Following an exchange of victories in games 4 and 5, an off day for travel and three idle days because of rain in Boston, the Red Sox squared the Series, 7-6, when Fisk poled a 12th-inning home run.